Christine Laidlaw holds a Ph.D. from the University of Edinburgh. Following an itinerant career in the Diplomatic Service she has settled back in Scotland.

THE BRITISH IN THE LEVANT

Trade and Perceptions of the Ottoman Empire in the Eighteenth Century

CHRISTINE LAIDLAW

TAURIS ACADEMIC STUDIES
an imprint of
I.B.Tauris Publishers
LONDON • NEW YORK

Published in 2010 by Tauris Academic Studies,
an imprint of I.B.Tauris & Co Ltd
6 Salem Road, London W2 4BU
175 Fifth Avenue, New York NY 10010
www.ibtauris.com

Distributed in the United States and Canada
Exclusively by Palgrave Macmillan,
175 Fifth Avenue, New York NY 10010

Library of Ottoman Studies 21

ISBN: 978 1 84885 335 5

A full CIP record for this book is available from the British Library
A full CIP record for this book is available from the Library of Congress

Library of Congress catalog card: available

Camera-ready copy edited and supplied by
Oxford Publishing Services, Oxford
Printed and bound in India by Replika Press Pvt. Ltd.

For my parents, Frank and Isobel
in grateful and loving memory.

Contents

CONTENTS

Illustrations

Acknowledgements

The Department of Islamic and Middle Eastern Studies of the University of Edinburgh sowed the seeds that produced this book during the years 1996 to 2000, and for this I am grateful to the then head of department, Professor Carole Hillenbrand, and her colleagues.

I owe a special debt of thanks to Dr John Chalcraft, whose enthusiastic support and encouragement never wavered, and whose sure-footed guidance with the thesis on which this book is based was invaluable.

My thanks go also to Anne and Edward Clay, Ann Malamah Thomas and Malcolm Dexter for their hospitality in Cyprus and Beirut as I contemplated getting started, and for the useful contacts they gave me. Juliet and Norrie Boulting kindly showed me their home, Braidshaw, where the Russells of Aleppo once lived. The Crellin family have taken a helpful interest in my enquiries into their ancestor, Ambassador John Murray. Michael Norman generously gave me a copy of his unpublished work on Colville Bridger's letters from Aleppo.

I much appreciated the assistance I received with my research from staff at the Public Record Office, the British Library, the National Library of Scotland, Edinburgh University Library and Manx National Heritage.

Finally I would like to record my gratitude for the patient help and advice I have received from Selina Cohen of Oxford Publishing Services, and my thanks to Kayleigh Woods for her assistance in the final stages of this work. Because of eyesight problems, I have been more dependent on them for proof-reading than I would have wished but any errors must be regarded as mine alone.

Preface

The motivation to write the dissertation on which this book is based arose from my own background in the British Diplomatic Service. A chance conversation in a Beirut restaurant during Easter 2000 refreshed a longstanding curiosity about those who served British interests in the Levant before the formation of the Foreign Office, and led me – via several visits to Syria – to this study of the Levant Company factory communities, which were the forerunners of today's embassies and consulates in the region. The focus of this work is not on the merchants engaged in 'the Turkey trade', but on the large and hitherto unstudied supporting cast of officials, chaplains, physicians and accompanying family members, whose presence at the Levant factories aided and facilitated that trade. Although I cast a backward look at the seventeenth century for purposes of comparison, this book is essentially about the eighteenth century, a period of fluctuation and overall decline in the company's fortunes, which led to its eventual demise. It was a time too that saw the beginnings of greater European involvement in the region, and the assumption by the British crown of full responsibility for its diplomatic representation there. My aim is to look beyond the company's commercial achievements to provide some insight into the social structure of its factories in the Levant, with an emphasis on the 'invisible imports' that accrued to Britain through the efforts and experiences of some of the non-traders who lived there alongside the merchants.

EDITORIAL NOTES

The versions of *place-names* used in the text are those most common in modern English, except in direct quotations from primary sources. Where *dates* appear uncertain (for example February 1644–45) this reflects the use in Britain until September 1752 of the old-style Julian calendar in which the year began on 25 March. In the footnotes, full details are given when a work is first mentioned, and thereafter an abbreviated version is used. This book contains a number of quotations from *The Natural History of Aleppo*, the footnotes for which require some additional explanation. Alexander Russell's original text (1756) is contained in a single volume, for which only page numbers are quoted, whereas for the later 1794 edition (edited and expanded by Patrick Russell), which is in two volumes, each reference quotes both the volume number and the page number. The few *Ottoman words and titles* that appear in the text are spelt as found in the Western primary sources used.

1

Introduction and Background to the Levant Company

That relatively little has been written about the Levant Company is perhaps a reflection of its modest importance as a trading company when compared with its contemporary and hugely successful rival, the East India Company. But, for more than two centuries, it played a pivotal role in English (later, British) relations with the Ottoman Empire and had a political impact in the Levant far beyond its commercial achievements. From its creation in 1581 until 1804 – just 21 years before it was disbanded – the company bore the total cost of English representation in the Ottoman dominions of the Levant, paying all the expenses of the ambassador at Istanbul and of the wide network of consuls throughout the region. During this period, the ambassador had a dual role as both the diplomatic envoy of the crown to the Sublime Porte and guardian of the company's commercial interests. The many thousands of individuals who served the company at its overseas establishments in the Levant, whether as traders or non-traders, between them paved the way for the increased political interest in the Ottoman Empire of the nineteenth century. The relations they forged in the Levant, and the information they garnered on the territories where they operated, were the building blocks for future British policy towards the region. Moreover, the Levant Company enjoyed massive prestige in England, particularly in the first century of its existence, and attracted as members some of the richest and most powerful men in London. Elitist policies, and the high cost of investing in a business where years might pass before any return on the money was had, kept membership relatively small throughout its existence, but the company was with justification regarded as a maker of fortunes and involvement in it was highly prized.

Most of the limited amount of writing on the Levant Company to date has, not unnaturally, concentrated on the trade it carried out and on the merchants involved. To the eye of the present writer, with much personal experience of working at British missions overseas, there is insufficient recognition of the chorus of personnel of all ranks and functions who were present at the Levant factories, operating for the most part off stage, in support of the merchants and the company's interests. The writer sets out in this book to look beyond commercial statistics and political objectives, and to focus instead on the contributions of those other British men and women who were also constituent members of the company's factories in the Levant. Administrators, clergymen, physicians and accompanying women and children, they all lived and worked alongside the merchants, underpinning the trading activity in their different ways and combining to form close-knit communities that did their best to replicate the lifestyle they would have known at home.

The focus of this study will be on the eighteenth century, and in particular on the second half of the century, which saw the incumbency of John Murray as ambassador at Istanbul from 1766 to 1775. Murray held the post at a time when the Levant Company was in its terminal decline, following a long slow downturn in its fortunes, and when Britain's political relations with the Porte were at a low ebb because of British support for Russia against the Ottomans in their war of 1768–74. This period has been chosen for two main reasons. First, it can be seen, with benefit of hindsight, as representing the end of an era. Englishmen in the Ottoman lands in

Murray's time had none of the power and less of the consequential arrogance that Europeans would acquire in the nineteenth century. Unlike their compatriots in the rival East India Company, they were in no position to dominate in the territories where they traded, and survived precariously – as they had done for the previous two centuries – by accommodating themselves as best they could to local practice and to the terms of the capitulations.

The second reason is that the lack of any previous study of Murray's embassy, or of any biography of him, has aroused my curiosity. Despite Murray being a well-connected and apparently well-regarded career diplomat who served as British Resident in Venice for 12 years before his nine-year posting to Istanbul – and all of this without any home leave in Britain – he received little tangible recognition of his service and scant mention in the history books. In this work the writer searches for the possible reasons for this and considers whether the decline of the Levant Company, together with Britain's poor bilateral relations with the Ottomans during Murray's tenure, might have been instrumental in blighting his career. Murray's letter book of correspondence on company issues for the first three years of his tenure at Istanbul (1766–69) has, however, survived.[1]

These previously unpublished letters, mainly to the company in London and to Murray's network of consuls throughout the Levant, give a more vivid and rounded picture of the role of an ambassador to the Sublime Porte than any formal political reports could illustrate. They reveal his wide range of preoccupations and responsibilities as overall head of a diverse cluster of his fellow countrymen over whom he had only limited control. The ambassadors to Istanbul must of course themselves be numbered among the non-trading factory residents. Because of the timing of his incumbency, the richness of his surviving letters, and the absence to date of any work relating specifically to him, John Murray's experiences provide a convenient and appropriate starting point for this book, which includes in the following chapter a section devoted to him.

Some preliminary explanation is necessary here of the composition of the company's overseas communities, the three largest and most important of which were at Istanbul, Izmir and Aleppo. The Levant Company was a body of merchants who traded independently and in competition with each other subject to a process of self-imposed regulation. It was run by officials elected from within its own ranks who formed a company court that made all policy decisions. At the heart of each of its overseas factories – the 'English nations', as these communities of expatriates called themselves – were the young agents or factors who carried out the mechanics of trading on behalf of their merchant masters in London.

Each factory also had its population of non-traders, who were in their different ways also servants of the company, and played an important role. There were the salaried officials such as the consuls and – in Istanbul only – the ambassador with his unique dual role, all of whom were forbidden to engage in trade (but who often found ways around this and other means of supplementing their salaries, such as financial speculation). The three larger factories had resident chaplains, elected by the full membership of the company in London and also in receipt of an official salary. On a less formal basis, there were also from time to time physicians present in the factories who were freelance, earning their living from the fees they collected for services. Until the mid-eighteenth century, it was relatively rare for any but the ambassador or an occasional consul to be accompanied by his family, but thereafter the factories might also include some wives and children, there in support of their menfolk and thus indirectly of the company too.[2]

All the constituent members of the 'nations' – merchants, officials, chaplains, physicians and families – were present because of the Levant Company, although not necessarily on behalf of it. They had to rub along together, and their totality supported the company's activities and facilitated its trading. They all in their way served the company in the sense of operating directly or indirectly on its behalf. The merchants were concerned with financial gain; the ambassador and his officials represented and protected its interests (as well as those of the British crown); the clergymen and physicians provided spiritual and physical support to the communities; and the families supplied domestic comfort to their menfolk. The company was a common denominator that linked them, along with their common nationality and their shared experience of a foreign place and isolation from things familiar. But, just as each merchant followed his own path to prosperity by means of the company (and making money was the overwhelming driving force for all of them), so did many of the non-traders – particularly those who served as chaplains and doctors – find it a convenient vehicle for the pursuit of their own professional, literary and scientific interests. Some discussion will follow on how the company was thereby instrumental, albeit indirectly, in bringing back to Britain a great deal more than Persian silk and gallnuts.

To summarize, the writer will aim, through a study of both official records and contemporary personal accounts of experiences *en poste*, to illuminate the living, breathing diversity of 'the English nations' of the Levant. Given that the company's fortunes peaked in the seventeenth century and thereafter were in overall slow decline, a further aim will be to consider how conditions in the factories, and the attitudes, objectives and fortunes of the community members may have changed and adapted in reflection of this. Especially important here is the period of Murray's tenure in the latter half of the eighteenth century, just before Napoleon's incursion into Egypt opened the door to increased European interest and involvement in the region.

OUTLINE OF EXISTING LITERATURE

The seminal work on the Levant Company, published in 1935, is by

A. C. Wood; his *History of the Levant Company* was the first general history of the company and no other has emerged since. Wood's declared objective was 'to suggest the many-sided importance of the company', and in this he succeeds; it is a wide-ranging and largely factual account, lively and very readable, if, inevitably, a little dated in some respects. Wood has, for example, chosen to use throughout, and without clarification, the Western nomenclature commonly used in company records, so that we read of Constantinople and Smyrna, of the Turkey trade, and of Turks as a loose collective noun for all Ottoman subjects. Equally inevitably, he also reveals some of the prejudices prevalent in his own period, which grate a little on the ear of a contemporary historian. Wood was aware that, because of the dual character of the company already described above, he could not avoid being drawn into both its economic and its diplomatic history, and ran the risk of inadequacy in both. He attempts – successfully – to achieve a fair balance between the two, and his work is a pleasingly rounded account of the company's trading activity against a rich background of the political upheavals, wars, piracy and pestilences of the seventeenth and eighteenth centuries. The human beings who served the company are not ignored by Wood, who includes a chapter on the embassy in Istanbul and its various occupants, and another on life in the factories. His sources were the Levant Company records, contemporary government papers, the accounts of travellers to the region during the period of the company's existence and biographical works – and Wood makes good use of them.

Ralph Davis provides a fascinating account of the Levant Company's trading activity at Aleppo in the mid-eighteenth century in his work *Aleppo and Devonshire Square*, published in 1967. He points to the inadequacies of using only company records (dry, methodical) and pamphlet literature (polemical, ill-informed) as sources, and bases his work on private correspondence between merchants and their factors, using primarily the surviving papers of the Radcliffe family, who traded under the Levant Company from the middle of the seventeenth century and throughout the eighteenth. Operating from a family property in Devonshire Square near the port of London, a location much favoured by the Levant Company's wealthier merchants, generations of Radcliffes engaged in trading through their factors based in Aleppo. His book contains only an essential minimum of general description of the Levant trade and of the company, and gives its main attention to the methods of trading individuals used, the problems they faced and the role of the factors during the period 1730–60. It provides an insight into the experiences of a wealthy company trading house coping with the disruption of the great trade in Persian silk[3] – traditionally the mainstay of the Aleppo factory – at a time when the Levant trade as a whole was slipping into decline and, with it, the company fortunes. The book gives a good account of the silk trade and of the complicated financial arrangements in which factors had to engage in the Levant.

Wood and Davis have written the only two books dealing exclusively with the Levant Company that later interested scholars seem to regard as authoritative and they are regularly quoted. Gwilym Ambrose's excellent article 'English Traders at Aleppo (1658–1756)' written in 1932 covers the practical aspects of trade there as experienced by the young factors. It contains clear descriptions of the competition between them to strike a good bargain and to find shipping space for their purchases. Ambrose describes also their wheeling and dealing with Jewish and Armenian brokers in the marketplace, the difficulties of negotiating prices and then of getting paid, and the dangers the camel trains carrying goods to and from the port of Iskenderun faced. Ambrose's article is dated 1932, and thus predates Wood. In 1987 Norma Perry published a useful article based on the surviving papers of the Bosanquet family who traded in Aleppo in the early to mid-eighteenth century. In a recent booklet, produced privately in 1998 and unpublished, Michael

Norman reproduced extracts from the private correspondence from Aleppo of Colville Bridger, a trader who served there from 1754 to 1766. Bridger's letters reveal much that is of relevance to this book and will be incorporated into it.

If relatively little has been written about the Levant Company's trade and traders, even less attention has been given to the non-traders, no doubt because the great majority of them went unrecorded, unless notoriety or tragedy earned them a mention in the official archives. There are biographical works, mostly written in the nineteenth century, on only a handful of the men who served as ambassadors at Istanbul and also represented the company, and these consist largely of their official correspondence taken from company and state papers. Sonia Anderson's excellent book (1989) on Paul Rycaut (albeit a consul rather than an ambassador) and Daniel Goffman's *Britons in the Ottoman Empire 1642–1600* (1998), a lively and fascinating account of the embassies of Sackville Crowe and Thomas Bendysh during the period of the disruption in England, represent the seventeenth century well. Bruce Masters includes a section on the European communities in eighteenth-century Aleppo in his book *Origins of Western Economic Dominance in the Middle East* (1988), and there is also much of general interest on the communities in Eldem, Goffman and Masters's *The Ottoman City between East and West: Aleppo, Izmir and Istanbul* (1999).

There has been nothing substantial at all on the chaplains the company paid and who resided at the larger factories, although many of the works mentioned above make reference to them either generally or as individuals, since Pearson's *Biographical Sketches of the Chaplains to the Levant Company, 1611–1707* was published in 1883. It is discussed in Chapter 3 below.

The question of medical care for the company's overseas communities has never been addressed, and very little is known about the freelance physicians who attached themselves to the factories. The only exceptions to this are the Russell brothers, who were physicians at the Aleppo factory in the eighteenth century and whose epic study *The Natural History of Aleppo* is known to all with an interest in that city and is much quoted, although no work exclusively about the Russells *per se* has as yet been produced. Anita Damiani, in her book *Enlightened Observers: British Travellers to the Near East* (1967), which consists of four mini-biographies including one of Alexander Russell, gives a useful criticism of *The Natural History*. Sarah Searight's *The British in the Middle East*, first published in 1969, is a fascinating and wide-ranging account of Britons who lived in or were associated with the Middle East between the middle of the sixteenth century and the outbreak of the First World War. It includes a chapter on 'the Turkey merchants' in which she too quotes from *The Natural History*. The Russells are the subject also of a recent article (2001) by Barbara Hawgood in the *Journal of Medical Biography*, which focuses on their achievements in the medical field. Nothing at all has hitherto been written about the Russells' successor at Aleppo, Adam Freer.

As far as the writer has been able to establish, only one account survives by or about any accompanying family member who served in the Levant in support of a father, husband or brother before the nineteenth century. This is in the form of the letters of Lady Mary Wortley Montagu, who accompanied her husband during his brief spell as ambassador to the Sublime Porte in 1717–18. Lady Mary's writings are well-known and have been much picked over. She was clearly an enthusiastic, intelligent and articulate observer, and she wrote copiously to friends and family in an extravagant style, awash with classical allusions, revealing a lively interest in issues above and beyond the domestic aspects of her life. It must be borne in mind, however, that Lady Mary intended her letters to be published and wrote accordingly. Both she and her husband Edward rapidly became so enthralled with all things Ottoman that his masters in London regarded him as having 'turned Turk' to a degree that clouded his judgement on political issues. Although under the terms of his appointment Edward Wortley Montagu should have remained at his post until 1721, within a year of taking up his position he received his official letters of recall from Secretary of State Joseph Addison. For some months he argued and battled against being withdrawn from his post, but this merely hardened hearts in London and, on 5 July 1718, he and his family, together with an entourage of 19 servants, departed reluctantly on board the English warship *Preston*, which had been dispatched to bring them home.[4]

Lady Mary thus spent only 16 months in what she called Turkey. It is arguable whether her highly privileged position gave her the exceptional access to local society she claimed or if it had the opposite effect of insulating her from all but what the local authorities chose to let her see. She was young – only 28 years old when she arrived – and came from a wealthy, aristocratic family in an age when class barriers in England were rigid. These facts should not of course be held against her in assessing the value of the observations and judgements contained in her letters from Istanbul, but they need to be borne in mind, for they surely cast doubt on the amount of exposure she could have had to ordinary subjects of the sultan. Nonetheless, for the purposes of this book, there is much of interest in Lady Mary's writings about her personal experiences as a woman supporting her husband and young children in early eighteenth-century Istanbul.

The relative paucity of literature on the Levant Company is evident from the above and is a sharp contrast with the wealth of material written about its contemporary, the East India Company, though perhaps not disproportionately so. The latter was of course a much larger and more powerful organization than the Levant Company, and drew far greater numbers of Britons to its overseas establishments. It was a centralized joint-stock company in which all the merchants were salaried employees trading for the company rather than as individuals. There was a recognized hierarchy with prospects for promotion up through the ranks, and the head of each factory was the senior representative of an employer common to him and to all his subordinates in that factory, and was therefore in a position of real authority. From the very outset in the late sixteenth century, married company men could be accompanied by their families, and were allowed to take houses in the merchant quarters of the cities, whereas bachelors were obliged to live within the confines of the factories. While far more wives and families lived in India than they ever did in the Levant factories, most of our knowledge of them comes from nineteenth-century material. The East India Company, moreover – for long effectively the British government in India – survived until 1860, rather longer than the Levant Company, which was wound up in 1825 after several decades in the doldrums.

Levant Company factories were established in the territory of the enormous and powerful Ottoman Empire and, for the duration of the company's existence, were dependent on their hosts' concessions and tolerance. The East India Company began in the same way with four principal settlements at Madras, Surat, Calcutta and Bombay. By the second quarter of the eighteenth century, however, the decay of the Moghul Empire and the growing presence and prosperity of the British in India combined to allow the company, remarkably, to metamorphose into a powerful political and military body. This body virtually ruled India from the 1750s until 1858, the year after the Indian Mutiny when the British government formally assumed political control. This vastly higher profile enjoyed by the East India Company, together with its voluminous and meticulously maintained records, is a further reason why so much more has been written about it than about the Levant Company.

SOURCES AND PROPOSED METHODOLOGY

The primary Western sources for any study of the Levant Company are very similar to those that Wood found in the 1930s. Contemporary researchers have the obvious advantage of information technology, so their whereabouts and some time-saving guidance on their contents can more readily be ascertained, allowing for a wider field of examination. Moreover, during the seven decades since Wood was writing, growing recognition of the political and economic importance of the Middle East has given rise to much scholarly study of the region's history, and to the concomitant emergence of a vast body of relevant literature. For Ottoman historians, the Ottoman archives, held mainly in Istanbul, are now accessible to researchers, allowing contemporary writers such as Daniel Goffman and Bruce Masters to correct through their works some of the distortions and 'Orientalist' misunderstandings that resulted from the use of only Western sources.

For the purposes of this book, consideration was given in the early stages of research to utilizing the Aleppo judicial records for the eighteenth century (written in Arabic, rather than Ottoman Turkish, and now held by the National Museum of Syria in Damascus). However, the advice of custodians and Western scholars working on the records at the time was that the potential findings would not justify the year or more of residential study necessary. There were very few references to the Levant Company and to the Europeans who lived and worked in Aleppo under Ottoman rule because – under the terms of the capitulations – they were rarely obliged to submit to the Ottoman judicial system. Since most of the *dramatis personae* of this book are Englishmen and Scots who played an ancillary role in the factories, and were therefore least likely to warrant any mention in official Ottoman records, the writer has chosen to base this work only on the Western, predominantly British, sources that are the natural quarry for research material.

The surviving records of the Levant Company, which are mainly held by the Public Records Office, remain the richest source on the company. A major source consulted was John Murray's letter book, mentioned above, which covers his Levant Company business during the first three years of his tenure as ambassador at Istanbul from 1766 to 1775. Also studied were other letter books containing correspondence on both company and diplomatic issues of ambassadors at Istanbul between 1582 and 1779; various surviving minute books of the assemblies of the factories at Istanbul, Izmir and Aleppo, along with the letter books of the factors. Details of the specific records used are included in the bibliography. Other writers and researchers have no doubt also looked at some of these papers, but so great is the volume of documentation that it still produces riches, particularly when approached from a different angle and with a different purpose. Alongside official reporting, these records are peppered with references to the daily concerns of factory communities – the many pleasures, as well as the fears and sorrows – including *inter alia* recreation, social intercourse, health worries and natural calamities. These reveal the diversity, drama, humour and dangers of life in the 'English nations' and have been extracted and used in this book as valuable illustrations of how the constituent members of these communities interrelated in good times and bad.

Such private papers and contemporary biographical material as have survived (including, for purposes of comparison, earlier works such as the life by his brother of Dudley North, a merchant at Izmir and Istanbul at the end of the seventeenth century), have similarly been scrutinized for relevant information on the factory communities. Biographical information was sought on the chaplains of the eighteenth century, on their writings and on the outside interests they pursued while in the Levant. One of the aims was to ascertain what motivated them to seek appointments as clergymen to their compatriots' small and distant communities in an age before proselytizing was writ large on the Protestant agenda. For the physicians, who seem to have been mainly Scottish, sources include the Scottish university records, the various medical societies, the archives of the Wellcome Foundation, and – perhaps less obviously – the libraries of Kew and Edinburgh Botanical

Gardens, both of which received input on plants of the Levant with potential medicinal value.

One of the aspects addressed in relation to these doctors was the extent to which their purpose in working in the Levant was to further their expertise by learning from local practitioners of medicine. They would have been aware that Western medical and scientific knowledge had passed into Europe via Islamic scholars who had not only carried on the practices of the great Greek physicians but had also translated their works into Arabic, so that they passed into the West through the Muslim conquest of Spain. Finally, the writings of eighteenth-century travellers to the Levant like the explorer James Bruce and the eccentric Edward Wortley Montagu Jr, both of whose paths crossed that of John Murray in Istanbul, have been trawled for what they reveal of life at the factories.

BRITAIN'S RELATIONS WITH THE OTTOMAN EMPIRE IN THE EIGHTEENTH CENTURY

The Ottoman Empire, or Turkey as it was known to the English throughout the time of the Levant Company, was of importance to British foreign policy throughout the seventeenth century primarily, and almost exclusively, for trade. The cultural and geographical distance between London and Istanbul, and the practical difficulties of communication, made any close relationship virtually impossible. A short-sighted comment by one of Charles II's secretaries of state, who wrote that Istanbul was a place 'so remote as any intelligence from hence hither [sic] ... can be of little use here',[5] reflected the lack of political contact beyond that which the Levant Company clearly needed to pursue its mercantile interests. Even the trading relationship, substantial though it was, did less than it might have done to further cultural exchange and increase understanding, for the commercial activity was enacted virtually exclusively in the Ottoman territories. This does not reflect any lack of interest in commerce on the part of the Ottomans, but rather different attitudes towards its implementation. Although in the fifteenth century there had been Muslim merchants resident in Venice, there occurred thereafter what Masters calls 'Muslim commercial retreat' from the West, leaving trade in the hands of Christian subjects of the sultan and the shah[6] (and also, of course, Jewish subjects, although Masters does not mention them).

This is not to say that the Ottomans did not welcome trade with the northern Europeans. They needed it, not least for provisioning, and indeed they sought it out, originally as a means to reduce Venice, their rival in the Mediterranean, and they chose with care the countries to which they granted capitulations. But, perhaps through a distaste for travelling to Christian countries or a reluctance to venture with their ships out of the Mediterranean, they preferred European merchants to come to them. All Levant Company trading was done by British merchants in British ships, with parallel arrangements for the French and Dutch. Although the capitulation agreements allowed for reciprocity, no Ottoman factories were established in Britain and Muslims did not customarily travel there to do business (though occasional non-Muslim individual Ottoman subjects reached Europe, arriving in ships as sailors or slaves, and possibly as independent traders).

Bruce Masters puts this down to a lack of any state-controlled or self-imposed organization among Ottoman merchants. Whereas in countries such as Britain and the Netherlands, merchants emerged as important economic and political pressure groups, and mercantilism came close to being state doctrine, he claims that Ottoman merchants seldom acted in a unified manner, or formed any corporate body. Masters asserts that Aleppo's merchants, for example, had no guild, and anyone who had money to spare dabbled in trade, the sign of success being that a merchant no longer had to travel with the caravans, but could afford to stay at home and pay others to do it for him.[7] There was not even an

Ottoman diplomatic or other representative in London or elsewhere in Europe until the very end of the eighteenth century, perhaps because the lack of Ottoman communities there in need of protection made this unnecessary. Thus, while the European merchants based in the Levant had the undoubted advantage of a much closer acquaintance with Ottoman culture than vice versa, it was always they – as Goffman points out – who had to accommodate to the strong and self-confident Ottoman state and society.[8]

Britain's relations with the Ottomans became entwined with Anglo–Russian relations around the middle of the eighteenth century by what became known as the 'Eastern Question'. Horn shows that before then the two ran curiously parallel. Both the Ottoman Empire and Russia were seen – at least by London bureaucrats – as remote and alien realms, ruled by autocrats, which were of little interest to Britain except in terms of commercial opportunity, and where political and social conditions in both made it preferable to do business by means of the 'factory' system, through monopolistic trading companies.[9] (In the case of Russia, the Muscovy Company, a body of English merchants with a monopoly of Anglo–Russian trade, was set up in 1555, thus predating the Levant Company, which followed in 1581. It traded as a joint-stock company until 1630, then changed to operating – like the Levant Company – as a regulatory body for its members. But, it had a shorter life than the Levant Company; Tsar Alexis withdrew its privileges in 1649 and, at home, it lost its monopoly of the Russian trade in 1698.) There was effectively no political cooperation with either during the seventeenth century, and any attempt by the tsar or sultan to enter into political alliance with Britain was rejected or evaded.[10]

From the early eighteenth century, however, the Hanoverians brought Britain into a closer political and commercial alliance with Russia and, in consequence, it became embroiled in Russia's quarrels. This was to be a stormy alliance, which created for Britain a conflict of interests arising from Russia's deeply inimical relations with the Ottomans. Throughout the eighteenth century, Britain's political and commercial popularity at the Porte fluctuated in accordance with the state of Russo–Ottoman relations, with the Ottoman Empire's many European wars and with its own ever-changing relationship with other European powers, in particular with Britain's old enemy, France. Russia came to be regarded as a more promising ally for Britain than the Ottoman Empire, but a constant obstacle to political cooperation was Russia's insistence that Britain must commit to Russia's hostility towards the Ottomans. Britain had no wish to jeopardize further its Levant trade, which was already in decline, and, while a friend of Russia, had therefore to tread carefully at the Porte. Moreover, both Russia and the Ottoman Empire controlled overland routes to Persia and India, and Britain needed to keep on good terms with both.[11]

The *raisons d'être* of British ambassadors to the Porte in the eighteenth century were to maintain tolerable relations with the Ottomans so as to preserve Britain's trading foothold in the Levant, to protect the capitulations and to facilitate the practicalities of commerce. Their function was thus more consular than diplomatic, in that their dealings with the Porte related almost entirely to protecting British commercial interests. British ambassadors put much of their energy into fighting off French attempts to undermine British interests at the Porte. France had been a political ally of the Ottomans for two centuries, and into the eighteenth century, it continued to make maximum capital out of being the only European power to side with the Ottomans in the war against the Austrians, which ended with the siege of Vienna in 1683. With Britain and the Netherlands thereafter the main allies of the Ottomans' arch enemy, the Austrian emperor, and thus in the opposite camp from the Ottomans and France, France's influence at the Porte rode high, giving it both a political and commercial advantage over its traditional rivals. To the great detriment of British trade in the Levant, which competition from the East India Company also adversely affected, France retained this supremacy into the middle of the century, with its trade bolstered by government subsidies and cheaper transport costs. The French gained a further valuable advantage in 1740 when, as a reward for negotiating peace between the Ottomans and an Austro-Russian alliance, the Ottomans granted French imports exemption from the misteria duty, a privilege that was not extended to the British until 1784.[12]

British trade with the Levant suffered in the latter part of the century when the focus of diplomatic interest moved to the American colonies and naval ships were deployed there, leaving none available to escort the merchant vessels to the Levant. Political relations with the Ottomans were severely damaged in 1770 when British cooperation with the Russians helped the Baltic fleet achieve the humiliating destruction of the Ottoman fleet at the Battle of Çesme, near Izmir; it was not until four years later, when peace was declared between the Ottomans and the Russians, that there was some *rapprochement*. In the 1770s, the attempts of individual Britons (James Bruce and George Baldwin) to open up the Suez route to India further undermined British influence at the Porte. This plan flew in the face of the traditional Ottoman prohibition of navigation by Christian vessels in the Red Sea north of Mocha, as well as threatening the commercial monopoly of local Ottoman merchants. Britain's defence of Egypt against the French incursion of 1798, however, finally gave the British and the Ottomans a common interest apart from trade, and the bilateral relationship moved into the nineteenth century on a more confident note.

BACKGROUND TO THE LEVANT COMPANY

By the beginning of the eighteenth century the Levant Company was past its prime. Although still powerful and active, it had begun a decline that would see it gradually emasculated as the century progressed and finally disbanded completely in 1825. A combination of

changing trade patterns, increased competition and growing resentment among other English merchants of its monopoly of trade
with the Ottoman dominions in the Levant eventually brought the
company down, exacerbated by its own rigid conservatism and
refusal to adapt to changing circumstances.

A few individual English merchants are known to have traded
directly with what they called the Levant from as early as the
fifteenth century, pushing beyond Venice, which had long been a
great clearing house for imports from the east. These commodities
were distributed from Venice throughout Europe, and were
conveyed to England from about 1317 in a fleet of merchant
vessels dispatched annually from Southampton and known as 'the
Flanders galleys'. Early in the reign of Henry VII (1485–1509)
English vessels were making regular visits to Venetian
dependencies, including the islands of Candia (Crete)[13] and Chios,
to pick up wines.[14] Hakluyt records that by 1511 'diverse tall ships
of London ... and of Southampton and Bristow' were carrying
English cloth to Crete, Cyprus and Syria in exchange for silks,
spices, oils, carpets and mohair yarn.[15] In 1530, Henry VIII
appointed an Englishman, Dionysius Harris, to be consul for life in
Crete (where an Italian had for ten years previously looked after
English interests). Hakluyt records that several other Englishmen,
whom he names, were living in the Levant about that time.[16]

As the power of Venice waned in the following decades and
Ottoman sea power grew, English trade reduced and then virtually
ceased. The dangers of the sea journey to the eastern Mediterranean, the very real threat to the trade route from Barbary pirates
bent on plunder, and the frequent warring between Venice and the
Ottoman Empire were all discouragements. With the discovery of
an alternative route to the east around the Cape of Good Hope, the
Dutch had come to take the lead in bringing eastern commodities
to Europe. By the 1530s Antwerp had outclassed Venice as a depot
for these goods, a very convenient development for English

merchants who found it considerably cheaper to buy from the Netherlands than to mount expensive and hazardous expeditions to the Mediterranean. The last fleet of 'Flanders galleys' sailed from Southampton in 1532.[17]

It was not until the reign of Elizabeth I (1558–1603) that circumstances began to point to a resumption of trade with the Levant. Commercial disputes with the Dutch led to the severance of the comfortable trading through Antwerp, and England had to look elsewhere for goods from the east. This, along with a recognition that the Ottomans were there to stay and were possibly open to commercial cooperation led to a reconsideration of the Levant market. It also led to what Wood describes as 'the expanding and ambitious mercantile spirit of the time, eager to develop new avenues of trade and profit in any quarter of the globe, known or unknown'.[18] A small group of London merchants succeeded through William Harborne, a factor to one of them, in obtaining from Sultan Murad III a grant of 22 rather generous capitulations defining the liberties and privileges accorded to English subjects trading in Ottoman territories. Because of the difficulty of ensuring that the Ottoman authorities would actually implement and adhere to the terms of the capitulations, and to give themselves some collective protection, the merchants applied to form a company. The queen strongly supported the project and, in 1582, granted to the merchants – who were not to number more than twelve – the sole right to trade with the sultan's dominions for seven years. This newly-formed company was from the outset loosely referred to as the Levant Company, but by the eighteenth century the terms 'Turkey Company' and 'Turkey merchants' were also in common use.

The company immediately proposed to station William Harborne at Istanbul as its representative. Queen Elizabeth agreed to the appointment, although she astutely insisted that the company pay the expenses of maintaining Harborne there and, on 20 November

1582, he received a royal commission appointing him 'our true and undoubted orator, messenger, deputie and agent' at the sultan's court, and thus the first English ambassador at Istanbul. As Wood points out,[19] from its inception this post had a dual aspect in that the incumbent was both a royal representative, commissioned by the sovereign and employed in diplomatic duties, and a commercial agent, paid by a company of merchants and pledged to safeguard and promote its commercial interests. In agreeing to pay the costs of the embassy (and later also consuls' expenses) the company set a precedent that effectively obliged it to foot the entire bill for English (later British) diplomatic representation in the region until 1825. The situation thus created was to be entirely unique.

A new charter, granted in January 1592, extended the Levant Company's monopoly of trade with the Ottoman dominions for a further 12 years and granted them also the exclusive right to trade with Venice. At the same time, the company was authorized to expand to 53 merchants with the option of a further 20, and was granted full incorporation under the title of 'The Governor and Company of Merchants of the Levant'. The first governor the company elected was the London merchant Edward Osborne, one of the founding members. Although the company started life under its original charter on a joint-stock basis, by 1595 merchants were trading individually to the Levant, albeit under company regulation. The merchants did not travel to the region, but appointed factors to trade on their behalf at Istanbul, and later at the other 'factories' the company soon established in the eastern Mediterranean, of which Izmir and Aleppo emerged as the two most important. Each factory was placed under the charge of a consul, whom the company paid and whom either the company in London but more usually the ambassador appointed. A consul was answerable to the ambassador in the first instance and, like him, was not permitted to engage in trade on his own account.[20]

The factors were on the whole young single men, who served

about three years under training with the company in London, and then four years at least – and often ten or twelve – at an overseas factory, before returning to London to set up as merchants on their own account. Alternatively, they could if they wished opt to stay in post at the end of their apprenticeship and switch to trading for themselves. Apprenticeship to a company merchant did not come cheap and the high cost meant that factors were very often the sons or young relatives of company members or younger sons of the aristocracy, all of them hopeful of making their fortune in the Levant.

Under a further charter of 14 December 1605, James I granted the company – now with the expanded title of 'the Governor and Company of Merchants of England trading into the Levant Seas' – the right to enjoy its privileges in perpetuity and declared it open to 'all our loving subjects'. In the event, certain conditions of membership the company imposed, together with the great wealth required to invest in the Levant trade, kept the number of participating merchants in tens rather than hundreds. It thus became an exclusive and elitist organization, with great prestige attaching to membership.

THE COMPANY IN THE SEVENTEENTH CENTURY

Despite setbacks and disruptions too numerous for inclusion in this brief history, English trade with the Levant grew and the company prospered during the seventeenth century, reaching its peak in the 1670s when membership approached an exceptional 400. (By 1731 this had dropped back to 80 or 90.) Following the disruptive period of the Cromwell protectorate in England, when civil war shook confidence in trading speculation and the company fortunes temporarily flagged, the Restoration in 1660 re-established order in the country and provided a new charter granted in 1661, under which the company was to trade until its demise in 1825. As England settled down, the company too was reinvigorated and took steps once again to impose discipline and strict bureaucratic order in its overseas factories, which, in view of the political disruption back home, had fallen into some disarray. In 1675 the process of rehabilitation was completed when ambassador Sir John Finch negotiated favourable additions to the capitulations with Sultan Muhammad IV, which gave the English certain advantages over other European traders.[21] There was a bonus too in that a grand vizier whom the English regarded as being of unusual integrity – Ahmet Köprülü – was in power in Istanbul from 1661 to 1676.

English trade with the Levant was based overwhelmingly on the export of English woollen cloth, which was exchanged for raw silk, cotton, mohair yarn and goats' hair, all for use in the English and European textile industries, as well as spices, currants, gallnuts (used in dyeing), drugs, coffee and some silk and cotton textiles.[22]

Since the early part of the sixteenth century, competition from the East India Company in drugs and spices had been troubling the company, but by the 1660s this competition had spread to the massively more important area of silk and had begun to pose a serious threat. The Levant Company protested long and loud, taking its complaints to parliament in a battle that was to rumble on for decades, with the crown consistently favouring the East India Company. To add to the Levant Company's woes, French trade flourished again under Colbert's protectionist policies, and the Levant was his special passion. Under his patronage, the French cloth industry was revived and modernized to produce lighter and more colourful woollen fabrics, which found great favour in the Levant over the drabber, heavier English products. France also gained political favour and influence at the Porte. European wars made the shipping routes more dangerous. Then, in 1688, a great fire in Izmir destroyed valuable company assets (and killed two English merchants). In May 1693 French fleets in the Bay of Lagos destroyed a huge convoy of more than 400 vessels belonging to English and Dutch merchants and carrying cargo to the Levant worth more than £4 million sterling. Wood quotes a contemporary report of the receipt in London of news of this disaster:

> Never within the memory of man had there been in the city a day of more gloom and agitation than that on which the news of the encounter in the Bay of Lagos arrived. Many merchants went away from the royal exchange as pale as if they had received sentence of death.[23]

After this rain of blows, the company entered the eighteenth century badly bruised, although by no means mortally wounded.

THE COMPANY IN THE EIGHTEENTH CENTURY

In the early part of the eighteenth century, the Levant Company began to attract hostile criticism in England for its strict monopolistic policies from manufacturers, parliamentarians, rival merchants and even from within its own ranks. After operating for more than 100 years, its business was narrowly based on only three overseas factories, Istanbul, Izmir and Aleppo, the result of a deliberate policy to develop these centres above others to facilitate the provision of shipping and to simplify administration.

The company's monopoly covered all 'Turkish' goods sold in the English market, which was kept hungry by limiting supplies, a policy that also ensured high prices and maximum profit. With some justification, the East India Company accused its rival organization of conducting its operations entirely for the personal profit of member merchants and with no care for the needs of the English nation. Wood found evidence that the Levant Company authorities in London were indeed loath to expand beyond their familiar narrow bounds, and rejected recommendations from some of their own members and factors to do so. The company's firm grip on shipping was a major weapon in its favour. Although for most of the seventeenth century merchants were from time to time allowed to ship their goods privately at a time of their own choosing, many – often for reasons of security – chose not to do so. They preferred to use the 'general' ships the company chose and dispatched in convoy, usually once a year, at a time when the cargoes might be expected to fetch the best prices.

The latter option denied individual merchants the freedom to gamble on shipping privately to steal a march on each other in the market place, and the opportunity to ship independently was therefore highly valued in principle. There was thus much protestation when in 1718 the company passed a by-law ordering that in future all goods should be transported in the annual general ships. Some company members appealed to parliament, but to no avail for the ruling remained in force until 1744, despite continuing protest and accusations that the company was deliberately controlling the market for selfish profit and, moreover, facilitating thereby the growth of French and Dutch trade in the Levant.[24]

Further competition to the Levant Company's monopoly arose in the first decades of the eighteenth century from the increased importance of the Italian port of Livorno (Leghorn) as an entrepôt for all the European 'Turkey trade' where merchants of the large Jewish community became middle men. In 1719 the company petitioned for only 'Turkish' goods direct from the Levant to be landed in England, but got its way only in respect of silk and mohair. Although silk, predominantly from Persia, had long been the mainstay of the English trade with the Levant, the supply would very soon begin to dry up as Persia fell into decades of political disarray from 1722 and the growing areas were either destroyed or cut off from traditional export routes.[25] Around the same period, demand in England was falling for mohair yarn and for other traditional Levant commodities, including drugs and gallnuts. These developments worsened the effect of the Leghorn involvement and by 1730 the company's trade had dropped sharply. With its income plummeting, and the cost of maintaining the ambassador and the consuls still to be met, it was obliged in 1744 to raise to an all-time high the charges levied on imports and exports.

Competition from the French remained the company's biggest problem at this period. Their fabrics had gained and retained favour in the Levant over English cloths, and were cheaper because of French government subsidies. The port of Marseilles offered easier, faster and thus safer and cheaper access to the Levant ports, and they benefited also from continuing diplomatic advantage in their relations with the Porte. By 1744, they had 200 large vessels and twice as many smaller ships engaged in the Levant trade, while the English were sending no more than ten ships a year. The English trade fell victim to yet another disadvantage when in 1753 parliament passed the Quarantine Act, obliging any ship carrying cargo or passengers from an area suspected of harbouring the plague to spend time in quarantine in a Mediterranean lazaretto (quarantine station) before it could be permitted to dock at an English port. This period often lasted many months, giving advantage to less meticulous rivals such as the Dutch, who were subject to only 40 days' quarantine, loosely enforced and in a Dutch port.

In England, its critics claimed that the company's troubles were largely the result of its own greedy, narrow, monopolistic policies. There were waves of complaint in 1729 and again in 1743 from cloth manufacturers countrywide, who resented among other things that the policy of general shipping effectively limited trade to the port of London, adding greatly to their costs as well as depriving other ports of a share in the business. In 1744 a proposal to enlarge membership of the company was thrown out of parliament by a tiny margin, and it was not until 1753 – the same year as the Quarantine Act and after another surge of widespread protest – that an act was finally passed that relaxed the conditions for membership. Nonetheless, it still left all members subject to the company's by-laws and, despite the abolition of general shipping in 1744, the Levant trade remained concentrated in London.

After 1753 there was a flurry to join the company, although it also lost a few existing members who left in protest, but trade remained sluggish, and in 1767 came the humiliation of having to apply for government aid to stay afloat. A grant of £5000 was made the following year and, with one or two exceptions, this became the pattern for the next 20 years. By 1794 only five factors remained at Istanbul and six at Izmir, while the factory at Aleppo was even worse hit. When the consul there died in 1783 he was not replaced, and the posts of chaplain and treasurer were suspended; then, in 1790, the factory closed completely and remained so until 1803. By this time, Napoleon's invasion of the Ottoman province of Egypt had – arguably – launched a new age in which the relationship between the Western powers and the Ottomans would change forever. The post of ambassador at Istanbul began to be seen as crucial to British foreign policy and, in June 1804, it was taken out of company hands to become solely an instrument of government, concerned primarily with politics and diplomacy. Simultaneously the company was advised to appoint a consul-general at Istanbul to take care of its commercial interests.

Although the company was much diminished in its declining years, with the reduced trade in the hands of far fewer merchants, it still remained possible for those few to make sizeable profits. In response to the fluctuations of French trade that the revolution of 1789 and then Napoleon's incursion into Egypt had virtually ruined, its fortunes see-sawed in the early years of the nineteenth century. The huge expansion of industry in England gave the company a final period of prosperity, so that by the year of its demise, 1825, membership had grown to an unprecedented 800. The great factories did not grow again and the company was soon to pass out of existence because it had become an anachronism; the nature of diplomatic relations had changed so that it was no longer appropriate for them to be funded by a private sector commercial organization, and contemporary political thinking had come to abhor monopolies. Finally, in 1824, parliament made it clear to the company that there was no longer any justification for the retention of its monopoly of trade with the Levant. Seeing that it had no future, the company's last governor, Lord Grenville, persuaded the company to disband of its own accord and, on 19 May 1825, all of its authority passed to the crown.[26]

2

The Administrators

As we have seen above, ambassadors to Istanbul throughout the eighteenth century and for most of the seventeenth century as well, served two masters in that they were appointed by the crown and paid by the Levant Company. It had not always been so. For the first few decades after the company came into existence in 1581, its envoys to the Sublime Porte were elected from within its own ranks and were leading merchants with a background of service with the company and personal experience of trading in the Levant. An application was then made for crown endorsement, which was effectively automatic. As the reputation of the post as both powerful and highly lucrative spread, however, a rivalry developed between the crown and company over the right to appoint the incumbent. Although the charter of 1605 clearly confirmed the company's right to appoint consuls, it was ambiguous about the appointment of ambassadors. In July 1625 Charles I went into battle with the company on this issue, seeking to impose his own candidate for the post, who happened to be a courtier with no knowledge of the company or of trading. The company protested long and vehemently, but by November of the following year were obliged to surrender, and thereafter (with only two exceptions)[1] the office remained in the gift of the crown and went to men who qualified in terms of social rank or diplomatic experience rather than to seasoned merchants.[2]

COMPANY ORGANIZATION AND FINANCES

In addition to picking up all the costs of maintaining an ambassador at Istanbul, the Levant Company also paid the emoluments of consuls and other British officials, as well as of the many locally-recruited support staff of its factories throughout the region. Earlier writers, especially A. C. Wood and Sonia Anderson, have provided admirable accounts in their works of the organization and financial management of the company. These are readily accessible and it would be tedious to reiterate them in any great detail,[3] but for ease of reference in this present work, it is convenient to include here some brief explanation of how the company exercised control over, and financed, its operations both in London and overseas.

Although it was conceived of in 1581 as a joint-stock company, by 1595 it had already changed to become instead a regulatory body whose members traded independently and at their own expense on agreed common terms. This was a form it was to retain until its demise in 1825. A group of elected dignitaries and officials – some honorary and some salaried – administered the company from the City of London. Policy decisions were usually taken at plenary assemblies of company members known as 'general courts'.[4] The record books of these assemblies for the seventeenth century have survived, but sadly not those for the eighteenth century. To raise money for a central treasury, the company obliged each of the individual merchants who were its members to pay, in London, impositions on all their exports and imports. The overseas factors of these same merchants similarly paid consulage[5] on any goods that passed through their hands, this consulage being collected by the treasurer at the overseas factory in question. Money thus collected overseas was used to fund the factory payroll and for other local running costs, any surplus being remitted initially to the treasurer at Istanbul and ultimately to London.

Further income was raised overseas by charging a higher rate of 'strangers' consulage' to any foreign merchants who, being without diplomatic representation of their own in the region, sought the protection of the English authorities. Fines levied on those who broke company regulations were also a source of funding. Money also came into the treasury from new members' joining fees. This included the charges levied on apprentice factors who, having served their seven-year apprenticeship, could within one year of completion buy their 'freedom of the company' – namely the right to trade on their own account – for a fee usually set at £25. The fees paid for apprenticeships, however, were a matter for personal negotiation between a merchant and his proposed apprentice, and were retained by the merchant. Apprentices had to be recruited in England, and could not be taken on overseas.

THE SALARIED OFFICIALS

In addition to the emoluments of the ambassador, and the wages of locally-recruited servants and support staff (such as dragomans, janissaries and messengers), the company paid salaries to its principal consuls and to two other categories of British officials stationed at each of the larger factories, namely the chancellor (frequently referred to also as *cancellier*) and the treasurer. The factory chaplains, who are the subject of a later chapter, also received company salaries.

At Istanbul, despite the ambassador's burden of responsibility to both the crown and the company, there was no member of his staff bearing the title of consul or fulfilling the practical aspects of the job until 1804, when the ambassador's role was redefined and became entirely diplomatic. At the smaller factories, the post of consul was usually honorary, the incumbent being chosen by the ambassador and commonly Levantine (namely of European extraction but born in the Levant) rather than a Briton. Honorary consuls were allowed to keep a certain percentage of the consulage collected on company transactions at their posts. The appointments of consuls at the important factories of Izmir and Aleppo were, however, weightier matters and were decided by the general court of the company in London, although nominations often came from the ambassador, or from the gentlemen of the factories proposing one of their own number. Although a consul generally contracted to do the job for three to five years, he could opt to stay on beyond the expiry of this period provided he continued to give satisfaction; some, such as Anthony Hayes who was in Izmir from 1762 until his death there in 1794, held their posts for decades. The position of consul, particularly at one of the larger outposts, was a prestigious one, carrying with it both practical and representational responsibilities. The consuls were charged primarily with maintaining order in the factories, implementing company instructions and regulations, and protecting British interests; but they were also the social and ceremonial heads of the factory communities, and their appointments were formalized by exequaturs, or *berats*,[6] issued by the ambassador and endorsed by the Porte. All consuls operated under the supervision of the ambassador, and in consultation with him, and reported to him in the first instance rather than directly to either company or government in London.

The general court of the company appointed chancellors too, often in consultation with the ambassador or the relevant consul, and they held their posts for as long as they gave satisfaction. The role of chancellor combined those of a notary and an archivist. The chancellor witnessed and registered all the official company business of his factory, including trading contracts and shipping records; prepared and preserved reports of assemblies; kept custody of 'Order Books' containing instructions and regulations received from London; administered oaths; prepared inventories and received wills. The post of chancellor at Istanbul was a particularly important one because the incumbent acted also as secretary to the embassy and deputy to the ambassador. He could be called upon to act as chargé d'affaires in the absence or illness of the latter,[7] but not in all cases.

Sir Everard Fawkener's chancellor-cum-secretary, Stanhope Aspinwall, acted as chargé for more than four years until the arrival of Fawkener's successor in 1747. In 1765, however, William Kinloch, the consul at Aleppo, became chargé at Istanbul for nine months, which was a rather odd choice given that Kinloch's future with the company was at the time in doubt and he was on his way to England to give an account of himself. Further, in May 1775, when ambassador John Murray left for England, Anthony Hayes, consul at Izmir, was appointed as chargé and held the post until October of the following year. In this last case, it is on record that Murray asked for Hayes, whom he held in high regard, to deputize.[8] Some years previously, Murray had demanded the recall of his chancellor, a Mr Lone whom he much despised, and he perhaps retained some prejudice against later holders of the office. Wood found that, because of the potential for a chancellor to act as ambassador, also taking on responsibility for state affairs, in the seventeenth century two ambassadors suggested that the post should carry a royal commission, but this was never implemented.[9]

The post of treasurer too was filled by the general court of the Levant Company. From 1658, candidates had to have completed a full seven-year apprenticeship to a company merchant and to have already served five years at the factory of their desired appointment. As for chancellors, the appointment lasted as long as service was found satisfactory. The treasurer kept the factory's accounts and handled all financial matters relating to company business; it was up to him to calculate expenses and liabilities and to ensure that funds were available to meet them. He paid the salaries of local employees, dealt with the outgoings necessary to fund bribes or meet extortion demands, and paid bills for the factory's ordinary running costs. To fund all this, he relied on dues such as consulage and, when any shortfall in income or extraordinary expenditure arose, he turned to the factors for loans.

The treasurer could, with the ambassador's or consul's

authority, call an assembly for the purposes of raising funds on negotiated terms. The treasurer submitted his accounts, together with any surplus funds, at regular intervals through Istanbul to London. He was expected to make up his books every three to six months; they were then audited by four people chosen at an assembly of the factory, one of whom had to have been a factor there for at least five years. The company in London checked them again, while reserving the right to reject any charges it considered inappropriate. In February 1642 a payment for removal expenses to a Mr Durant, whom the ambassador had ordered to remove himself from Istanbul to Izmir 'for the peace of the factory', was summarily reduced from $430[10] to $200. That same month the company also refused to accept a charge of $1400 for building a chapel at Istanbul on the grounds that it had not commissioned such work or even been informed of it.[11]

The company's reliance on raising funds from the gentlemen of the factory to tide it over until money could be remitted from London was awkward, depending as it did on goodwill. The factors could not be coerced into lending and were not always ready to oblige. In addition, the sums involved were not insignificant. In September 1768 the ambassador wrote to the company welcoming a remittance he had received from London because it would 'greatly ease your debt, as ... by this means, it will be reduced to 40,000 dollars'.[12] Six months later, when the Istanbul treasurer was obliged to call two assemblies to raise yet more funds, on each occasion only two people turned up besides himself, and an exasperated Murray was moved to complain bitterly to London of the factors' impertinence.[13] But, in fairness to them, circumstances at the time were such that the factors were perhaps exhibiting sensible financial judgement rather than impertinence. The company clearly already owed them a great deal of money. Murray on his arrival in 1766 had found the embassy accounts in great disorder, with irregularities going back many years;[14] trade was in the doldrums, and in 1767 the company had for the first time become dependent on an annual government subsidy in order to make ends meet.

EMOLUMENTS

The salaries paid to the ambassador and his consuls, chancellors and treasurers are interesting because none of them was permitted to trade while in office, yet, despite the emoluments appearing in some cases to have been modest, the jobs were much sought after and many a fortune was made. Incumbents were required to deposit substantial sureties[15] in London and to take appropriate oaths of loyalty that they would conduct themselves with integrity. Nonetheless, perquisites clearly bolstered official income, as did ways of making money that did not overtly contravene the ban on trading. Although the company's general court records have not survived beyond 1706, later correspondence to and from the factories indicates that salaries remained virtually unchanged from then until the end of the eighteenth century, when they had to be raised to reflect the greatly increased cost of living in the Levant.

Comparisons are problematic because of the range of different currencies cited in references to salaries and other financial transactions during the period of the company's existence. Davis points out in his work on the merchants trading at Aleppo that exchange rates were arbitrary and of limited importance because few commercial transactions were done in cash.[16] They mattered only when money was being transferred to or from England, usually done by Bills of Exchange or through the factory accounts. For the purposes of this book, we need only know the approximate value in sterling of amounts quoted in the sources in other currencies; these are most commonly in dollars, which exchanged at around four to the pound sterling in the seventeenth century, and between five and eight in the eighteenth century, depending on the purity of their metal content.[17]

From 1616 ambassadors were forbidden to trade, and in 1637 the salary set for Sir Sackville Crowe was 5000 chequins[18] (about £2500) per annum, payable half yearly in advance, plus payment on appointment of a £600 allowance towards outfitting and travel expenses. From 1660 to 1681, ambassadors were paid a salary of 10,000 Spanish dollars or 'pieces of eight', plus an annual gratuity of $2000. It was then reduced to 8000 Spanish dollars, plus the gratuity of $2000, for Lord Chandos (in post 1681–87). In 1698 the £600 outfitting and travel allowance, which had become the norm, was discontinued and salaries were thereafter paid in less valuable Dutch lion dollars, a move by the company that ambassador Sir Robert Sutton (in post 1702–17) protested reduced his salary by one-third. By 1745, Sir Everard Fawkener was complaining that his salary – ostensibly the same as that paid 100 years previously – had been reduced in real value from £2400 to £1856.[19] John Murray received a lump sum of £500 on his arrival in 1766, and was also granted a daily allowance of £3 (perhaps as a cost of-living supplement to his basic salary) and an unspecified amount of money to cover official entertaining, both of which were to be paid to him quarterly.[20] Moreover, the Ottomans, who traditionally regarded all foreign ambassadors to the Porte as guests of the sultan, accorded each a daily living allowance.[21]

When John Murray took up his post in 1766, the Levant Company was in deep financial difficulty following many years of sluggish trade, and within a year had to be subsidised annually by the government in order to survive. By this time, too, living costs in the Levant were rising steeply and the English public image in Istanbul had become a little down at heel. Murray's immediate predecessor, Henry Grenville (in post 1762–65), had complained to the British government soon after his arrival that he was the poor relation among foreign residents,[22] and four years later Murray found little improvement. He found that the ambassador's residence at Pera – known as the 'British Palace' – was shamefully shabby and in great need of repair.[23] Also, the dragomans the embassy employed were underpaid compared with those of other Western nations and in relation to 'the great increase in the prices of all necessaries.'[24] Murray's official correspondence to the Levant Company contains many references to his personal problems in making ends meet, although written in rather muted terms and implying sorrow rather than anger. The issue was no doubt a sensitive one, not for the eyes of his secretaries, and therefore dealt with in private letters, for he did squeeze the occasional *ad hoc* subsidy out of the company and even on at least one occasion, in 1772, out of his political masters in London.[25] No permanent increase was agreed, however, until Robert Liston took over as ambassador in 1795; by which time inflation had reduced the value of the salary to just £1000 per annum and Liston was allowed a further annual payment of £1000.[26]

In matters of official expenditure, Murray shows considerable sympathy and consideration for the company's predicament, fretting when he has to inform 'their Worships' that some heavy cost must be incurred, especially when that related to his diplomatic responsibilities rather than to purely company business. The closing months of 1768, when the Ottomans had just embarked on war with Russia, provided examples of the latter. The grand vizier would shortly be marching with the armies to Edirne (Adrianople) to set up camp there, and the Porte expected each foreign minister to station a dragoman there, perhaps for many months. This entailed great expense, for the man – as the ambassador's representative – had to be splendidly equipped with horses, tents and fine clothing, and given servants and janissaries to attend to and protect him. In the event that Murray should have to go there himself, he too would need fine trappings if the English nation were not to be shamed and, although suitable items such as tents and saddles were on the embassy inventory, they had vanished in the confusion of the recently sacked Chancellor Lone's incompetence.[27]

Despite such problems, Murray reveals fortitude alongside a certain weariness when he writes, to his consul Hayes at Izmir:

I flatter myself we shall see this drooping Trade hold up its Head, before I quit the Levant, which must be in a few years, for an honest man can scarce bring both Ends to meet in this Country, and a Beefsteak by my own Fireside in my own [country], I prefer to all Ministerial Honours.[28]

At this point Murray had been out of England for a continuous period of 14 years, but his moments of homesickness did not lead him to demand withdrawal from Istanbul and his proclaimed shortage of money did not bring him to bankruptcy. Clearly, the job had professional, social and financial compensations. In respect of the latter, Murray, like others before and after him, no doubt found ways of augmenting his salary. The earliest ambassadors, who were company men, had been allowed to trade and to take a percentage of the consulage on company trade. Although these privileges had been removed by the mid-seventeenth century when the crown started to appoint ambassadors, there were still rich pickings to be had from the strangers' consulage collected from foreigners shipping their goods on English vessels or sailing under the English 'flag of convenience'. The company ban on trading, moreover, could be interpreted rather loosely as relating only to company business, leaving a financially embarrassed ambassador plenty of scope for dabbling in private enterprise. There were opportunities, too, for currency speculation and for abusing diplomatic privilege by selling goods (especially alcohol) imported free of duty. Moreover, we read much in the company records about the expensive gifts it was obliged to present to the Porte, through the ambassador, to mark special occasions. These included English pistols, silver bridles and fine clocks, but there is little mention of the many fine

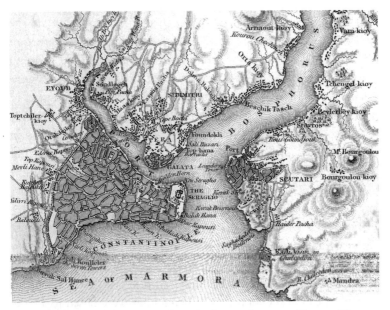

1. Map of the Golden Horn in the early nineteenth century. Thomas Allom,
Constantinople and the Scenery of the Seven Churches of Asia, 1839 (Edinburgh
University Library Special Collections Department S.16/1/64/1).

gifts such as horses and sable furs that the ambassadors and
consuls routinely received in return, and which, in all likelihood,
the recipients retained for their personal use.

A common source of additional income for ambassadors right
up until the end of the eighteenth century was selling *berat*s, or
patents, to Ottoman subjects in the employ of the company, such
as dragomans. A *berat* was much coveted, for it conferred on the
holder valuable exemptions from local taxes and dues; those
holding *berat*s therefore tended to work until they dropped and also
tried frantically to ensure that the *berat* would pass to a relative.
*Berat*s for the entire region where the company operated were in the
gift of the ambassador at Istanbul, who was entitled to charge a fee
for them. Murray decided soon after his arrival to charge a fixed
rate of 2600 piastres (around £330), although he had heard that his

predecessors had charged 3500.[29] In theory, the Porte limited the number of berat-bearing appointments permitted to any foreign embassy, so a new berat could be issued only if an existing appointment fell vacant. But this was hard to police and berats were much sought after, so less scrupulous ambassadors, if tempted to raise funds by exceeding the limit permitted or charging excessive amounts, could do so with impunity. Wood records that when Liston became ambassador in 1794, he reported that his pre-decessors had earned between £2000 and £3000 each year from the sale of berats. The system was eventually pulled into order in 1809 under the Treaty of the Dardanelles.[30]

The company's two most senior consuls, at Izmir and Aleppo, were each paid $2000 a year, plus an annual gratuity of a further $1000. These amounts were set in 1649 and remained unchanged until the last few years of the eighteenth century, when, due to steep increases in the local cost of living, they were raised to $4500. The salary of the chancellors at Izmir and Aleppo were – in 1746 – $400 and $200 respectively. The chancellor at Istanbul, who doubled as secretary to the ambassador, was rather better paid, receiving $600 in 1673 and $800 by 1790. For the treasurers of all three posts, the salary paid from 1699 until 1790 remained unchanged at $400.[31] As will be discussed in Chapter 5 below, these relatively modest rewards did not deter individuals from remaining in their posts for long periods, even decades.

ORDER AND DISCIPLINE

The dual nature of the ambassador's responsibilities have already been highlighted. As we have seen, the Levant Company paid him and he was required to support and promote company commercial interests, not just in Istanbul but also throughout the Ottoman dominions. He was in overall charge of other factories in the region and responsible for overseeing – and in some cases appointing – other consuls and officials. As well as being the centre of Ottoman power, Istanbul was also the seat of British power in the region. Remoteness from Istanbul and the slowness of communication inevitably diffused ambassadorial control over the provincial factories[32] – distant Aleppo in particular – but in Istanbul he was required to manage and directly discipline the resident community, albeit without having much in the way of enforcible authority over the great majority of its constituents.

These 'English nations' consisted of an assortment of people gathered together at a distant and foreign location for a variety of purposes, with dissimilar conditions of service and without any real motor for cohesion save the need of a minority group to stick together for its own protection. They had no common paymaster. The ambassador and his appointed consuls were charged with keeping order in the factories; this could prove an unenviable task, for, although they had the formal right under company regulations to impose discipline, it was often a problem to enforce it, especially in the case of the young factors who formed the overwhelming majority in each community. As we have seen, the factors were individuals, each employed by a merchant master in London.

There was no all-encompassing Levant Company hierarchy or internal career structure, applying to officials and merchants alike, as existed in the rival East India Company. At an East India Company factory the governor in charge was almost invariably the oldest and longest-serving of the traders there, a man who had attained seniority over his colleagues by working his way up through the ranks. Immediately below him were a few senior merchants, appointed councillors, who – together with the governor, whose power was restricted to a casting vote – formed the ruling body of the settlement. Each of these men had gained his promotions from the directors of the company and had risen through the grades of writer, factor, junior and senior merchant to achieve a seat on the council. They shared the same employer as the junior traders under their command and the same single-minded preoccupation with commerce; even the governor in the eighteenth century was actively engaged in trade, preparing cargoes for shipment and receiving goods from Europe. Despite the advantage that the governor and councillors had in coming from the same stable as their juniors and thus in theory having direct authority over them, they still had problems keeping order among the wilful young company men of the factories, which the presence of young British soldiers and a sprinkling of free merchants exacerbated.[33]

The position of the Levant Company ambassador at Istanbul (and of his provincial consuls) was more difficult than that of his opposite numbers in the East India Company. While he could pull rank on his officials and demand their obedience, he did not have the personal power to hire and fire the Levant Company's independent factors, to censure the unruly by demotion, or to offer advancement as a reward. He did, however, have authority to suspend or blacklist a merchant who offended.[34]

The ambassador, with the help of his consuls and other company officials, was also expected to enforce the regulations and instructions the company laid down, but factors were young and wilful and resentful of authority. Discipline therefore depended largely on an ambassador or consul's ability to win the personal loyalty and respect of the individual factors in his charge; notwithstanding the prestige of his official position, he could not easily command it. For the discussion of important matters of general concern to a factory, plenary meetings or 'assemblies' of the traders were called, but again an ambassador or consul could not enforce attendance at these. The young factors went along only if they were so inclined, which, as we have seen above, could leave officials in an embarrassing position, if the purpose of the assembly were – as was often the case – to request loans to meet company expenses.

Control over the chaplains should in theory have been easier given that they were salaried employees of the company, recruited in London and appointed to a specific factory. But this too caused problems since, under the terms of his contract, a chaplain had to be provided with board and lodging in the residence of his ambassador or consul, and this situation understandably gave rise to friction from time to time. In 1664 the company rescinded the right of an ambassador to sanction the sending home of any disturber of the peace after the Reverend John Broadgate – 'a fiery haire-brained zealot' – was sent packing by Ambassador Heneage Finch and his consul at Izmir, William Cave. More than a century later, John Murray, arriving to take up his post as ambassador, found that he had inherited not only a disreputable chaplain, but also a 'back-biting old Curr' of a doctor, as sitting tenants in his residence in Istanbul.[35]

TRAVELLERS, HOUSEGUESTS AND HANGERS-ON

One hazard of the ambassador's job was that he suffered from having his residence regarded by British visitors passing through – official and otherwise – as a hotel in which they had a natural entitlement to be accommodated, sometimes for periods of many months. One such traveller, the prison reformer John Howard – albeit writing in the early nineteenth century – actually refers to the 'hotels' of the British ambassadors on whom he descended.[36] Privacy was thus hard to come by and, for the representational aspects of the job at least, there was no clear definition between working hours and off-duty periods.

For example, when John Murray arrived at Istanbul in June 1766, he found his house there anything but a haven of peace from the rigours of the job. Not only did he inherit as co-habitants the factory chaplain, the doctor and the chancellor, but he also found installed there William Kinloch, who had been consul at Aleppo from 1759. Kinloch had been acting as chargé d'affaires at Istanbul since the departure of Murray's predecessor Grenville in October 1765 and, although a company official with some right to be accommodated, might have been expected to effect a polite and prompt withdrawal from the house and the city on Murray's arrival.

However, he showed himself to be in no hurry to do so and proceeded to enjoy a lengthy holiday there, while continuing to stay at the ambassador's residence.

Uncertainty about his future can partially explain Kinloch's reluctance to move on. It is evident from Murray's letters that correspondence about this was underway between Kinloch and the company, which culminated in his receiving notification of his dismissal from his post at Aleppo for misconduct, including sending the company an offensive letter.[37] Nonetheless, his cavalier exploitation of Murray's hospitality must have been hard to bear. Kinloch was still in Istanbul at the end of October 1767 lodging with Murray. In a letter of 1 October to the company, Murray tells them:

> Mr Kinloch's behaviour cannot be more extraordinary to you, than it is ridiculous to me. He spends his time chiefly in the Country, and comes and goes to and from my House as if it were his Inn; however I shall have sufferance with him as long as he is my Guest.

Writing to the new consul at Aleppo on 28 October, having by then been obliged to tolerate more than four months of Kinloch's unwanted presence, Murray reports: 'Mr Kinloch still has his apartment in my House, where he comes and goes at his Pleasure, but he spends most of his time with the foreign Ministers as he thinks every one of them of consequence but his own.'[38]

The second half of the eighteenth century was the era of the grand tour and Murray would have had plentiful experience during his time in Venice of 'gentlemen travellers' who had come to regard the tour as an essential part of their education. Among those he encountered there was Robert Wood, who as a tutor accompanied the Duke of Bridgewater and who was later to become famous for his works on the ruins of Palmyra and Baalbek. Murray seems to have been less than sympathetic to adventurers. When in 1767

44

James Bruce was pressing him for help to obtain various permits from the Porte to travel in Syria, he was moved to comment tetchily to his consul in Izmir: 'What Scheme he [Bruce] can have in going to Palmyra, I can't conceive, as Mr Dawkins and Mr Wood have given so satisfactory an account of it.'[39]

Bruce's approaches to Murray, who knew Bruce only by name as a former consul in Algiers, were legitimate and not unreasonable, and he would have known that the process of obtaining such permits could be slow and tedious. He may not, however, have been aware that complying with his demands would be made doubly difficult for Murray by the fact that all the senior Ottoman officials who had to sign the required permits had decamped to Moldavia with the sultan and his armies. Although Murray had stationed one of his own dragomans at the camp, the practical difficulties of communicating with him, and of his getting the attention of any Ottoman official in time of war, were immense, and greater, perhaps, than Bruce realized.

But travel beyond the European heartlands was relatively rare before the Napoleonic wars; only intrepid explorers and adventurers such as Wood and Bruce, and the occasional eccentric, ventured into the Ottoman territories. A notable example of the latter category was Lady Mary Wortley Montagu's remarkable son, Edward Jr. Most famous because, as a child at his father's embassy in Istanbul he was given a ground-breaking inoculation against smallpox,[40] Edward grew up a rebel and a source of bewilderment, embarrassment and disappointment to his parents. Horace Walpole observed of him that his mental parts 'were not proportional, his characteristics ranging from linguistic brilliance to profligate squalor'.[41] No doubt influenced by his childhood experiences and by his parents' enthusiasm for foreign travel and for 'Turkish' culture, Edward was a restless spirit who drifted for decades around Europe and the Levant. In this respect, he conformed to the pattern of many children of officials and merchants of the

Levant Company who inherited and carried forward their parents' attachment to the region.[42]

But Edward Wortley Montagu was an example of an apple that fell rather further from the tree than most. Leaving behind in England his first two wives (the second of whom he had married bigamously) and two sons, he set off in 1761 on years of travel that would eventually take him to the residence of John Murray in Istanbul, the very house in which he had lived as a child. By the following year he was in Leyden, reportedly studying Arabic, and wearing a turban and long beard. Sometime in 1762 he reached Alexandria where he married a third wife, Catherine Dormer (Mrs Feroe). He arrived in Venice in September 1765, where he became one of the sights of the city: 'his beard touched down to his breast, being of two and a half years' growth, and the dress of his head was Armenian.'[43] By this time Edward's mother had already been back in England for four years, but Murray was still in Venice as Resident and the two must have been known to each other there.

Murray's correspondence reveals that Edward Wortley Montagu subsequently turned up in Istanbul where he resided in Murray's house as his guest for a period of seven months from September 1767 to April 1768. This can hardly have been very welcome to Murray, who would have been unable to refuse hospitality to the son of one of his predecessors, no matter how bizarre his appearance and behaviour. It was no doubt with some relief that he waved him off to the Dardanelles in mid-April. There are indications that he had irritated Murray. Edward Jr had shown himself to be, in Murray's view, strangely unenterprising for such a restless spirit. In a letter to Hayes, his consul at Izmir (in whose patch Edward lingered for many months more, although it is unclear whether or not he was a guest of the consul), Murray says:

As to his ramblings abroad, you may be assured he will never stir out of his House, wherever he takes up his Abode. He was seven months here, and had he not been dragged out by some noble Venetians, he would never have seen Constantinople. He is so void of Curiosity, that he never once saw the Canal to Bujukdere, which is undoubtedly the most worthy of being seen.

As a further irritant, Murray, writing again on 27 June to Hayes, reveals that he had still had no letter of thanks from Edward, although others in the capital had heard from him. It was clear that, although Murray considered he and Edward had parted friends, Edward was in fact angry with the ambassador, who must have commented adversely on Edward's rather loose marital arrangements. Murray confided to Hayes:

I imagine he is unwilling to let me know that he is going to meet his Fair one, as he has denied it to me, though I was pretty sure it was his Intention, he having bought an infinite number of Women's Baubles. He was angry at me for not calling her his wife.

It would seem that in Venice Edward had asked Murray to effect divorces from earlier wives so that the marriage to 'his Fair one', presumably the lady he had acquired in Alexandria, might be deemed legal.[44]

Edward Wortley Montagu eventually left the Dardanelles for Scio in September 1768, having at last written an apologetic letter to Murray that explained how offended he had been.[45] By the end of the year, the two are once again in correspondence, when Edward is back in Izmir and in need of a permit from the Porte to return to Egypt. He is at this stage accompanied by his 'wife', and Murray comments that 'Mr Montagu must be happy to be in possession of a Treasure that has cost him so much Toil and Trouble.' Later letters from Murray to Hayes reveal intriguing glimpses into the relationship between Edward and the 'treasure', and make the non-availability of Hayes's replies the more regrettable. Hearing that Edward was planning to leave Izmir in February 1769, Murray – clearly enjoying a bit of gossip – tells Hayes: 'I do not wonder at his locking up his wife *à la Turque*; my surprise is that she submits to it.' By April 1769, Edward had clearly achieved some kind of divorce from his previous wives, for Murray writes further to Hayes that:

> I am very glad to hear Mr Montagu's lady is with child, if it gives him pleasure; but I greatly fear that he has omitted very many material circumstances to entitle the child to so large a Share of his Father's Estate, for should the divorce be deemed a legal one, I apprehend he should have undergone the ceremony of another Marriage, after the Divorce was obtained, and I heartily pity every Child that has a Law Suit entailed upon him.

By May 1769, Edward has taken a house in Izmir, perhaps awaiting the birth of the expected child. Murray writes approvingly of this, saying 'I am persuaded he has found an agreeable Society, which is much more pleasing at his and my Time of Life, than wandering in the Deserts of Arabia.'[46]

There are no later letters from Murray that mention Edward Wortley Montagu. We know that he passed his final years from 1773 in Italy, having at some stage spent a period in quarantine in Zante.[47] Howard records in his report on the Zante lazaretto that:

> Here the late Mr Montagu performed his quarantine; after which he resided for some time in the convent of the friars. But there being an earthquake while he was there he afterwards lived in a tent in the garden of these friars, and would never enter a house on the island.[48]

Edward Wortley Montagu, the son of one of the Levant Company's ambassadors to Istanbul, a great nuisance to a later incumbent of the post, and himself a colourful part of the company's social history, died in Padua in 1776, aged about 60.

AMBASSADOR JOHN MURRAY

That Murray was an engaging and colourful character is clear from the correspondence in his surviving letter book and from the personal descriptions of him that have come to light in the course of my research for this book. His letters on company issues are written in a robust and direct style, which is very different from the one he used in his official dispatches on government business to the secretary of state. His company correspondence gives a much more vivid and rounded picture of the role of an ambassador to the sultan's court than is routinely illustrated by his political reporting, encompassing as it does the wide range of more personal difficulties and frustrations that preoccupied Murray alongside his official duties and responsibilities. His more open and informal communications to the company and to the officials at the other factories within his massive parish contain asides that portray with great colour and much humour the harassments of his daily life. These include the medical problems, domestic squabbles, physical dangers, humiliations, financial difficulties and tedious visitors that were all part and parcel of his job as envoy to Istanbul.

Nothing has hitherto been written of this man, John Murray, who held the very senior diplomatic appointment of British ambassador to the Ottoman Empire for nine years at a time when bilateral relations were tense and the Levant trade was in deep difficulty. There is no record of his background, performance in the job, reputation with his employers, or explanation of why the British government failed to honour him in any way, as it did so many other incumbents of the prestigious Istanbul post. It is therefore relevant to this book, with its focus on those who resided at the Levant factories in support of the company's commercial purpose, to include here the results of research into the background and career of a man who occupied the highest position in the hierarchy from 1766 until his death nine years later.

Murray's letters reveal a man of considerable personality; he was outspoken and irascible, impatient of fools but supportive of loyal employees, a strong, sensible and conscientious man striving hard in difficult circumstances to control his widespread parish and massive workload. He arrived in Istanbul to take up his new post with 12 years' experience of diplomacy gained as British Resident in Venice. With no previous direct involvement in Levant Company business, however, he took every opportunity in his earliest letters to his new paymasters to court their confidence, and wrote with rather untypical self-righteousness of his determination to battle constantly on the company's behalf against extortion and corruption. He sent frequent verbose and rather pompous reminders of his own good character to his wide network of consuls also, and was fierce as he worked to establish his authority over them and win the confidence of the company in London. Sycophancy was not his style and from the outset Murray, who was thoroughly articulate and had a fine line in sarcasm, wrote openly and naturally, so his letters remain fresh and lively more than two centuries later.

It seems unlikely that Murray was known personally at the headquarters of the Levant Company, for he went to take up his appointment at Istanbul in 1766 directly from Venice, where he had served as the crown's representative for the previous 12 years. He could be said to have thus been a genuine career diplomat. Commenting on Murray's appointment, his old friend and colleague Horace Mann, who was the British crown's representative in Florence from 1740 until his death there in 1782, observed: 'I most surely do not envy him, but in the eyes of the diplomatic world this is a vast stride above Resident.'[49] Murray did not want the job. In a grumpy letter to his consul at Aleppo in September 1767 he con-

2. John Murray, attributed to Benjamin West, Venice, 1763. Courtesy of
Manx National Heritage.

fessed that he went to Istanbul 'much against my Inclination,
having refused the Embassy in repeated Letters'.[50]

After 12 years spent in a declining Venice, Murray could hardly
have been seen as one of England's top diplomats. Professor Horn
observed that British diplomats and consuls at Venice in the second
half of the eighteenth century had ceased to play a political role and

busied themselves with collecting pictures and books, and smuggling antiques out of Italy in the diplomatic bag.[51] It is interesting therefore to speculate why this apparently grand assignment was unappealing to him and indeed why it was offered to him. Murray could well have found it unattractive for purely personal reasons, perhaps because his wife would not or could not accompany him, or simply because he was happy in Venice. But it seems possible that the Istanbul job, at that time when Britain's interest in the Ottoman territories had gone off the boil in favour of Russia, was regarded as a thankless task in a distant outpost and was therefore difficult to fill.

Before the creation of the Foreign Office in 1782, great nobles filled diplomatic posts and British diplomatic representation overseas was limited to the countries of Europe. The ambassadorship at Istanbul, paid for as we have seen by the Levant Company, was an anomaly. Horn states that Palmerston's acid nineteenth-century comment that 'no climate agrees with an English diplomat, excepting that of Paris, Florence or Naples,' might equally have applied to the eighteenth century.[52] Whatever the thinking behind Murray's appointment, it is worth noting that the French at the time fielded a man of much higher standing as their ambassador to the Porte. This was Charles Gravier, Comte de Vergennes, who served there from 1754 to 1768, and went on to replace the Duc d'Aiguillon as France's foreign minister in 1774 on the accession of Louis XVI. In 1769, the equally prestigious Comte de Saint Priest replaced Vergennes at Istanbul and held the post until 1785.

Not a great deal is known about Murray. No biography of him has come to light; he gets no mention in the standard dictionaries of biography and he left no memoirs, perhaps because he died on his way from Istanbul to England in 1775 at the fairly early age of 61. A clearer view of his background is, however, necessary if one is to measure his achievements and establish the extent to which the decline of the Levant Company, and Britain's troubled relations with the Ottomans during his time in Istanbul, may have combined to cast a shadow over his personal standing with his masters.

Most recently, Murray gets a mention in a dictionary of British and Irish travellers in Italy.[53] The scant information it provides on his background includes an indication that social connections were certainly instrumental in his being awarded the post at Istanbul. Murray, who was born in 1714, married in 1748 Bridget Milbanke, the widow of Sir Butler Cavendish Wentworth, and in his letters refers to her always as Lady Wentworth. She was the only daughter of Sir Ralph Milbanke, 4th Baronet of Halnaby Hall in North Yorkshire, and his first wife, Elizabeth Darcy, the eldest sister of Robert, 3rd Earl of Holderness. Bridget was thus a first cousin of the 4th Earl of Holderness (Robert Darcy, 1718–78) who became Murray's patron. Her first husband, to whom she was married from 1731 until his death without issue in 1741, held the baronetcy of Howsham, also in North Yorkshire.[54] Bridget's cousin, the 4th Earl, Lord Holderness, was sent to Venice with the title of British Ambassador Extraordinary on 17 October 1744 and served there until 23 August 1746.

Since 1736 there had been no British Resident in Venice following the republic's reception of the Young Pretender. Holderness's appointment, and that of Joseph Smith as British consul there the same year, marked the resumption of full diplomatic relations. When Holderness left Venice, his secretary Sir James Gray stayed on as Resident. It would seem certain that Holderness, who from 1751 held the powerful post of Secretary of State for the Northern Department (in other words he was one of two secretaries of state sharing direct responsibility for foreign affairs), later influenced the appointment of his cousin's second husband, Murray, to the post in 1754 replacing Gray. Murray effectively admits as much in a letter to Holderness from Venice in October 1756, writing 'In short, my Lord, you have put us into so good a pasture that if we don't change the soil we shall all burst.'[55]

Murray's position as Resident did not equate to an ambassadorship. In the eighteenth century an ambassador was often an
envoy sent overseas to accomplish a specific task, but whose
mission could last months and even years because of the slowness
of doing business and of communications. Residents or consuls
provided a permanent presence. Thus, Holderness re-established
relations with the Venetian republic and returned to England, his
mission completed. Another clear example of this was the appointment of Charles Compton, 7th Earl of Northampton, as
ambassador extraordinary to Venice in 1762, during Murray's time
there as Resident. Northampton, aged just 25, was sent to recipro-
cate the dispatch of a Venetian embassy to London to congratulate
George III on his recent accession. His story is a tragic one, for
both he and his young wife, Lady Anne Somerset, became ill from
their travels and died, she in Naples in May 1763 and he in Lyons in
December that year while on his way back to England, leaving their
three year-old daughter Elizabeth an orphan.[56]

John Murray's wife, Bridget, accompanied him to Venice, where
they arrived on 9 October 1754, together with his unmarried sister
Elizabeth. The three seem to have settled happily there; in October
1756 Murray writes contentedly to Holderness 'my wife laughs and
grows fat, my sister the same.'

Within a year of that, Murray had married his sister to the
elderly British consul, Joseph Smith. Smith, who had moved to
Venice in 1692 at the age of 18 and been consul there since 1744,
was 83 years old at the time of the marriage, and had lost his first
wife, an opera singer named Catherine Tofts, two years previously
after nearly forty years of marriage. He had long been an
enthusiastic patron of the arts (and particularly of contemporary
artists, including Canaletto) and had accumulated a magnificent
private collection of books, paintings, sculptures, medals and
cameos. It was rumoured at the time that Murray had induced his
sister to marry Smith to get his hands on this collection.

3. Elizabeth Murray (Mrs Joseph Smith), attributed to Benjamin West, Venice 1763. Courtesy of Manx National Heritage.

If this were indeed the case, there is no record that he was successful, for many of Smith's treasures were purchased from him in the early 1760s by George III (who reigned from 1760 to 1820) and passed into the Royal Collection. The Consul Smith Collection (which includes 40 works by Canaletto, a wide representation of paintings by Venetian artists and a Vermeer) remains in royal ownership and is of great interest to contemporary art historians; it was the subject of a special exhibition at the Queen's Gallery in London in 1993.

Smith was still alive and tolerably well, though aged 91, when Boswell called on him at his 'elegant villa' in Venice on 14 July 1765 and was introduced to 'the curious old man'.[57] Smith died there in 1770. His wife Elizabeth had nursed him during his final years, aided by her niece, Catherine Murray, daughter of her brother, Thomas, a clergyman in London. Elizabeth Smith stayed on in Venice after her husband's death. She sold his *palazzo* in 1775 and for several years up until 1777 there are records of her selling items from his collection. In 1778 she returned to England with her niece and by 1789 she is known to have died. It is clear, however, that she was still in Venice when her brother, John Murray, suffered his terminal illness and died there in 1775 while on a journey to England from Istanbul.[58]

Very little is known about Murray's life prior to his marriage in 1748, by which time he was apparently settled in York. Such information as has been discovered in the course of research for this book is included as an indication of the man's background and consequent social standing in an era when advancement depended largely on one's connections. He was born in 1714 at Douglas in the Isle of Man to John Murrey (*sic*) and Susannah Patten and was the eldest of their eight children – four sons and four daughters. He was baptised at St Matthew's church there.[59] As one would expect given his later advancement, his family were comfortably situated, with land and property both on the Isle of Man and in Cheshire. His paternal grandfather, also John Murrey, a merchant, achieved fame as the issuer of the first Manx coinage, known as 'Murrey's Pence'. Ambassador Murray's father (1671– 41) was also a successful merchant who traded with the West Indies; he lived in a house called Murrey's Court in Douglas, and in 1721 bought the substantial estate of Ronaldsway. Murray's mother Susannah (who died in 1739) was related to a local dignitary, Bishop Thomas Wilson.

A short work by A. W. Moore, entitled *Manx Worthies* and published in 1901, claims that Murray went to England when quite young and became a member of the English Bar. Moore, whose account of Murray contains several clear inaccuracies,[60] claims also that Murray had 'an estate called Landican in Cheshire'.[61] In fact his father's will[62] indicates that this was a farm that was left to Murray's youngest brother, Robert. Oddly, the father bequeathed his house and estates to Murray's three younger brothers but nothing to his eldest son.[63] It is reasonable to assume, however, that John Murray had already been well provided for, perhaps by his mother's family. Certainly, he must have been sufficiently secure, financially comfortable and well enough educated to embark on a career in the service of the crown, and to move in social circles that allowed him to meet his wife, Bridget, whose father and first husband both held modest titles. At the time of their marriage in York Minster on 3 October 1748, he was inscribed in the register as 'John Murray, of the City of York, Esquire', and Bridget as 'Dame Bridget Wentworth.' It is perhaps fair to suspect that Murray's family was not especially well connected or influential, since we hear nothing of them from him, and all the career support he enjoyed seems to have come from his wife's family.

Such personal descriptions as we have of Murray come mostly from his time in Venice; it is therefore to these that we must look for a picture of the future ambassador to Istanbul. They reveal a rather colourful individual, physically large and heavy, sociable and hospitable, a *bon viveur*, fond of good food and drink and of the ladies, and an art collector. Boswell records that Casanova (who was engaged in his own disreputable activity in Venice in 1755–56) once described Murray as like 'a handsome Bacchus, painted by Rubens'.[64] In his autobiography, Casanova further observes that Murray was

'prodigieusement amateur du beau sexe, de Baccus et de la bonne chère ...
sautant de l'une à l'autre il avait toujours les plus jolies filles de Venise'.[65]

A further personal description of Murray is provided by Lady
Mary Wortley Montagu. The wife of a former ambassador to
Istanbul, and by this time aged 67, she took up residence in Venice
in 1756, where she initially spent much time in the company of the
Murrays and of Consul Smith and his wife, describing them as
'worthy, friendly people'. However, some months later, for reasons
that seem to have been related to political rivalries in Britain, she
developed a great dislike of the family, and of John Murray in
particular. In letters to her daughter, Lady Bute, she refers to him as
a 'scandalous fellow, in every sense of that word, ... not to be
trusted to change a sequin, despised by this government for his
smuggling, which was his original profession, and always surrounded with pimps and brokers, who are his privy councillors'.[66]
She made some disobliging comments also about Murray's sister
Elizabeth on the occasion of her marriage to Consul Smith,
describing her as 'a beauteous virgin of 40, who after having refus'd
all the peers in England because the nicety of her conscience would
not permit her to give her hand where her heart was untouch'd, she
remain'd without a husband till the charms of that fine gentleman
Mr Smith, who is only 82, determined her to change her
condition.'[67] Robert Adam commented, in 1757, more kindly of
Elizabeth that she was 'facetious, frank, and of a sweet turn of
behaviour'.[68] Her portrait, as might be expected, shows her looking
pleasant, if unexceptional.[69]

Lady Mary's animosity must be seen in context, for she and
Murray were on opposing political sides. His official position of
course obliged him to support the monarch, George II, who
reigned from 1727 to 1760 and in whose name he had been
appointed. He was thus unable to receive certain friends and
relatives of hers who had Jacobite connections, and she found his
views disagreeable. From the security of her own aristocratic

background, she further commented to her daughter that it was unfortunate that, with few exceptions, England's foreign ministers were of such low birth and behaviour. As an example of this, she accused Murray of discourtesy in not sending the English newspapers to her or visiting her.[70] Lady Mary's letters indicate that her feud with John Murray continued until she set out to return to England in September 1761, but we have no evidence of his behaviour towards her and so should not judge the fairness of her criticism. Her comments are included because they provide one of the few surviving personal descriptions of Murray.

Some further explanation of their poor relationship can be found in the background of Murray's patron, Lord Holderness. Holderness had long been close to the crown. Before his appointment to Venice he had held the post of Lord Lieutenant of North Yorkshire and was also a Lord of the King's Bedchamber. Following his return from Italy, he spent two years as minister plenipotentiary at The Hague before beginning a ten-year stint in London during which he was, as noted above, one of the two secretaries of state who served King George II, switching several times between responsibility for the northern department and the southern department.

On 12 March 1761 the new king, George III, dismissed Lord Holderness and replaced him with John Stuart, third Earl of Bute (1718–92), thus reducing Holderness's influence. John Stuart was married to Lady Mary Wortley Montagu's only daughter, and he had long been a confidant and personal favourite of the new king.[71] Rivalry between Holderness and Bute may well have been an underlying cause of the friction between Murray and Lady Mary. Although she had a difficult relationship with her daughter (also named Mary) whom she found disappointingly dull, Lady Mary was hugely impressed by her aristocratic and much prized son-in-law, who gave her 11 grandchildren and whose success was everything she had hoped for in vain from her son. It is a little ironic that some years later in Istanbul, John Murray was obliged to tolerate the extraordinary and unorthodox Edward Wortley Montagu Jr as a guest in his house.

Casanova's description of Murray as a ladies' man ties in with a footnote in Moore's work.[72] Moore claims that a descendant told him that John Murray had a daughter, Catherine, born *c*.1762, from his relationship with Catterina Podrimolli during his time in Venice and that Catherine[73] subsequently married Count Felice Lombardo. A document in the Manx National Heritage Library[74] substantiates this information and gives details of the line of descent from Catherine, whose descendants now live in Vienna. From the evidence provided below, it would seem that she, however, was born later than 1762.

Murray's last Will and Testament, written in Italian, in the presence of a Venetian notary public, on the very day he died in Venice, provides absolute confirmation of his parallel domestic arrangements. The document[75] shows that Murray and Catterina Podrimolli had not just a daughter but also three sons and, furthermore, that Murray had an older fifth child, presumably from an earlier relationship. Murray bequeathed everything to his Italian family. To his natural[76] son Giorgio Giovanni he left 1200 zechins; this boy was about sixteen years old and living in Naples. To 'my Beloved Friend' Catterina Podrimolli, Murray gave 600 zechins a year for life. He named as his heirs the four natural children – three boys and a girl – procreated with Catterina Podrimolli, and bequeathed to them 'the residue of all that is belonging to me or which shall hereafter belong to me whether in Stocks Effects or otherwise nothing reserved or excepted and all and every my Estate at any place whatsoever existing'. The eldest of these four young children – who are named in an annotation to the will as Giovanni Battista Murray, a minor, and Catterina, Gulielmo and Giorgio Murray, all infants – was only eight years old when Murray died in 1775 and must therefore have been born during his time in Istanbul.

There is no record or indication that Murray and his wife Bridget had children. It would seem likely that his relationship with the mother of his eldest son was the reason for Murray's unwillingness to go to Istanbul and Bridget's decision not to accompany him there. In 1766, when Murray was appointed to Istanbul, Giorgio Giovanni would have been about seven years old, but Murray must already have been in a relationship with Catterina Podrimolli, for the evidence points to her having gone there with him. It is unlikely that Murray would have mentioned an extramatrimonial family in his correspondence with his employers, or that the company would have formally condoned their living with him in the ambassador's official residence. They may, however, have turned a blind eye to it, or the family could have been accommodated separately, perhaps in one of the villages on the Bosphorus where most Europeans kept country houses. We know from his correspondence that Murray did not leave Istanbul during his nine years there, and he could therefore only have fathered his four younger children if Catterina were in residence there.

Certainly, there is no indication that Lady Wentworth accompanied her husband Murray at any stage of his stay in Istanbul. When Murray was transferred there from Venice, she travelled back to England, arriving there on 22 June 1766. On her return, the Levant Company presented her with a piece of silver plate, a customary gesture to a wife on her husband's appointment as ambassador.[77] Her father had died in 1748, but her stepmother was still alive (she was to die during 1767) and Lady Wentworth, recognizing that her marriage had no future, may have gone home to spend some time with her own family. Meanwhile, John Murray left Venice on 11 May 1766 and made his way directly to Istanbul, where he took up his new appointment as ambassador on 2 June. He frequently refers in his letters from his new post to the large 'family' he was obliged to support there, a term that could refer to an ambassador's usual large household of servants, lodgers, visitors and hangers-on, but in Murray's case it seems to have included his mistress and, later, their young children. Murray was to spend nine years there.

In *Manx Worthies*, Moore claims that Murray's service at Venice and Istanbul spanned the reigns of George I, George II and George III. He also says that he left at his sister's house in Venice 'three silver boxes ... containing the seals of his appointments as ambassador under those sovereigns'. This is clearly incorrect, since George I died in 1727 when Murray was still a boy. But Moore goes on to say that two of the boxes, together with portraits of Murray and his sister Elizabeth, were (1901) in the possession of a descendant of Murray in the Isle of Man. One of these boxes[78] is on display at the Manx Museum and a search in the museum's vaults brought to light the portraits. They were unrestored, unsigned and with little explanatory pedigree, but the curators identified them as John and Elizabeth Murray.[79] Murray is recorded as having sat for the artist Benjamin West in Venice in 1763, and it is believed to be this picture, along with a contemporary portrait of Elizabeth, apparently by the same artist, that are in the museum's possession.[80]

Murray also features in a picture by Richard Brompton of the Duke of York and his friends, painted in May 1764 when the duke was visiting Venice for the Feast of the Ascension. Brompton (1734–82) was in Venice from January 1763 to August 1764, and he exhibited his picture of the Duke of York and friends at the Society of Artists in 1767.[81] While Brompton's painting provides us with a clear visual image of Murray, the composition of the work, together with the young artist's account of the commissioning of it, reveals something of Murray's personality. Like Consul Smith, although on a smaller scale, Murray was a collector[82] and he and his wife were supportive of young artists such as Brompton who came to work in Venice. During the Duke of York's brief visit, Murray, no doubt recognizing this as a heaven-sent opportunity to have himself recorded for posterity in the company of royalty, persuaded the duke to sit for Brompton. The 'friends' with whom the duke was painted were the courtiers who formed his entourage, together with two greyhounds and Murray; the other subjects are so positioned that Murray is the most prominent figure after the duke. He is shown full length as a splendid, portly figure in a fine and lavishly embroidered coat. His face is plump, florid and full of character, and his short chubby legs are clad in dark, knee-length breeches, light stockings and buckled shoes.[83] Murray's protégé Brompton has done his sponsor proud in his composition of the painting.[84]

Although the death of Bridget Murray, Lady Wentworth, on 3 September 1774 was reported in the *Gentleman's Magazine*, the publication did not carry any notification of Murray's death the following year. She never took his name and it would seem that, despite his considerable career achievements, he remained right up until his death her social inferior.[85] Nonetheless, Murray ultimately attained superiority, albeit posthumously, in that the original portrait of him with the Duke of York still hangs in the state rooms at Windsor Castle, accessible to public view, while a copy of it is at Hampton Court Palace.

There can be little doubt that Murray would have ordered a copy of the painting for himself, and that it would have been a much-prized possession that he might have been expected to take with him for prominent display in his residence at Istanbul. There was a version of it in a sale of Consul Smith's collection at Christie's on 16 May 1776, which Millar suggests might have belonged to Murray.[86] Although Murray left all his possessions, wherever located, to his mistress Catterina Podrimolli and their four children, many of his personal effects, including some paintings, were nonetheless shipped back to London. This might account for his copy of the painting coming to be owned by the Smiths (although it seems unlikely that Elizabeth would offer it for sale just a year after her brother's death).

4. Edward, Duke of York with his friends in Venice (John Murray second
from right) by Richard Brompton, 1764. Royal Collection © 2009
Her Majesty Queen Elizabeth II.

To return to Murray's career as a diplomat, there can be little doubt that he had a rough ride during his time as ambassador in Istanbul, and not only because of difficulties facing the Levant trade. The Ottomans were at war with Britain's ally Russia from 1768, and Murray was fortunate to escape the fate of his Russian colleague, who was thrown into prison with all his diplomatic staff. The most dangerous moment of Murray's incumbency came in July 1770 as a result of British involvement in the humiliating defeat of the Ottomans at the Battle of Çesme, of which the ambassador had received no advance warning. The real physical dangers the factory communities faced in Istanbul and Izmir for several years after the event are described in Chapter 5. Since the circumstances of the battle had a very adverse effect on bilateral relations during Murray's incumbency, and also affected him personally in that they led to his staying on at Istanbul for five years longer than he would have wished, they are described here in some detail.

According to Saint Priest's contemporary account of the battle, Catherine the Great's Russian fleet had been under the command of Count Alexis Orloff, the brother of one of the empress's favourites who knew nothing of naval matters.[87] Orloff had, however, at his side an English admiral, Elphinston, a naval man who had brought with him four Russian vessels equipped in England and manned by English officers and sailors. The two fleets engaged in a number of inconclusive skirmishes in the Aegean off the coast of the Peloponnese and finally confronted each other in the channel between the island of Chios and the coast of Asia Minor. In a fierce battle between the two flagships carrying the Russian and Ottoman admirals, both vessels caught fire and exploded, killing most of their crews, though the two admirals escaped. Both fleets scattered, and the Ottomans took refuge in the small mainland harbour of Çesme, where the Russians blocked them in and forced them into submission. It was said to be Elphinston's idea to destroy totally the defeated fleet by setting it ablaze. Murray was puzzled when rumours reached him from local sources of his own country's involvement in this affair. He wrote to London reporting them, commenting angrily that Britain was supposed to be neutral in the Ottoman–Russian war, and asking for an explanation. A mealy-mouthed reply from Secretary of State Weymouth claimed that the government had known nothing of this and had indeed refused a request from Lord Effingham to accompany the Russian ships. Nonetheless, Weymouth confessed, it was true that several English transports did accompany the Baltic fleet (for reasons he explained to Murray in a secret code).[88]

The aftermath of Çesme and the continuing war were to affect the remainder of Murray's posting. About this time, he wrote a private letter to his political masters in London to say that he wished to retire 'with a competency'.[89] In September 1770, there was a sign of restlessness on his part when he wrote to the British consul in Venice about his concern for the financial security of his sister Elizabeth, whose husband, the elderly former consul Joseph Smith, was selling off his valuable collections of books and art works. 'I have been a long while acquainted,' he wrote, 'with the folly and vanity of this old man. I was sure somehow her marriage settlement has been lost or spent.'[90]

The reply from London to his request for retirement came in October 1770 when he was advised that the king agreed that Murray might leave but not until Russia and the Porte had settled their differences. On quitting the embassy, Murray was to have a pension of £1000 a year, 'till some equivalent provision is made for you by any other mark of His Majesty's favour which may be agreeable to your wishes'.[91]

In October 1772 Murray again asked to leave Istanbul, but was told that the king was not yet ready to name a successor and did not want an inferior character to Murray in the job. Murray offered to stay on until peace was declared and the king responded by inviting him to stay as long as he liked, and to let the secretary of state know when he was ready to move.[92] These are clear indications that Murray was trusted and respected in London and that his performance in Istanbul was regarded as entirely satisfactory. There is also an implication that he was to be well rewarded on his return, perhaps with a baronetcy or knighthood.

In the event, the war between the Ottomans and Russia did not end until 1774 and, for the duration of his time in Istanbul, Murray was scarcely able to stir beyond his own walls. He was also short of money, due mainly to spiralling local inflation resulting from Russian naval blockades and consequent shortages in the marketplace. He complained to this effect to Rochford, and in February 1772 the king granted him a special gratuity of £500.[93]

Murray had another problem of which he was blissfully unaware – espionage. In accordance with the practice of his predecessors, Murray had a large household of personal staff and servants. It was not unusual for some of these to be brought from home, but most had to be recruited locally. Murray brought some with him from Venice, but, not coming to Istanbul direct from England, would have had more need than most to find staff from local sources. These locally-engaged employees were often unreliable and there were instances of individuals being found spying for other governments. Murray was a victim of one of these. One of his servants, a Pole, was discovered to be a spy the French had introduced into his household and who had been privy to all Murray's correspondence from early 1770 until the end of his tenure in 1775.

This was revealed in the memoirs of the Comte de Saint Priest, the French ambassador at Istanbul during that period, who agreed to the planting of the spy. Murray liked Saint Priest, who had arrived at Istanbul in January 1769, and wrote in May of that year that Saint Priest 'upon all occasions shows great readiness to assist me. ... I should be happy to serve him, as I have very great esteem for his many good qualities, and with whom I live on the easiest of footing.'[94] France and Poland were at the time allies, and Saint Priest records that a Polish agent approached him with an offer to help procure the correspondence of the English ambassador. The plan involved a Polish manservant in Murray's employ, whom Saint Priest described as a bit of a simpleton. It was this man's job to sweep the ambassador's office while the latter was at dinner, an occasion that never lasted less than two hours. Saint Priest described Murray as an '*homme de plaisir*' who liked being at table and would never interrupt his enjoyment for even the most important matter. Each day when there was a courier, the servant took from a drawer in Murray's office both the mail he had just received and the letters he proposed to send by return. These were taken to Saint Priest, who quickly copied down extracts of each, then replaced in the drawer before Murray had risen from the table.

The extracts were dispatched with a French courier and read in Versailles even before the originals reached England. Saint Priest observed that there was rarely anything of interest learnt from Murray's correspondence, but that it was already something just to know that there was nothing going on of importance. He admitted that such spying would be shocking behaviour between private individuals, but given that ambassadors to the Porte were forever at war among themselves, he could not possibly therefore have turned down such an opportunity. The Polish servant, whom we are told, was acting for purely ideological reasons, believing England to be scheming against Poland, was rewarded after Murray's departure with what he most desired, a pilgrimage to Jerusalem and a pension from the French court.[95]

Information that Murray had been betrayed through the latter half of his time in Istanbul is unlikely to have come to the attention of his political masters in London until some time after his death, and could not therefore have had any bearing on his reputation or career in his lifetime. Saint Priest's memoirs were not published until 1929, though word of his espionage against Murray must have become public knowledge much earlier. Certainly, it was not known in July 1774 when Rochford sent Murray a new set of credentials for presentation to the Porte, reiterating his full power to represent the British crown there. Rochford also assured Murray that George III continued to regarded him with much approval.[96]

When peace was declared in 1774, Murray requested and received permission to take some leave from his post at Istanbul to set his private affairs in order. His departure was delayed because no frigate was available to transport him home, but he was finally able to leave in May 1775. Anthony Hayes had arrived from Izmir to act as chargé d'affaires *ad interim*, and Murray departed on 25 May for Venice aboard a merchant ship, the *Crown Galley*. On arriving there on 27 June, he entered the lazaretto to spend the 42 days in quarantine required of all arrivals from the Levant. Several years previously, while stationed in Venice, Murray had included in a report to the Earl of Halifax, then (May 1765) secretary of state for the southern department, descriptions of the two lazarettos in the city. Murray wrote of the older of these two, a 'hospital' on the island of San Lazzero:

> There is a noble building, erected by the State in the year 1423 on account of the Plague. It is used for the perform-ance of Quarantine of persons and Goods, and very commodious for that purpose; it is governed by a Prior under the Direction of the Magistrates of Health.[97]

It was here that Murray and presumably any travelling companions had patiently to await their due release date of 8 August.

Murray's quarantine was a privileged affair. In recognition of his earlier years as British Resident in the city, he was accommodated in the apartments of the lazaretto usually reserved for returning Venetian ambassadors and treated with great politeness and con-sideration. Not only were his sister Elizabeth and niece Catherine permitted to visit him every day, and the British officials in the city permitted to attend him, but (uniquely, he was told) some of the Venetian nobles were also permitted to call on him.[98] Murray was granted the king's permission to remain a while in Venice to help his sister and niece tie up their affairs there, his plan being that the two ladies would then travel back to London with him. Sadly, this was not to be. On 4 August, just as his period of quarantine was coming to a close, Murray was suddenly taken ill 'of a feverish disorder', which four days later became 'putrid and malignant' and he died on the evening of 9 August.

On the day of his death he was still entirely lucid, but summoned no one to his bedside except three lawyers, to whom, in his last few hours of life, he dictated his last will and testament, bequeathing (as we have seen above) everything to his Italian children and their mother. Murray further placed all four of his younger children under the guardianship of the former Venetian *bailo* (ambassador) to the Porte, authorizing him to remove the children from their mother if he saw fit, and see to their upbringing and education himself.[99] For each child so removed, Catterina's annual allowance would be reduced by 50 zechins, so that, even if she lost all four, her allowance would never be less than 400.

While he was alive and well, Murray enjoyed the respect due to his exalted status from colleagues in Venice and London, but his unexpected death in their parish and the terms of his will embarrassed local officials and threw them into confusion. The Resident, John Strange, hustled Catterina and her four young children into a house in the city and gave them money for their immediate needs. Nowhere in the records is it made clear whether they too had just arrived from Istanbul and had been in the lazaretto with Murray, although that seems probable. On the second day after Murray's death, before he had even been buried, Strange wrote to Rochford, enclosing a copy of the former ambassador's will and asking advice on what to do about Catterina and the children; Strange recommended taking them away from Catterina to spare them the fate of being brought up as Catholics. This evoked the prompt and frosty reply that the government could not get involved in Murray's personal affairs.

Any loyalty, respect and consideration Murray had enjoyed in his lifetime clearly died with him. A funeral – decent, but not extravagant, in accordance with Murray's wishes – was arranged by the British consul, John Udney, for Sunday 13 August, and took place 'in the most honourable manner' at the Lido Protestant cemetery. It was attended by 'the English Gentlemen, and Captains of Ships now here, and all the Foreign Protestant Merchants'. There is no indication that the people Murray loved were there; perhaps in the case of his sister and niece that was because it was not customary for women to attend funerals. His Catholic family were no doubt banned from attending a Protestant ceremony, so could not be there even had they so wished.[100]

No further comment from Murray's political masters about his death has come to light, nor has anything been found in the Levant Company records. He vanishes from the files; his wife Bridget had predeceased him and we do not know if any pension or death benefit for his long years of service was paid to surviving relatives in England. The attitudes shown to his Catholic family in Italy make it unlikely that they would have received any official help. John Udney wrote to London that he proposed to sell some of Murray's belongings locally for the benefit of Catterina and the children, and to freight back for sale in England the many cases of pictures and books that had remained on board ship during the quarantine period. An inventory taken just after Murray's funeral shows that he had been travelling with a huge quantity of baggage, including household goods, jewels and alcoholic drinks (all of which an ambassador could bring into England free of duty).

The inventory (for which Udney must have had help from

Elizabeth Smith and Murray's young private secretary, Riddell, who was travelling to England with him) valued Murray's entire estate, encompassing property in Venice, Istanbul and England, at £8000, a sum that Udney observed would not raise sufficient interest to pay Catterina her annual allowance. The amount shown for his English property was £3000, which included his late wife's effects and made no mention of any houses or land. Udney reported that Murray's English family, who were not beneficiaries of the will, did not propose to contest it. Although Murray had made it in a great hurry in his dying hours, it was properly signed and witnessed and matched an earlier will he had made in Istanbul that was found among his papers.[101] Two years later, by which time the Venetian *bailo* had declined guardianship of his friend's young children, a note was added to Murray's will to the effect that Murray appointed Catterina Podrimolli – who meanwhile had married Francesco dall' Arqua – as the lawful guardian of her four young children.[102]

The Levant Company subsequently appointed Robert Ainslie as Murray's successor, a man 15 years his junior. That George III knighted Ainslie (another of the king's favoured Scots whose father owned an estate near Edinburgh) on the occasion of his appointment underlined the absence of any honour for Murray and could be interpreted as a slight to the man who had held the post for nine years before dying in harness. Horn, however, argues that Ainslie's appointment and knighthood were rewards for earlier successes in the field of espionage. Apparently, at a critical stage in a dispute with Spain over the Falkland Islands in 1770, Ainslie stole copies of some French correspondence to the court at Madrid from the office of the Duc d'Aiguillon, the then French foreign minister, and the contents of these letters encouraged the British to adopt a firm stance against Spain.[103]

It is worth noting here that Ainslie received only a routine briefing on his appointment as ambassador; there was no change in either policy or emphasis that might have implied criticism of his predecessor Murray.

CONCLUSION

Rather than suffering any intended slight from his king, Murray would appear to have been simply unfortunate in dying before he reached England, where, there seems every reason to believe he might have expected to be fêted and honoured for a job well done.[104] Life must have seemed good to Murray as he made his way to a long-awaited reunion with his family in England before resuming his post in Istanbul. His wife had died, and – although Catterina's Catholicism would always prevent their marrying – they were blessed with their young family. He, by contrast, was dealt a shabby hand. Having swept his beloved but embarrassing Catholic family swiftly under the carpet, his masters in London seemed quickly and quietly to have forgotten him. His old friend failed him by refusing to care for the children as Murray had wished, although, in fairness, John Strange observed that such an arrangement would have been impracticable for legal reasons; and within two years of his death, his Catterina had remarried. Moreover, although he did not die a poor man, Murray's residual estate was little enough to show for 21 years of unbroken public service.

Following the difficult years of Murray's incumbency, bilateral relations warmed in 1774 with the accession of Sultan Abdul Hamid I, who saw that the Russian war was going against the Ottomans and rather favoured British mediation. He is said to have been advised against it, however, by his foreign minister, who did not like Murray and had warned the previous sultan in 1773 that 'the English Ambassador will do nothing for the Porte.' Murray was sufficiently confident of his own reputation to report this unfavourable comment to the secretary of state, Lord Rochford, in London. The war ended in a disastrous defeat for the Ottomans in 1774 without any foreign mediation, but the hostile foreign minister was to remain in place until a year after Murray's departure.[105] Sir Robert Ainslie's arrival at Istanbul in October 1776 to replace Murray coincided happily with the appointment of a new minister and Ainslie was well received. Personal descriptions of Ainslie – pompous, boring, vainglorious and ill-tempered – depict him as a much less attractive personality than Murray, but his early bonding with the foreign minister stood him in good stead throughout his 23-year tenure at the Istanbul embassy, the last of the eighteenth century.

3

The Chaplains

In this chapter we turn our attention to the Levant Company's provision of salaried chaplains to its three principal factories at Istanbul, Izmir and Aleppo. As we shall see from this, and from the following chapter on doctors, the company's policy of including clergymen but not physicians on its payroll is puzzling. While it might reflect an age in which men placed their faith over-whelmingly in God rather than in science, the very different policy of the contemporary East India Company seems to suggest otherwise, particularly since, in the early days at least, the two companies had a number of directors in common.[1]

At the Levant Company's inception in the late sixteenth century, England was a Protestant country and the London-based company was a thoroughly English and Protestant institution. Unlike the East India Company, it did not initiate the provision of religious support to its overseas communities, but when asked to do so it readily agreed and was happy to pay the costs involved. Throughout the entire period of its existence, the Levant Company recruited and financed these chaplains regardless of the vagaries of trade and the resulting effects on company fortunes. As we shall see, the Church of England had no hand in choosing candidates, in dictating their job description, or in monitoring their performance. The company's interest lay in keeping the factory communities within the Protestant fold and safe from alien, particularly Roman Catholic, influences. It did so by installing English clergymen to provide religious discipline and the usual services of marriage, baptism and burial. Protestant proselytization did not begin in any concerted way until the early nineteenth century and it was never a function of these chaplains.

Pearson's work on the seventeenth-century chaplains provides enough inspiration to carry his study forward through the eighteenth and into the early nineteenth century when the Levant Company ceased to exist. We shall look at how they fared in an increasingly materialistic age and consider the experiences and achievements of some individual chaplains who served in this later period during the company's slow but steady decline. By the second half of the eighteenth century, moreover, when trading was much reduced and the government in London's foreign affairs priority was veering towards the American colonies, the small factory communities remaining in the Levant were becoming more settled and had begun to include many more English women and children. This presented the chaplains with a very different group of parishioners from the young, largely unattached, bachelor communities of earlier years.

THE SEVENTEENTH CENTURY

For information on seventeenth-century chaplains, we have John B. Pearson's *A Bibliographical Sketch of the Chaplains to the Levant Company Maintained at Constantinople, Aleppo and Smyrna*, which was published in 1883 – 58 years after the company was wound up – and which covers the years 1611 to 1706. As he explains in his introduction, Pearson, a doctor of divinity and fellow of Emmanuel College, Cambridge, wrote his account in the belief that these chaplains' 'dry and forbidding' records 'furnish information which throws much light on the religious ideas and usages prevalent among our countrymen at the period in question'. While fully recognizing that a system followed in the seventeenth century could not be regarded as appropriate for the nineteenth let alone twentieth centuries, he suggests that it might be interesting for modern churchmen to see how the goals for which they were aiming were achieved in the past. Pearson's book does not, in fact, achieve that objective. It contains virtually nothing on the religious ideas and usages of the seventeenth century or on the Church of England's policy and objectives at the time he was writing. Its value lies rather in that it provides factual detail on an aspect of the Levant Company about which relatively little is known; other literature on the company consists in the main of accounts of its trading activity and of the wealthy English merchant families involved.

There is no doubt that the Levant Company unreservedly accepted that it had some responsibility for the spiritual well-being of its overseas communities. The Church of England did not impose chaplains on the company's overseas establishments and no religious authority in England controlled or supervised the individuals who served in that capacity. The obvious such authority would have been the Bishop of London, under whose jurisdiction a royal order of 1634 placed the English church at Delft, and by implication English churches in other overseas settlements. No evidence has been found that this was ever interpreted to apply to the Levant chaplaincies. The company was not bound by its various charters to supply its agents in the field with the services of the church, and there is no indication that it took the initiative in imposing clergymen on the factories.

Information is scarce on the appointment of the earliest chaplains, but requests for the formal provision of them as part of the establishment seem to have come from the overseas communities. This is certainly so in the case of Aleppo, which applied in 1624 and Izmir followed suit in 1635. The first recorded chaplain at Istanbul, William Foord, is known to have been at his post on 31 July 1611 when he preached at the funeral of Lady Glover, the wife of Sir Thomas Glover, then ambassador to the Porte. Istanbul was always a little different in that the chaplain was often a member of the personal entourage of an ambassador, who was granted the courtesy of being able to choose a candidate, though the company paid his salary and reserved the right to a final say in the matter. This ambassadorial privilege seems to have been bullied out of the company by 1633, when a court assembly held on 16 January recorded that 'Sir Sackville Crowe, ambassador to Constantinople, is taking a Preacher chosen by himself, contrary to usage.' Crowe later enquired what salary the company allowed for the post, so clearly had no intention of paying for the man of his choice.[2] It is clear that at no time did the company raise any objection in principle to requests for resident clergymen and, from the outset, took on the recruitment of chaplains in London, and paid their salaries and travelling expenses. Moreover, as Pearson points out, the company seems never 'to have been led by the vicissitudes of trade ... to grudge the salaries required'.[3]

Levant Company chaplains were chosen from clergymen who applied independently for the posts. There is no evidence that the jobs were advertised or any suggestion that these men were recommended by the Church of England, belonged to any kind of umbrella organization or were connected to each other in any way. They were, in their way, adventurers, enterprising individual clergymen who would have heard of the Levant Company's requirements by word of mouth from earlier incumbents, church colleagues or contacts in the company. Pearson shows that there were often four or five candidates for a post, who were each required to preach a sermon before a plenary assembly of the company's officials and merchants in London. Personal references were required as well as references from the candidate's university. The man chosen for the job would have his sermon printed at the company's expense. The amount allowed for this was £5 and, in one case in 1664 – presumably typical – it was agreed to print 500 copies of such a sermon for the governor to distribute to the company.[4] Copies of many of these sermons survive, although none later than 1724.[5]

While ambassadors were granted the privilege of travelling at company expense by the safer overland route to Istanbul via Vienna and Edirne (Adrianople), chaplains (unless accompanying an ambassador) were – like factors – usually obliged to travel by the more dangerous sea route and were given free passage out to their post in one of the ships the company owned or hired. If they chose to travel overland, wholly or partially, it was at their own expense, though there were occasional instances on record of the company making a donation towards a chaplain's travelling costs. For example, a Mr Curtis, the chaplain at Izmir, who was obliged by circumstances to travel overland from Leghorn to England in 1641, was granted £20, albeit reluctantly, for he had left his post without permission. Then, in 1689, £30 was allowed to Mr Edward Smyth, who had been 'forced to leave Ireland', for his expenses in getting to Izmir.

Chaplains were paid an annual gratuity and, on appointment, were given a grant towards books and equipment. They resided with the ambassador at Istanbul or with the consuls at Izmir and Aleppo, who received an allowance from the company for the chaplain's board and lodging. No letter of appointment or contract, if such were issued to the chaplains, is recorded as having survived, but individuals were expected to give a number of years' service before qualifying for a return passage. In 1645 a Mr Browne was appointed to Izmir for five years, with the company reserving the right to withdraw him sooner if they saw fit, but he did not in the event take up the post. In the seventeenth century the period of duty was for most around four to six years, with a number of stalwarts staying more than a decade. The company required one year's notice of resignation to find a suitable successor, but there are several instances on record of breaks in continuity brought about by an incumbent dying in post, discharging himself from his duties or being expelled locally for being in some way unsatisfactory. Anyone who abandoned his post without authority was denied the customary goodwill gratuity paid to a returning chaplain; an example of this was a Mr Pritchard, who discharged himself from the chaplaincy at Aleppo in 1640.

As a salaried employee on the company payroll, a chaplain was an official member of the factory and, as such, under the jurisdiction of the ambassador or consul at its head; he was also, as we have seen, entitled to his board and lodging within the personal household of the ambassador or consul. Levant Company chaplains did not, however, enjoy the social standing of their opposite numbers in the East India Company (EIC). At English trading settlements in India into the eighteenth century chaplains ranked second after the official in charge, who was known as the president or governor. This reflected their standing as educated professionals in these EIC factories, where everyone else from the governor down was a man of trade, and where most were of relatively humble origins compared with the well-born adherents of the elitist Levant Company.[6]

The EIC, which like the Levant Company was a thoroughly Protestant organization, had from its earliest days taken a proactive interest in its employees' spiritual welfare and voluntarily supplied chaplains to its factories and ships. Ships were in the early years of trading hired on an *ad hoc* basis as required, with no new voyage commencing until the previous one had returned to England. The early chaplains were appointed for one or more return voyages. In February 1601, Thomas Pulleyn went as a chaplain on the EIC's 'First Voyage', a group of four English ships that sailed from the Thames for the Indies under the command of Captain James Lancaster and that was away for two years. Pulleyn died in Madagascar in February 1602 while on the outward voyage. Henry Levett MA was offered £50 in 1601 to travel on a ship bound for the east, presumably as part of the same voyage, since the second did not leave England until March 1604.[7] Given the dangers of the undertaking, and its unpredictable duration, this was not an especially generous emolument (chaplains residing at the Levant Company factories were receiving £50 a year plus board and lodging for much less hazardous positions) but there may have been a final gratuity for chaplains who survived the ordeal.

As early as 1619, a chaplain named Matthew Cardrow – described as a Lutheran[8] – was stationed at the East India Company's outpost at Isfahan. At that time Isfahan was the Persian capital and was important not only as the centre of the company's trade with Persia but also as a staging post on the overland route to India. As the coastal factories in India became more established, ships' chaplains began to stay on there as residents, one of the first being George Coluns, who was appointed to Surat in 1631 and later transferred to Isfahan. It is unclear whether such posts were open to married men in the seventeenth century, but McNally shows that by the eighteenth century it was usual for EIC chaplains to be officially accompanied by their wives and children, details of whom are included in the company records.[9] There is, however, no evidence to suggest that Levant Company chaplains were normally so accompanied.

Pearson observes that the low salaries paid to the chaplains in the early years must have made it impossible for any but single men to accept an overseas post;[10] indeed, there are instances of candidates being rejected on the grounds that they were married. In 1614 a Mr Whetstone, applying for the chaplaincy at Istanbul, was turned down for this reason, as was a Mr Pindar in 1647. There seemed to be no objection to successful applicants taking along a male companion or manservant, for both Cadwallader Salisbury in 1619 and Christopher Newstead in 1622 were 'given leave to take a youth with him' to Istanbul.[11]

In fact, accompanying families were not the norm for any of the constituent members of the English communities in the factories, nor were they encouraged. There was a period from the 1650s, however, when several factors in Izmir had their wives with them[12] and this might have been reflected elsewhere. Ambassadors at Istanbul were usually accompanied, as on occasion were the consuls at Izmir and Aleppo, but as we shall see in Chapter 5 it was not until the mid-eighteenth century that it became more common for some of the more senior traders of the company to be married. In addition to the requirement to be unmarried, there must also have been some professional disadvantage in overseas service for an ambitious young cleric in that he was removed for a period of years from the mainstream of his calling and from the eyes of those senior clergymen on whom he would have depended for advancement. If he did well in his company assignment, however, the reflected glory of the high prestige in which the Levant Company was held would probably negate this latter disadvantage.

THE LURE OF THE LEVANT

Pearson found that in the seventeenth century clever and competent men, some of whom went on to attain high office in the Church of England or to become distinguished academics, sought employment as a chaplain at a Levant Company factory. All applicants were educated men who had attended the universities of Oxford or Cambridge, although by no means all had qualified specifically in divinity; several graduated BD or DD after their return from the Levant, with some apparently being granted the degree on the strength of their service overseas. It does not immediately spring to mind that a major attraction of the chaplaincies would lie in the expectation of great financial reward. More obvious incentives might include an interest in learning something of the Eastern churches, or the possibility of visiting the Holy Land. Edward Pococke, for one, freely confessed that collecting manuscripts was one of his chief aims in seeking appointment to Aleppo in 1630.

Nonetheless, the posts were reasonably well paid by the standards of the time, offering a salary that rose from $200 (£50) a year in the early part of the century to $400 after 1654, and then to $500 in 1724. Thereafter there was no further rise until 1794, when it was decided to increase the pay of the chaplain at Istanbul to $1000 a year, and at Izmir to $700; these rises reflected local inflation and currency debasement rather than offering real increased spending power. By 1817–18, in the dying years of the company, the chaplains at both places were in receipt of £250 per annum.[13]

When comparing these salaries with those of the consul and other salaried officials, which are contained in an earlier chapter, it should be borne in mind that the chaplains were generally accommodated and fed, free of charge, by either the ambassador, in the case of Istanbul, or the consul at Izmir and Aleppo. In 1651, for example, when the salary of the chaplain at Aleppo, Nathaniel Hill, was $200 a year, the consul's allowance for 'the Minister's diet' was $300.[14] A chaplain's real earnings were thus more than double the amount he received in cash.

Moreover, a number of fringe benefits augmented his income. It was, for example, regular practice during the seventeenth and eighteenth centuries for factors to bequeath sums of money to both the chaplains and the physicians who had served alongside them. During Paul Rycaut's time as consul at Izmir (1667–78), when company business was booming and the chaplain was paid at the rate of $400 a year, the merchant Thomas Thynne left $100 to the minister. References to the trader John Temple's will mention what are described as 'commonplace legacies' of $100 to the chaplain, $30 to the poor of the city, $300 towards the redemption of slaves[15] and $50 to the doctor.[16] Both chaplains and doctors received gratuities from departing merchants, either in addition to or instead of legacies. The doctors, who were not salaried employees of the company, could legitimately have regarded such windfalls as personal gifts, but we have no way of knowing whether chaplains saw them in a similar light or used them for church work; there was no doubt some variation of approach between individual incumbents.

Many, perhaps the majority, of the men who served as chaplains

5. The church of St John at Bergama. Thomas Allom, *Constantinople and the Scenery of the Seven Churches of Asia*, 1839 (Edinburgh University Library Special Collections Department S.16/1/64/1).

in the seventeenth century took advantage of their situation to follow up a personal interest in the Levant.

It is indeed reasonable to assume that many who sought a position would, like Pococke, have done so with exactly that in mind. They were drawn not only by a desire for adventure and a less conventional life, but also by the prospect of proximity to the Holy Land, or the opportunity to learn something at first hand of Islam and the Eastern Churches, or an interest in classical antiquities. A favourite excursion from Izmir, and almost *de rigueur* for any resident or visitor with the time to spare, was a tour of the seven churches of Asia. These are mentioned in the Book of Revelations and one of them was at Izmir and the other six within a few days' journey.[17]

Henry Denton, chaplain at Istanbul for about three years from 1664 to Ambassador Heneage Finch, was a Greek scholar. The then compiler of the *Magdalen Registers* described his successor, Thomas Smith, to Pearson as 'perhaps the most learned man that Magdalen College ever sent out'.[18] Smith's accounts of his voyage to the Levant and of Istanbul and Bursa were later published by the Royal Society. Pearson comments that the inclusion of such as Smith in the list of chaplains 'is an interesting proof that persons who cared for Oriental studies could use the post as a means of forwarding their pursuits'. John Covel (or Covell)[19] who served at Istanbul after Smith from 1669 to 1676, published shortly before his death in 1722 a folio work on the Greek Church on which he had been working since his time in the Levant.[20]

Among the chaplains who served at Aleppo in the seventeenth century, we have the prodigious scholar Pococke, who went there at the age of 26 in 1630 and remained five years, later returning independently to Istanbul for two years, where he collected 'oriental' books, and acted as temporary chaplain to ambassadors Wyche and Crowe. In 1683 Pococke became the first professor of Arabic and later of Hebrew at Oxford and is recorded as knowing also the Samaritan, Syriac and 'Ethiopic' languages.

In 1655 the Aleppo chaplaincy was taken by Robert Frampton, another proficient linguist who learnt Arabic and Italian there, and who went on to become Bishop of Gloucester. In the intervening years he was a popular preacher in London, earning an admiring mention in the diary of Samuel Pepys.

From 1670 to 1681 Robert Huntington was at Aleppo. While there he made an excellent collection of 'oriental' manuscripts, now in the Bodleian Library alongside those of Pococke and, in Pearson's words, he 'distinguished himself in the study of Oriental literature and as an indefatigable traveller.'[21]

William Hallifax, chaplain at Aleppo from 1687 to 1695, visited Palmyra during this period along with two companions. An account of their journey, together with their sketch of the ruins, was printed in 1695.[22]

In 1703 Henry Maundrell's famous 'travels' were first published.[23] Maundrell served as chaplain at Aleppo from 1696 until his death there in 1701 at the age of only 35. There, he records, he found an English colony of about 40 for whom he had a high regard, and performed daily services every morning to a devout and large congregation. In February 1697 he set off with 14 other residents from the settlement on an Easter pilgrimage to Jerusalem, returning to Aleppo in May. Pearson, commenting on Maundrell's premature death, suggests that he probably 'fell a victim to the fevers generated by the want of proper sanitary arrangements so common in oriental cities'.[24]

The Izmir chaplaincy too had its share of talented incumbents, among them John Luke. He was there from 1665 to 1669 and was later elected professor of Arabic at Cambridge, a position he held from 1685 until his death in 1702. From 1697 to 1701, the chaplain at Izmir was Edmund Chishull, a classical scholar and antiquary who was later appointed chaplain to Queen Anne. Chishull kept diaries of recreational excursions he made from Izmir to Ephesus and to Istanbul, and of his journeys to and from his post, which were published posthumously to considerable acclaim; they are both scholarly and entertaining. His account of his homeward journey in 1702, as a member of the entourage of Lord Paget, returning from his post as ambassador to the Porte, paints a vivid picture of the lavish treatment accorded to a departing ambassador by the Ottomans, and of the honours heaped on Paget and his party at every stage of the journey through Europe.[25]

As Pearson discovered, there is little about these chaplains in the company court records that tells us much about their personalities or their performance in the field, but, among the many admirable men who served the company were a few who were less of a success. We know that their profession did not automatically bring the chaplains the high position in the factory hierarchy that the chaplains of the East India Company enjoyed. Since the factors of the Levant Company were themselves well born and well educated, they accorded the clergymen no unquestioning respect.

The biography of the Hon. Dudley North, a factor at Izmir and later at Istanbul from the 1660s, indicates that those chaplains who gained the respect of the lively young men of the factories were honoured and revered by them, and could live well and grow rich on the generous gifts they received. If, on the other hand, the young factors felt themselves patronized by a fool, the offender could expect a rough ride.[26]

One such unfortunate, hounded out of his post after incurring the ridicule of the community, was John Broadgate, who was elected to the post of chaplain at Izmir on 4 December 1662 and whose case was sufficiently troublesome to be recorded in the court records. Pushed in the direction of the unsuspecting company by a previous employer 'offended at his unfitness and ill carriage' and anxious to be rid of him, Broadgate had within his first year so upset the consul at Izmir[27] with whom he lodged (in accordance with usual practice) that the consul, with the ambassador's backing, had turned him out. It would seem unlikely that Broadgate was blameless in this incident (though indications are that he was no more than a pompous fool), but the company's sympathies were clearly with him. In January 1664 it is recorded in the minutes that, in response to a letter of complaint received from Broadgate in Izmir, they thought fit to send him a letter of encouragement. This informed him of a gratuity of $200 for his first year of service and a further allowance at the rate of $300 per annum, presumably for his board and lodging 'for such time as the Consul has turned him out of doors'. Nonetheless, by October 1664 he was back in England, following 'his removal as a prisoner from Turkey', where he presented his complaints to the company court, which judged the actions of the consul at Izmir irregular, contrary to the company's orders, and prejudicial to its interests. The consul was reprimanded, fined and obliged to pay Broadgate the very substantial sum of $600 in compensation. Thereafter, until 1702, by which time he would have been in his mid-seventies, the records are peppered with references to charity payments made to him by the company.

An earlier example of a chaplain who did not meet with approval, was the man appointed to Istanbul following Sir Sackville Crowe's insistence on having someone of his own choosing. The person the ambassador designate had picked having fallen out for some unknown reason during the five-year period between Crowe's appointment as ambassador and his eventual departure to take up his post in 1638, Mr Nathaniel Durant – 'recommended for his learning and life' – was accepted to travel with Crowe. Durant had graduated with a BA and MA from Jesus College, Cambridge, but it seems he became the cause of disruption at Istanbul, for, in 1642, Crowe advised the company that 'for the peace of the factory' he had told Durant to go to Izmir. Durant refused to budge until he had received a written instruction from the company telling him to comply. He remained two years at Izmir, a replacement for him being appointed in February 1644–45, but seems to have stayed on in some independent capacity for another five years until, in March 1650–51 – by which time Thomas Bendysh was ambassador – he was ordered to leave the country. Crowe's tenure at the embassy was notoriously troubled. It coincided with the Disruption[28] in England and throughout he was much at odds with the company and with the men of the factory. Although Wood writes that Crowe managed the merchants' affairs with ability and resolution,[29] aspects of his behaviour nonetheless caused them to rise in protest against him. This led in 1646 to the publication in England of a pamphlet on 'the abuses and oppressions exercised by him on the persons and estates of the English at Smyrna and Constantinople'. It may therefore be that Durant was simply a victim of this troubled period.

COMMERCIAL ACTIVITY

Pearson found evidence that it was not unknown for a chaplain in the seventeenth century to augment his income by engaging in trade. Trading was not permitted to the consuls, but there seems to have been no specific ban on it for chaplains, despite their being salaried employees of the company. The Reverend Sir George Wheler, an itinerant botanist who visited the English factory at Izmir in 1675, observed that among the perquisites enjoyed by the English chaplain was the use of a warehouse in case he should wish to trade.[30] Company attitudes to the rights and wrongs of this no doubt varied, and there are indications that at times it was condoned grudgingly. Chaplains were not members of the company, and to buy and sell goods would have had to engage the sympathies of one of the legitimate factors.[31] Pearson refers to having found 'frequent references in the Minutes to commercial transactions on the part of the chaplains at the factories' but highlights only two such cases, both at Izmir.

Of Edward Smith (or Smyth), there from 1689 to 1692, he records that he was absent in the East for four years, 'to the great advancement, it is said, of his private fortune'. Smyth died at Bath in 1720, leaving a considerable estate behind him, the foundation of which seems to have been laid by him when at Izmir.[32] One of Smyth's successors at Izmir, John Tisser, who was elected to the post in December 1701 and was still there in 1706, was similarly engaged in business. Pearson writes of him:

> Like Dr Smyth, he does not seem to have thrown away the advantages which his position offered him in a pecuniary point of view, for in 1704 we learn that his father was investing the proceeds of his fellowship at Oxford in cloth, to be sold at Izmir on the son's account.

The Company Minutes for 18 October that year record that the sum in question was £200 and that Tisser was required to pay 'such duties as are paid by members of the company'. In the extracts from the company minutes for the seventeenth century that Pearson reproduced there are two other references to trading activity by chaplains on which he does not comment in his biographical notes of the individuals concerned. Thomas Curtis, the first recorded chaplain at Izmir, was granted permission in January 1637 'to adventure £100 yearly in cloths'. In September and October 1672, the company court sanctioned the sending of two 'adventures in cloth' to the value of £100 to Istanbul for the chaplain John Covel. The minutes further record that on four subsequent occasions between 1674 and 1677 Covel was with some reluctance permitted to have 'farther transactions in silk and cloth'. Clearly such trading activity as was permitted to chaplains was heavily regulated and strictly limited.

Wheler further commented in his account of his visit to Izmir in 1675 that the English chaplain had no chapel save a room in the consul's house dedicated for the purpose, and that this was a shame 'considering the great wealth they heap up here, beyond all the rest'.[33] While this rather ambiguous comment could conceivably be taken as referring to the wealth amassed by chaplains, it is more likely to be a criticism of the Levant Company and the factory community. No evidence has come to light that might indicate whether or not chaplains continued to engage in commercial activity during the eighteenth century, although the surviving inventory of possessions left by the Revd Thomas Owen, who died at Aleppo in August 1716, reveals nothing that could be regarded as trading goods.[34]

For the chaplains of the East India Company (EIC) the position on trading was equally ambivalent, oscillating in response to varying company attitudes. On the one hand, some of the respect in which they were held at the Indian factories stemmed from their being professional men who, alone in the communities, were not avowedly connected with trade. In 1692, one chaplain, John Evans, was dismissed from the company's service for private trading, although this ignominy did his clerical career no apparent harm, for he went on to become Bishop of Bangor and later Bishop of Meath.[35] That the chaplains' position in this respect was not clear in the seventeenth century is evident from its being regularized in the EIC's 1698 charter. Thereafter, chaplains were formally banned from engaging in most of the important trade with Europe, but could trade as they liked elsewhere, as long as they did not neglect their pastoral duties. Spear found that, into the eighteenth century, most continued with some kind of commercial activity, both to supplement their income and to fill in their time, and the company tended to turn a blind eye to the detail of it.[36] Others may have overstepped the mark. Around 1720, for example, Charles Long, chaplain at Fort St George (Madras) since 1713, was dismissed for private trading.[37]

PROSELYTIZATION

It is quite clear that it was never an official purpose of the Levant Company chaplains to attract converts to the Church of England or more generally to Protestantism. The role of the English chaplains at company factories was purely to look after the spiritual welfare of the English communities and to supply the normal services of baptism, marriage and burial. No detailed job descriptions (if such existed) have come to light, but instructions seem to have been simple and straightforward. Court minutes reveal, for example, that W. Gotbed, chaplain designate to Izmir in 1640, had agreed to the requirements that he should preach 'duly and truly', conduct himself well and not return home without giving a year's notice. That same year, Bartholomew Chappell, bound for Aleppo, was required 'to reside there to preach the word of God and administer the Sacraments, according to the Cannons [sic] and Constitutions of the Church of England'.[38]

There is no hint of any company encouragement or incentive

for chaplains, as learned professionals as well as company employees, to go beyond this basic brief and assist the company further. They were not, for example, expected to learn Arabic or Turkish while in post, record information on the region, or make contacts with local religious leaders that might lead to greater understanding and goodwill. In these pre-imperial times, the many who did learn languages and who took an academic interest in the Levant did so on their own initiative.

Although the doctors at the factories were prepared to serve anyone who sought them out – no doubt because they were self-employed rather than salaried employees of the company – no reference has been found to suggest that the chaplains similarly operated professionally outside the English communities to which they were assigned. They did, however, admit to their flocks any other European Protestants present in the factory cities. In Aleppo, for example, the Dutch consul and his family were regular members of the English chapel community. Given that the numbers on the ground in the Levant Company factories were tiny in relation to the population of an English parish, the pastoral duties of a chaplain – except in circumstances of crisis such as an outbreak of plague, or an earthquake – can hardly have been onerous.

We know that the three factories at Istanbul, Izmir and Aleppo reached the peak of their prosperity and size in the second half of the seventeenth century. Wood quotes figures that show that the number of factors at Istanbul held steady at about 25 during that period, although, as he points out, this number would be swelled by numerous servants and dependants who were not members of the company or in its direct employ. The figures for Izmir are a little woolly and contradictory, but seem to indicate that in 1675 there was a resident English community of around 100, a third to a half of whom were authorized factors and apprentices. At Aleppo in 1662 there were about fifty factors. In 1676 Henry Teonge (a chaplain on board several of His Majesty's ships between 1675 and

1679) recorded in his diary: 'I preacht a sermon in the factory ... and had an audience of above 50 English men – a brave shew in that wild place.' He goes on to mention the presence at the time of his visit of around 200 of his compatriots, some of them no doubt in transit like himself. As we have seen, in 1699, the Revd Henry Maundrell – chaplain in Aleppo from 1695 until his death there in 1701 – recorded that there were more than 40 of his countrymen resident in the city.[39]

From the 1730s, the company's fortunes began to decline for a variety of reasons (among them changing patterns of trade, competition from the French and from the East India Company, and the collapse of the silk industry in Persia), so that Istanbul's factors had dropped to fewer than ten by 1760 and to five by 1794. Izmir, which became the busiest port in the Levant in the eighteenth century, nonetheless saw its numbers reduced from 36 factors in 1704 to six in 1794. Of the three factories, Aleppo's traders dropped the most dramatically, being reduced to only two by the 1780s.[40]

As these figures show, at no time did the chaplains have large flocks to tend, but one cannot assume that this necessarily reflected the level of demand for their services. One needs to make some allowance for the difficulties the English communities faced, including extreme isolation. The uncertainties of shipping meant that they regularly went for months, even years, without news of their friends and family at home. They also faced the pressures of living in an environment that was alien to them and that must at times have seemed frightening, even hostile. Fears of fires, earthquakes and outbreaks of the plague were ever present, and there were occasions of very real personal danger from civil unrest, as in 1770 when news leaked of British involvement against the Ottoman fleet at the Battle of Çesme. These and other hazards are covered more fully in later chapters, but they need to be kept in perspective and seen in the light of life in Britain in the seventeenth and eighteenth centuries. However, there was undoubtedly much that was interesting and enjoyable to be found in the Levant to compensate for any homesickness, and many individuals and families chose to spend decades there.

Even if Levant Company chaplains had had the time and fire in their bellies to proselytize, a handful of Church of England individuals would have stood little chance of success against the army of Latin Catholic missionaries who had been active in the region since the fourteenth century and who had met with considerable success in converting the sultan's Christian subjects to Catholicism.[41] Masters observes that, from the sixteenth century, they were further driven by the fear of Protestantism to pull all Christians of the region under the umbrella of Rome, and took advantage of the protective wall of the capitulations to engage in proselytization. The French capitulations of 1673 accorded Roman Catholic pilgrims and priests the right to visit the holy places in Palestine, and French clerics the right to reside anywhere in which the French were established.[42] Jesuit figures for Aleppo in 1714 put the numbers taking communion from them at between 5000 and 6000. If this were indeed so, then almost half the city's Christians – Greeks, Armenians, Maronites, Suryanis – were by then Catholic. Under pressure from the established Churches to halt these defections, the Porte instructed the governor of Aleppo in 1709 to forbid local Christians from attending Latin mass, clearly without effect, for the instruction and others like it were repeated throughout the eighteenth century.[43] In the face of these Catholic missionaries who had a strong continuing presence in the Levant, and particularly in Aleppo, a major concern of the few European Protestants there was to protect their own integrity against Catholic infiltration.

The Protestant EIC communities in India felt themselves similarly threatened by the many converts of Portuguese missionaries. In the early seventeenth century the EIC chaplain,

Matthew Cardrow, found a Catholic mission of the Barefoot Carmelites already established at Isfahan, in Persia. Pope Clement VIII had dispatched them there in 1604, with a threefold brief to find out about Persia, investigate the possibility of political alliance and make known the Christian faith. The Carmelites called the EIC men 'heretics',[44] but gave lodging to the factory's Scottish Catholic doctor[45] when he fell out with the company. If the Church of England chaplains of the Levant showed no real interest in proselytizing, whether or not there were opportunities, it was partly because they predated any concerted Protestant enthusiasm for it. There were undoubtedly zealous individuals operating in the region. In the late seventeenth century, for example, Dudley North wrote about an Englishman, 'John the Quaker, [as] a sort of pilgrim to Constantinople, for converting the great Turk'.[46]

From the mid-eighteenth century, the Danes started to lead the field with their mission school in Copenhagen and mission stations established in India. Nevertheless, although the Reformation happened in the early sixteenth century, widespread Protestant missionary activity did not begin until the very end of the eighteenth century. Some explanation of this can be found in Hugh Goddard's *History of Christian–Muslim Relations*, in which he relates that there were four main reasons why Protestants did not launch into mission work. This was because they believed:

1. that Jesus's call to the apostles (Matthew 28:19–20) to 'Go ... and teach all nations, baptizing them' applied only to the apostles;
2. that the doctrine of divine election precluded the need for mission;
3. that the task of mission belonged to civil rulers rather than to the church on its own; and
4. that even if the principle was right, there were more urgent tasks to hand, such as the struggle against Roman Catholicism.[47]

THE CHAPLAINS OF THE EIGHTEENTH CENTURY

Pearson records that he was unable to continue his research into the eighteenth century because the surviving minute books of the company court, which were his major primary source, cover only the period up to 1706, later volumes having been lost or destroyed. Working as he was in the 1870s and early 1880s without benefit of modern technological aids to speed up the research process, his achievements in unearthing as much information as he did about the chaplains must not be underrated. Later company court records have not emerged in the interim for the convenience of the twenty-first century researcher and, in their absence information has been garnered relating to the later chaplains largely from surviving factory records and letter books, contemporary accounts by individuals such as the Russell brothers and private correspondence of the period.

Commenting on his inability to continue his study of the Levant Company chaplains beyond 1706 for lack of later court assembly records, Pearson suggests that the decline of the company's fortunes in the eighteenth century, together with 'the failing interest in religion usually ascribed to that epoch' may have put a stop to the provision of chaplains. This was not the case, however, and the company continued until its demise in 1825 to bear the cost of maintaining clergymen at its three main factories. As we have seen, there is no evidence that this expense was ever grudged, or that it was ever suggested that a factory might do without a chaplain for a while until fortunes improved.

That the company held to its religious principles and that successive factory communities continued to want the services of a chaplain, perhaps conceals a subtle change of attitude towards the Church during the eighteenth century. Greater confidence and increasing materialism had reduced God-fearing dependence on the Church to what Spear, in his work on the British in eighteenth-century India, calls 'true piety without enthusiasm'. Respectability was highly important in eighteenth-century British society and (Spear continues) a clergyman representing 'the most genteel of the professions' had become 'the indispensable adjunct of any gathering of gentlemen'.[48] It would seem probable that this applied equally in the educated and privileged factory communities of the Levant Company. Even if religious fervour was becoming less fashionable, the chaplains were still necessary for the comforting normality of their presence and the traditional services they provided to their flocks. While the social life of the more remote and closer-knit community at Aleppo revolved around the English chapel (which was never more than a room set aside in the consul's house within the Great Khan), there is little to suggest that at Istanbul and Izmir the communities had such a focal point. In neither place were they billeted together as in the Great Khan at Aleppo, so individuals had more personal freedom. The seventeenth century habit of starting the working day with morning prayers may have grown lax in the changing spirit of the eighteenth century, though it was apparently still in place at Aleppo as late as 1778 when the factory chancellor was paid from Levant Company funds for reading prayers during a gap between chaplains.[49]

The East India Company, too, became less religiously zealous and its traditional proactive concern for the spiritual and moral welfare of its servants waned as the eighteenth century progressed. Although its new charter of 1698 stipulated that every ship of '500 tons burthen' should carry a chaplain, for the next 60 years the increasingly mercenary directors were careful to ensure that the ships did not exceed 499 tons. During this period too they not always observed the rule that 'every garrison and superior factory' should have a chaplain.[50] This was a far cry from the earlier strict religious observance of the EIC factories, where attendance at prayers had been compulsory and the sabbath was very strictly observed. Britain's growing supremacy and imperialist interest in India allowed EIC chaplains to expand their activities in ways that were never at any stage available to their counterparts in the Levant factories. They became heavily involved in the education of local children, the care of orphans and other charity work, including raising money for asylums and famine relief. They thus had a role in paving the way for the Protestant mission societies that streamed into India from the early nineteenth century.

In terms of Western Christian religious activity in general and of the Levant Company chaplains in particular, Aleppo has been found to be the factory best documented. Alexander Russell, writing in the mid-eighteenth century when he was physician to the English factory there, records that the Roman Catholics were well represented in the city. The Terra Santa convent, which was under the protection of the French consul and run by 14 Franciscan friars, had a church that was attended by all the European Catholics and many native Christians, such as Greeks and Armenians. The Capuchins and Jesuits each had three brothers in the city and a convent containing a chapel, while in the Great Khan[51] there was a fourth convent with two or three Carmelite friars. Russell observed that 'all these missionaries wear the proper habit of their order'.[52] His near contemporary, Abraham Parsons, who served as consul and factor marine at Iskenderun, the port for Aleppo, for six years from 1767, records 20 years later than Russell did that, at Aleppo, there were four 'convents of missionaries'. These were all under the protection of the French consul and he lists them as La Casa de la Terra Santa, the Order of St Francis, the Carmelites and the Jesuits.

Parsons records an amusing incident relating to these assorted Christian clergymen that illustrates the strong presence of the Catholics. It happened during his time at Iskenderun (1767–73) when a new pasha who had previously been grand vizier was appointed to Aleppo. At that time, the French were supreme among the Franks in the city because their trade was greater than that of the English, Dutch or Venetians, all of whom had consuls in Aleppo. The French consul was thus first to call on the new pasha, accompanied by 18 merchants and 30 men of religion, followed by the English consul, who had only 12 merchants and a single chaplain. The pasha was said to have observed that if he ever became a Christian he would join the English church, where there was not so much religious supervision. He was joking, as Parsons points out, but the French were very cross.[53] Indeed, such a barbed comment by the sultan's local representative, made however jocularly, must have left the French fizzing with rage and embarrassment and their traditional rivals, the English, crowing with delight.

At the same time, in Iskenderun, Parsons tells us, there was a Roman Catholic church with a burial ground under the charge of a friar from Jerusalem. The English and Dutch (as Protestants who preferred anything to Catholicism) were traditionally buried in the graveyard of the large Greek church of St Nicholas – 'a church without steeple or bell' but with a seminary that could accommodate 12 students being educated for the priesthood. The students wore black gowns and trencher caps, and were instructed by three Greek priests, the most junior two of whom were very ignorant. He adds that the Greek church had a good church plate, which it always deposited with the English consul for security.[54]

Sadly, neither Russell nor Parsons says anything at all about the arrangements for worship in place for the Protestant English of the Aleppo factory other than to record that there was a chaplain present. Research for this book has brought to light the names of two chaplains who were contemporaries of Alexander Russell – John Hemming and Thomas Crofts. Hemming, who had been educated at Eton and then at King's College, Cambridge, arrived in Aleppo in 1742–43 when he was about 25 years old. Alexander Drummond, in his account of the travels he undertook in the region before ultimately becoming consul at Aleppo, writes about Hemming, who became a good friend of his and accompanied him on at least two expeditions from Aleppo.

On 17 August 1747, the two set off on a journey 'into the

desarts [sic] of Arabia, and other countries inhabited by savages' that took them as far as Beer on the Euphrates River. Three other Englishmen from the factory, Messrs Fitzhugh, Levett[55] and Chitty, accompanied them. The party was, Drummond tells us, a very happy and cheerful group. There were no disputes and no accidents, except to Hemming, who was stricken with an attack of gout 'but bore it with admirable good humour and philosophy'. Early in the outward journey, they visited the complex of ruins marking the place of Simeon the Stylite (whom Drummond irreverently referred to as 'this aerial martyr' and 'Saint Wronghead') where they all got rather sunburnt and Hemming copied out Latin and Greek inscriptions.[56]

The following year, Drummond again took Hemming and Chitty with him, together with the then English consul, Arthur Pollard, when he set off from Aleppo 'in quest of such antiquities as had escaped the blind fury of those wretches who are now in possession of Asia'. This time they first visited the ruins of 'Old Aleppo or ancient Chalcis'. To read some inscriptions they found there, Drummond and Hemming 'were obliged to lie on our bellies for a considerable time, and suffered a great deal in the flesh from the dry thistles upon which we lay'.[57]

Although not belonging naturally or exclusively to a chapter on chaplains, some reflection is appropriate here on Drummond's frequent disobliging comments on 'the Turks'. He travelled for the pleasure and fascination of it, and in the company of similarly enthusiastic friends, but his accounts of the Levant contain a certain dismissive arrogance towards its people. In a few instances he gives low-key praise to the local Arabs, commenting for example on their industriousness, 'the men and women working hard together in the fields, and none but infants unemployed'. His occasional passing references to the hospitality and kindness he encountered on his travels (such as the gift of an antelope from a local chief) are eclipsed by profuse and caustic criticism of 'the Turks'. It is

6. Hélène Glavani and the English merchant Mr Levett *c.*1741, by
Jean-Etienne Liotard (© Musée du Louvre/DR).

interesting to note, therefore, that Drummond claims that his fellow
travellers checked and agreed on all his written accounts.[58]

His travel accounts consist mainly of letters sent to his older
brother George, the Lord Provost[59] of Edinburgh, for the information of 'our learned friends' in that city. It is perhaps fortunate that
the more measured and objective writings of Drummond's contemporary at Aleppo, Dr Alexander Russell (also an Edinburgh man),
were published in 1756, just two years after Drummond's letters.
Unlike the more enlightened and sympathetic Russell, Drummond
seems gripped by hostility towards 'the Turks', apparently stem-
ming from a bitter resentment of the Ottoman occupation of the
Holy Land and of so many sites of classical antiquity. In his letters
he churns out vitriolic comment, ranting, for example, that the region
is 'governed and possessed by creatures who disgrace humanity'
and who 'are ashamed of nothing that is base or perfidious'.[60]

Commenting on the Koran, he describes it as 'a soil so fruitful of chicanery and deceit, that it may be expounded a thousand different ways, according to the caprice, villainy and injunctions laid upon the expositors'. If Drummond did indeed obtain the approval of his travelling companions, then this view would seem to have been shared even by 'my ingenious friend, the Rev Mr Hemming'.

Sarah Searight comments that Levant chaplains often seemed to share the view of most educated Englishmen of the period that Muslims were beneath contempt and made no attempt to bridge the gap between Islam and Christianity,[61] but there is insufficient evidence for us to judge just how common such an attitude may have been. It is a fact, however, that these seventeenth and eighteenth century Church of England clergymen had no brief to foster Christian–Muslim relations. Some of the bigotry and intolerance of the early seventeenth century is perhaps reflected in the writings of Charles Robson, one of the earliest of the Levant Company chaplains, who served at Aleppo from 1625 to 1630. In a letter to a fellow clergyman in England, he writes about an aqueduct bringing water to the city 'into curious cisterns, which are in the courts of their Mos'kehs or churches, where either it is fetched for private use, or forct to wash the stinking feet of the profane Turke before they enter into their bawling devotions'.[62]

Robson seems not to have been ideal chaplain material. His Oxford college (Queen's) had been glad, because of his laxity, to grant him leave of absence to take up his appointment in Aleppo. Then, in 1631, just one year after his return from the Levant, Queen's deprived him of his fellowship because of his dissolute haunting of taverns and *inhonesta loca*, and his neglect of study and divine worship.[63] Edmund Chishull, chaplain at Izmir 1698–1702, was more interested and less dismissive. He wrote vividly of attending a Sufi ceremony that had clearly fascinated him, although he was critical of the sermon he heard there and wary of the whirling.[64] By the eighteenth century, although Britons living in or visiting the Levant continued to voice plenty of criticism of 'the Turks', little of it seems specifically anti-Muslim, relating instead to the perceived defects of the Ottoman administration or to characteristics such as greed, avarice and corruption that were applied indiscriminately to the entire native population.

John Hemming must have left Aleppo fairly soon after his second journey with Drummond, for by 1750 he had taken up the first of two ecclesiastical appointments he was to hold in rural Norfolk over the next decade. For seven years before his death in 1765 he was Dean of Guernsey. His successor, Thomas Crofts, was certainly in post by January 1750–51 when he is recorded as having accompanied Alexander Drummond (who by that time had replaced Pollard as consul at Aleppo) on a recreational trip to Mount Lebanon. Crofts, who was probably still at Aleppo in November 1753,[65] has been identified as an Oxford graduate who matriculated in March 1740 at the age of 17 and graduated with a BA three years later and an MA in 1746. His time at Aleppo from the age of about 27 was an early adventure in the life of a distinguished antiquary and traveller of wide-ranging interests. At an early stage Drummond clearly recognized his talents, found him, like Hemming, useful for translating classical inscriptions, and called him 'my learned and valuable friend'.

Pursuing his own passion for collecting rare books, coins and medals, Crofts later acted as guide to Lord Fitzwilliam through France, Switzerland and Italy during the years 1764–68. Young William Fitzwilliam was sent abroad at the age of 16 to a warmer climate and Crofts, 'an excellent scholar and very agreeable companion', was recommended by the headmaster of Eton[66] to accompany him. In 1769 Crofts was appointed chancellor of the diocese of Peterborough, an appointment that he would hold until his death in 1783. This did not, however, prevent him from setting off on further travels some months after his appointment, and he spent the next two years travelling in Italy with another young nobleman, Francis, the Marquess of Carmarthen.[67] Crofts went on to become a fellow of the both the Royal and the Antiquary societies.

Following his death, his 'Curious and distinguished library' was sold in London at an auction that took place over 42 days from 7 April 1783. The catalogue, which was available from booksellers throughout Britain and Europe, listed 9000 books and manuscripts, many of great rarity and value, and on an extraordinarily eclectic range of subjects. Reflecting his early sojourn in the Levant, Crofts's collection included many books and manuscripts in Arabic and Turkish, as well as numerous accounts by travellers to the region such as Maundrell, Chishull and Crofts's contemporary at the Aleppo factory, Dr Alexander Russell.[68] His 'Curious and valuable collection of Greek and Roman coins and medals and other antiquities' had been sold at a three-day auction a few days previously.[69]

There is no indication that the Aleppo chaplain ever had any kind of chapel premises outside the consul house in the Great Khan, and it is clear that the consul usually accommodated him free of board and lodging, which formed part of his emoluments. There must, however have been some flexibility in the accommodation arrangements. When the chaplain Thomas Owen died in 1716, an inventory[70] was taken of the goods found in his chambers, gardens and stables, which is an indication that he lived outside the khan.[71] Robert Foster, chaplain from 1770 to 1778, who married an English lady he met in Aleppo, clearly had separate quarters – although perhaps within the khan – since he was from time to time granted company funds for furniture 'for his house'. On one occasion he was also reimbursed for 'a Reading Desk and Cushions for the Chappel'.[72] All of these items were added to the factory inventory as company property.

In 1756, Aleppo's chaplain was Charles Holloway, another Oxford man from Trinity College. There were a few English women and children resident at the factory by this time and in November that year Holloway performed the first christening in the English chapel for 30 years. This happy event prompted him to open a register of marriages, baptisms and burials that has survived to this day and covers the period 1756 to 1780.[73] No other such register for any of the Levant factories has come to light. The paucity of entries in the register reflects clearly the downturn in the fortunes of the company from the mid-eighteenth century and the consequent shrinking in size of the English community present at what had once been a major outpost.

The only entry for 1756 is the baptism 'in the English Chappel' on 7 November that year of a child, Thomas Edwards van Masegh, born on 10 October. His father is recorded as 'a German settled in Aleppo about Spring 1755' and his mother as an English lady who arrived there in September 1755. (From later entries in the register these parents can be identified further as Nicholas van Masegh, the consul of the Netherlands and his wife Elizabeth.[74]) There are no entries at all for 1757. For 1758 there is only one baptism, the deaths of two wives of English merchants and the death of the chaplain himself, at 9 a.m. on 22 September 1758 in Aleppo; he was buried 24 hours later and would have been no more than 39 years old. The cause of his death is not given, but his register was maintained by successive chaplains. Entries are recorded in their personal handwriting except on occasions where no chaplain was present and records were in the hand of the consul or a senior trader. It provides a fascinating quarry of information on the more personal aspects of factory life in the late eighteenth century, which the official records little reflect, and its contents are discussed at greater length in a later chapter.

Following the death of Holloway after only two years as chaplain at Aleppo, the factory community enjoyed a long period of continuity of religious support under Thomas Dawes, yet another Oxford man, who stayed with them for ten years from August

1759. Dawes seems to have followed tradition in, like John Hemming before him, suffering from gout and holding views of the region reminiscent of those of Alexander Drummond. A private letter from Dawes survives in which he commiserates with a friend in Latakia – similarly afflicted by gout – and blames his own suffering on 'the sedentary life I am obliged to lead in this villainous country'. Dawes was less negative than Drummond, however, for he goes on to relate that 'Almost all our gentlemen as usual at this season [May] are at Baballak where we pass our time very pleasantly and the country is in all its beauty, although we are a little cold, as the house has bare walls and wooden windows.' He further adds the cheerful news that the wife of the Dutch consul, 'the very amiable Mrs Maseyk', had given birth two weeks previously to a fine baby girl and was already so well recovered as to begin to receive company.[75] Despite his gout and his perhaps fashionable reference to Turkish villainy, the Revd Mr Dawes sounds from this letter to be rather contented with his lot. His comments would seem to support the evidence contained in Chapter 5 of this book that by the 1760s the community at Aleppo was becoming more settled, and more attractive to European wives and children, than it had previously been.

On 1 January 1765, Thomas Dawes opened a 'Chaplain's Book of Charitable Donations', which survives to this day and in which he recorded the receipt and disposal of charity money.[76] Records are kept in the chaplain's own script and cover a period of five years, the last entry being made in 1770 after Dawes's departure. It is clear that a charity fund was built up at the Aleppo factory from three sources – $180 per year from Levant Company funds, paid in by the factory treasurer; collections made at services and at the Christmas and Easter sacraments; and donations and bequests. The annual income of the fund over the five-year period ranged between $203 and $293. Charitable offerings were paid out on an *ad hoc* basis throughout the year and the specific sum of $8.20 was distributed at the gates of the factory regularly, twice a year, at Christmas and in the month of June.

The list of recorded recipients is very wide-ranging and includes Armenians, Jews, Maronites, Greeks and Catholics. Some 'Syrians' are mentioned also, who were probably Suryani Christians, since there is a noticeable absence of any reference in the list to Muslims, perhaps indicating that the latter were diffident about seeking Christian charity. Assistance was granted to *inter alia* people in prison, poor pilgrims *en route* to Jerusalem, and people who had been robbed of their possessions. A blind Arab girl, a poor Wallachian slave, a sick Maronite priest, and distressed families of former factory employees all benefited from the fund. On one occasion a distressed European was helped, as were an orphaned Greek girl and 'a poor Object in the road'. Payments were made also 'to Christina, and to the widow Mulenhaver, as instructed in the will of Mr Bobbitt'.[77] In addition, the fund financed the provision of a servant to take care of the chapel. In his book, Thomas Dawes recorded too the number of those who attended the Christmas and Easter sacraments. His clients numbered only between five and eight, the most faithful being Mrs Esther Rowles who never missed a service between Christmas 1764 and Easter 1769, and who gets further mention in Chapter 5 of this work.

Given the high proportion of Levant Company money in the charity fund, it would seem likely that such funding for charitable assistance was supplied also to Istanbul and Izmir where there were also chaplains on the company payroll. Aleppo Assembly records show that as late as 1783 a decision was made that the annual payment to the charity fund there of $180 would continue to be paid.[78] This distribution of charity money was thus one means at least by which even the most sedentary and least adventurous of the chaplains had some social interaction beyond what was available within the confines of the factories.

When Thomas Dawes left Aleppo in 1769–70 after ten years at his post, he was replaced by Robert Foster, a 23 year-old Cambridge graduate, who found himself a wife there and remained until 1778, transferring later to become chaplain at Izmir. In 1774 Foster married Leonora Parker, the daughter of an Englishman and his Italian wife, and Leonora converted from Catholicism to the Church of England on her marriage.[79] By the late 1770s, the fortunes of the factory had slumped to such an extent that only a few English families remained, long-term residents such as the Vernons and the Edwards about whom there is more in Chapter 5 below. Nonetheless, a replacement chaplain, John Hussey, arrived in June 1779 to replace Foster. According to Levant Company records, Hussey left just three years later. In 1783 the post of chaplain was suspended and from 1791 until 1801 the Aleppo factory was closed for lack of trade. It seems possible that Hussey may have returned there independently of the company. McNally's work on the chaplains of the East India Company lists Hussey as having been chaplain at Aleppo from 1788, prior to his moving to India in March 1799. Hussey, who by this time had an English wife and baby son, died aged about 48 at Allahabad in October 1799 while on his way to take up a post as an EIC chaplain at Fategar.[80]

ISTANBUL AND IZMIR

John Murray, who took up his post as ambassador to the Sublime Porte on 2 June 1766, seemed not to have exercised his option to take a chaplain of his choice with him. This was perhaps because he was transferred to Istanbul from Venice, where he had resided since 1754, but was a decision he possibly came to regret, for he found on arrival that he had inherited someone far from satisfactory. He lost no time in complaining to the company about the incumbent, whom he does not name. He wrote, rather bluntly, that:

'Your Worships have a very worthless fellow for a Chaplain,

who is gone or going to Poland to teach a Pole English. I should be glad you would send some other person in his room, for he is not to be born [*sic*] any longer. If you want an explanation I shall give it to you. ... All I will tell you at present is, that every reasonable man here is astonished at my patience.[81]

Murray's correspondence with the company about this chaplain, whom Murray had very promptly thrown out of the ambassador's residence, continued for many months. Before the end of July, the man had quit Istanbul, leaving behind him not only great debts but also his clergyman's habit, with instructions that it should be sold after his departure; Murray concluded from this that he had no intention of continuing his clerical career. The company claimed that the chaplain had told them nothing of any plans to go to Poland. On the contrary, he had written requesting a few months leave in England to deal with 'the melancholy situation' of his father's family there. The company had replied to him and assured Murray that 'he will show you the answer we gave him'. By the time Murray received this information the chaplain had long since gone and we do not know what that answer was. The chaplain later asked the company to allow him until November of that same year to decide whether to return to Istanbul from Poland, but the company assured Murray that they would not heed the request, since the ambassador clearly would not welcome him back.

Murray's fury at the behaviour of his chaplain was fuelled by the long delays in getting any replies to his letters. Initially reticent about reporting the more indelicate detail of the errant chaplain's shortcomings, he was provoked by December into revealing that the chaplain had been 'convicted by the evidence of several persons of having committed an insult in my house upon a Woman at a time when she was lying upon the ground in a most violent Hysteric Fit'. Referring to the man's duplicity in asking leave to return to England when he had already agreed to go to Poland, Murray added:

> Deceit is always abominable, but it is insufferable in a Clergyman when it is sure of being detected. I shall not enlarge further than to assure you that he is not worthy your Service, and to beg you that he may never have an opportunity of setting his foot within my doors as long as he lives.

It is evident that this was more than a straightforward personality clash between Murray and his chaplain because there had been other complaints both towards the end of Grenville's time as ambassador and during the period of Kinloch's interim charge. On both occasions the chaplain had written to the company to the effect that he had found himself 'under disagreeable circumstances with respect to board and lodging at the British Palace', so it would seem possible that they too found him uncongenial. Writing to Murray of this state of affairs before he left Venice to take up his post, the company said that such difficulties over a chaplain's accommodation were unprecedented and they were confident that Murray would comply with what had always been customary.[82]

Although, as we have seen above, Murray asked the company in 1766 to appoint a more suitable chaplain to Istanbul, no evidence has come to light that anyone took up the post. There is also nothing to suggest that Murray had any personal interest in religion whatsoever. He had married conventionally enough in York Minster, but his later acquisition of an Italian Catholic mistress with whom he had four children may have jaundiced any earlier loyalty to the Church of England; certainly no hint has been found in his correspondence that the factory gathered for prayer meetings during his time as ambassador. From August 1768 there were references in his outgoing correspondence to an English chaplain at Izmir, the Revd Mr Clendon, who paid a visit to Istanbul and whom the ambassador accommodated. Murray subsequently wrote of Clendon to his consul at Izmir, 'He may be the best and most orthodox Divine in the world. Wearing the long gown is quite needless; for if he was cloathed in scarlet, I could swear to his Profession.' Clendon's visit was not without incident. Having returned to Izmir he engaged in correspondence with Murray about the theft in Istanbul of a communion plate, an indication that he performed religious duties there and that his visit was not merely recreational. The ambassador replied that:

> I have made all possible Enquiry to find out the Servant you suspect to have robbed you of the Communion plate. I can find no Traces of him here. If I should meet with him, I shall endeavour to frighten him into a Confession; which is all I can do as you yourself have only a Suspicion, that he is the Thief.[83]

Just two weeks later, Jasper Abbott, a company man based in Angora (Ankara), was unable to find a clergyman there to christen his child. Murray wrote to him with pragmatic advice that seemed to reflect Murray's own low regard for clergymen, physicians and their like:

> I am sorry you could not prevail upon the Danish [this has been underlined, and in the same hand has been written above it 'Swedish'] Minister to go to Angora to christen your child, but for want of a proper person you can undoubtedly do that office yourself which will hold good both in the Eye of God and Man. If hereafter you find a proper qualified person you may have the Child christened over again conformable to the law of the Church.[84]

Of Clendon's predecessors at Izmir, one incumbent seems to

have been in post for at least 20 and possibly as long as 35 years. The Revd Charles Burdett, who arrived about 1724, was still there at the end of 1744 when Alexander Drummond visited for a few months *en route* to Aleppo. A list of the personnel of the Izmir factory dated October 1759[85] shows that, by that date, Burdett had been replaced by a Philip Brown and from 1760 he was back in England and rector of Guildford. It was during Burdett's incumbency, and under Consul Samuel Crawley, that Drummond established at Izmir during this short visit a lodge of freemasons, the first in the Levant and 'the first daughter of the Lodge of Drummond Kilwinning, from Greenock'. Drummond reported in his letters home that he had 'made many worthy brethren in this place', and that the 'native ladies' of the place – knowing of his freemasonry activity – were intrigued by him, and 'thought me a bit odd, some kind of priest or conjuror'.[86]

Robert Ainslie, who succeeded John Murray as ambassador at Istanbul in 1776, was a Scot and therefore unlikely to have exercised his right to choose a chaplain, given that the incumbent had to be a Church of England clergyman. The Istanbul factory was small during the embassies of both Murray and Ainslie, with the number of factors reduced to only five by 1794, the year of Ainslie's departure, and the post of chaplain may have been unfilled during much or all of that period.

New rates of pay were set in 1794 for the chaplains' posts at both Istanbul and Izmir, possibly with the dual purpose of recognizing the steep rise in the local cost of living and attracting candidates for the posts. That same year, Ainslie's successor, Robert Liston – also a Scot – employed James Dallaway (1763–1834) as chaplain to the factory. Like some of the earlier Levant chaplains, Dallaway had no formal clerical qualification, Church of England or otherwise. He had, however, accumulated three degrees, including one in medicine, prior to his employment by Liston. He is recorded as being appointed in the dual role of chaplain and physician, although it is not clear whether his medical responsibility was personal to Liston and his household or extended to general practice.

Liston, who was unmarried at that time, spent only two years at Istanbul, although he returned with his wife in 1811 for a much longer second stint as ambassador. Dallaway returned to England with, or soon after Liston, and was back there by 1797. He went on to follow a career path that was neither specifically clerical nor medical, becoming for more than two decades secretary to the Duke of Norfolk, Earl Marshall of England. He edited Lady Mary Wortley Montagu's letters and published an account of Constantinople as well as local histories of Sussex.[87] It may be that, in employing a man of Dallaway's calibre, Liston was merely taking advantage of the salaried position for a chaplain at Istanbul to fill it with a well-educated young man who might provide him with intellectual stimulus and congenial company. Liston, a graduate of Edinburgh University, was a career diplomat and an excellent linguist, who had at one time been tutor to the family of the Earl of Minto in the classics, law and – more surprisingly – dancing. He may have feared that social life with the small English community at Istanbul would prove dull.

The last chaplain of the eighteenth century at the Istanbul embassy, Philip Hunt, arrived in 1799 with Ainslie's successor, the Earl of Elgin. He was later to achieve notoriety as the man Elgin sent two years later to Athens (then, of course, part of the Ottoman empire to which Elgin was accredited) to arrange and personally supervise the removal of large parts of the Parthenon, which were shipped to England and would later become famously controversial as 'the Elgin marbles'. Although Elgin's appropriation of these sculptures is notorious because of its grand scale and audacity, there are indications in some of the private correspondence that survives among Levant Company records that the collection of more modest personal souvenirs was not uncommon. Grassby records that, in the late seventeenth century, at least one English merchant, Nathaniel Harley, dealt in the export of more exotic commodities, including Arabian horses, falcons and ancient statuary.[88]

In the 1740s, Alexander Drummond writes of shipping home as a gift to the Duke of Argyll an inscribed stone that had been picked up near Palmyra and later presented to Drummond by a fellow Scot. This was a Mr Munro of Culcairn, who found the stone while travelling towards Aleppo with a desert caravan from India. Drummond also mentions an inscribed stone kept in the factory library at Aleppo[89] and clearly many other such artefacts were brought to Britain during the lifetime of the Levant Company in the personal collections of officials, merchants and chaplains alike.

CONCLUSION

The initiative that led to the presence of clergymen at the principal English factories in the Levant for over two centuries came from the communities themselves. In the more God-fearing early years of the company this arose from genuine feelings of need for the protection and support of a church in these distant outposts. There was no shortage of Christian churches of Eastern denominations in the Levant, and there had long been a strong Roman Catholic presence in the region. However, England and the Levant Company were firmly Protestant and the communities wanted their own Church of England to be represented among them. By the eighteenth century, a clergyman had also become a drawing-room accessory in polite English society, a change in role that was reflected in the small groups of essentially privileged and well-educated Britons who resided at the Levant factories. He was by now required for the respectability he brought, as much as for the performance of the usual functions relating to baptisms, marriages, deaths and worship.

The motives that drove individual clergymen to seek overseas appointments with the Levant Company were various, but personal religious fervour would appear to have been low on their list of priorities. Upholding the spiritual well-being and Protestant integrity of such small flocks of parishioners can hardly have presented much of a challenge to any cleric alight with crusading zeal and, as we have seen, the chaplains made no attempt to operate in any professional capacity outside the confines of the factories. They did not get involved in charitable works apart from administering the distribution of small amounts of alms money. For many chaplains, the Levant Company posts, with their modest but regular salaries, provided a convenient vehicle for the pursuit of private interests, such as the study of the Eastern churches and visiting the Christian holy places in the region.

For its part, the Levant Company, anxious to keep its remote communities in order and to prevent any moral laxity that might be detrimental to the good relations with the Ottomans on which its trade depended, was only too happy to provide and pay for a chaplain at each of its three most important factories. There was recognition that some church presence was a reasonable request, unremarkable in the social climate of the seventeenth and eighteenth centuries, and that chaplains might be expected to serve company interests and preserve its Protestant ethos by providing a civilizing influence and by helping prevent any leakage towards the great enemy, Catholicism. Their inclusion on the payroll throughout the lifetime of the company was thus a form of insurance, well worth the small premium payable, rather than a humanitarian gesture towards the company's overseas communities.[90]

4

The Physicians

As discussed in the preceding chapter, the Levant Company made some provision at its three largest overseas factories for the moral welfare of the communities of Britons living there. This chapter covers the company's contrasting detachment from responsibility for their physical well-being, and consider both the health problems that the communities faced and how they coped with them.

Rather less has been recorded in the archives or written by historians on the physicians who served the Levant Company factories than on the chaplains. Because the chaplains were salaried employees of the company, there are a fair number of references to them in the official records of both the company in London and its factories in Istanbul, Izmir and Aleppo. As has been shown in the preceding chapter, the company accepted responsibility to provide for the spiritual welfare of its overseas personnel by both supplying and paying for chaplains at each of its three principal factories, but the company made no such arrangement in support of its overseas agents' physical well-being. Virtually no references to physicians appear in the formal records and it is clear that those who served the factories in that capacity were not salaried employees of the company. Rather, they were engaged locally in some private arrangement with the 'gentlemen of the factory', or simply attached themselves to the community informally and earned their keep by charging for their services. Wood, in his chapter on life in the

Levant factories, refers frequently to the preoccupations of the English communities with the dangers of local illnesses, including the plague, but fails to address the subject of medical services beyond a single reference to 'the resident doctors who were established in the largest factories'.[1]

This apparent lack of any Levant Company concern to provide healthcare might be explained away as merely a reflection of the times were it not in stark contrast to the policy of the contemporary East India Company (EIC). From its outset the latter recognized the need for medical support in its ventures and made provision for it. The earliest ships it dispatched to India in the first decade of the seventeenth century each had its appointed surgeon on board, and, once factories had been established in the east, they too were provided with salaried medical officers. The earliest EIC factory to be set up in Persia, at Isfahan in 1616, had a doctor on its payroll from 1619. This contrast in policy between the two rival companies is especially remarkable since, in the early seventeenth century, they had many senior members in common, rich London merchants such as Maurice Abbott, Hugh Hammersley and Henry Garraway, who had already made fortunes from trading and could afford to invest in both ventures.[2]

One possible explanation could lie in the companies' differing staffing arrangements. Whereas all EIC officials and factors were salaried personnel of the company, which thus took corporate responsibility for them, Levant Company factors, who formed the main body of its overseas personnel, were employed individually by their merchant masters in London. It could also be that the East Indies, because of its greater distance from England and more extreme climate, was regarded as presenting higher health risks than the Levant. Whatever the reasons for this difference in approach, the Levant Company's detached attitude has left us with no official documentation on medical arrangements at its overseas factories. Information is scarce on the doctors who tended the English communities at Istanbul and Izmir, although Aleppo is better documented, at least for the eighteenth century.

ISTANBUL

Given that an ambassador assigned to Istanbul usually had a sizeable entourage of personal staff, some of them brought from England, it would seem logical that this would include a doctor, who might reasonably be expected to care also for other company personnel and their dependants. That this was not always the case, combined with the Levant Company's corporate *insouciance* towards the provision of medical care, suggests that fear of disease was not a major concern of the factory communities. The greatest dangers to life and limb probably lay in the long journey from England. Once travellers were safely arrived, their health was most likely at no greater risk in the ports and cities of the eastern Mediterranean than in England during the seventeenth and eighteenth centuries.

Indeed, the softer climate of the region, together with the plentiful availability of good local produce – especially fresh fruit and vegetables – must have been positively advantageous. Diseases such as smallpox, cholera and typhoid could as easily be caught in England. The greatest risk in the Levant came from the plague, which still remained prevalent in the region, but, though an outbreak often killed large numbers of the local population, Europeans learnt to protect themselves by adopting self-imposed quarantine and only a handful succumbed. There is nothing in the history of the Levant Company that has come to light to suggest that the rates of death and sickness, from whatever cause, among the factory communities were such as to raise alarm. Certainly the region at no time acquired the aura of a 'white man's grave' that came to be associated with other areas of British overseas enterprise.

There is, on the contrary, evidence that by the second half of the eighteenth century the Levant was coming to be regarded as offering recreation and positive health benefits. When Henry

Grenville travelled to Istanbul in 1762 to take over the embassy there, Lord Warkworth, eldest son of the Duke of Northumberland, who was sailing around the Mediterranean for his health, joined him and his family in Naples and accompanied them on their voyage to Istanbul.[3] Grenville's successor, John Murray, reported to London in 1773 that Lord Algernon Percy had come to Izmir to take the air, and 'if he could he'll go to Egypt as he dreads the cold.' Murray went on to warn, however, that the Istanbul air was fatal in 'any Complaint of the Breast'.[4] A few weeks later, a merchant, William Luard set off for Istanbul, Izmir and Aleppo 'for the recovery of his health, as well as for trade'.[5]

Between 1772 and 1774, George, the 20-year-old 9th Earl of Winchelsea, enjoyed a grand tour of the Mediterranean, including a visit to Istanbul. He travelled on a British merchant vessel and a personal physician, the Scottish doctor Alexander Monro Drummond,[6] accompanied him. Also in holiday mode, in May 1774, the French ambassador at Istanbul took some local leave and travelled to Bursa for three weeks to drink and bathe in the waters there, although, as Murray rather acidly records, 'he does not seem to have the least occasion for them, and takes his family with him.'[7] That the Comte de Saint Priest felt able to leave his post and take his family on holiday at this time must reflect the end of the long war between Russia and the Porte. Peace negotiations had been under way for some months and were completed in July 1774.

To return to the question of ambassadors employing doctors, it has not been possible to establish how common it may have been for them to take a personal physician to Istanbul, because – as with the envoys' wives – a doctor's presence or otherwise is seldom recorded, and then only if he is in some way unusual. We know, for example, that Ambassador Bendysh had his own doctor in 1649 because he drowned while accompanying one of Bendysh's sons on a pilgrimage to Jerusalem.[8] Ambassador John Finch, MD (Padua), who took over the embassy in 1672, was a qualified physician but was accompanied during his nine years in Istanbul by his old friend and fellow doctor, Thomas Baines, who acted as physician to the 'embassy'. It is not clear whether this can be interpreted as covering the factors, or just Finch's household and company officials.[9]

Dr Charles Maitland (1668–1748), a surgeon engaged in England to accompany Ambassador Edward Wortley Montagu, his wife Lady Mary and their young son Edward on their posting in Istanbul, travelled overland with them, arriving in March 1717. He attended the birth of Lady Mary's second child, a daughter, in Istanbul in early February of the following year, assisted by Dr Emanuel Timoni[10] and, in a letter to her sister shortly after this event, Lady Mary commented wryly, 'I don't mention this as one of my diverting adventures.'[11] Maitland is on record as having at some stage graduated in medicine from Aberdeen University, but given that Lady Mary referred to him as a surgeon rather than a physician, this may have occurred after his return from Istanbul.

In the seventeenth century, and well into the eighteenth, surgeons and apothecaries, having learnt their trades by means of apprenticeship rather than academic study at a university, were generally worse educated than physicians. Lady Mary was to be instrumental in raising Maitland to modest fame later for introducing into England inoculation against smallpox. Herself disfigured as the result of an attack of the disease in girlhood, Lady Mary had observed, while in Edirne (Adrianople) on her way to Istanbul, the local practice of 'engrafting' or implanting a small quantity of the pox bacteria as a preventive measure. On 19 March 1718 (a few weeks after the birth of her daughter and without consulting her husband who had been away for many months attending the sultan at Sofia), Lady Mary had Maitland 'engraft' her son Edward against smallpox. Writing to her husband a few days later, she told him the boy – then aged about five – seemed fine, and she would have had the baby treated also but for the fact that her nurse had not had the disease. Ambassador Wortley Montagu's posting to Istanbul was curtailed and by early 1719 the family had returned to England, where Lady Mary's social connections ensured that news of her son's successful inoculation was spread widely.[12]

MACKENZIE AND MACKITTRICK

John Murray certainly did not employ a physician. The letter book containing his outward correspondence on company matters for his first few years in post reveals that he had a low opinion of medical men. Writing in March 1768 to the English consul at Izmir about the illness of a diplomatic colleague there, he says, 'I am heartily sorry for M. Hochpied's indisposition, but I don't think he will suffer much for the want of physicians. I have no great faith in that tribe.'[13] As we have seen in a previous chapter, Murray was transferred to Istanbul direct from Venice, where he had been resident since 1754, and took with him a considerable household, including an English postilion (coachman), but he apparently found no need for either a chaplain or a physician. For instance, when his postilion was mortally wounded in a fight with another servant, Murray sent 'a surgeon' rather than 'my surgeon' to him.

We know that on his arrival in Istanbul Murray inherited a resident doctor who lived under the ambassador's roof and was therefore, presumably, provided also with his board, although he was not part of the company establishment. The presence of this man in the house (along with that of a chaplain) was a remnant of an arrangement that Henry Grenville, Murray's predecessor, had permitted. Murray's letters indicate that the man was a Dr Mackenzie. For example, in July 1768, Murray asked the English consul at Aleppo to convey his compliments to Dr Russell (the resident physician at Aleppo) 'who was so kind to mention me in his letter to Dr Mackenzie'.[14]

Writing to the company a few months later, complaining that he has been 'surrounded with the most wrongheaded family [namely household] that ever poor man was plagued with', Murray declared that Dr Mackenzie and the company's chancellor, Mr Lone, were spying on him and that he was determined to get rid of them both. The situation regarding the physician was clarified vividly when in June 1769 Murray learnt from his consul in Izmir that a Dr Mackittrick was on his way to Istanbul. Revealing the extent of his exasperation with Mackenzie, whom he had by this time tolerated for three years, and his low opinion of the profession in general, Murray wrote an irascible response:

> Your letter by Dr Mackittrick is not yet come to hand, nor do I know how I can serve him. He writes me that Dr Mackenzie has resigned. If he means his Gallipots[15] I have no objection to his entering upon the Premises. What else he had to resign I can't find out. If he means to succeed him in his Lodgings, I beg leave to be excused; for I found his Predecessor in this House, and I have let him run about it like an old snarling Dog that is left without a Master and that Compassion won't suffer you to hang; otherwise he is certainly the most backbiting old Curr, that ever was permitted to live. He may have studied Galen and all the Tribe; but he knows as much of practical Physick as I do of the practical Part of making Shoes. I certainly upon your Letter shall do Mr Mackittrick no Harm, but I have many material Objections against these itinerant Scotch Doctors that run about the World without Recommendations. And I think if you have been a good Physiognomist, you might have discovered a Spice of Madness. There are some very ingenious Men of the Profession here, that don't get Salt to their Porridge, and I am afraid he will be one of the number.[16]

Dr Mackittrick got off to a bad start with Murray, who, prejudiced by his experience of Mackenzie, was in no mood to tolerate another Scottish doctor under his roof. The luckless Mackittrick distinguished himself by getting arrested on his arrival for lack of funds. In some exasperation, Murray further writes of him:

> To give you a slight Hint of this Gentleman's genius. When he first presented himself to me, in order to win my favour, he told me, that the Ship that brought him here, hurried him away from Marseilles, before he had Time to take his letters of Credit upon me. He told me, when he left the West Indies he quitted Business that rendered him £1000 p.Ann. And when I freed him from his Chains ... as soon as my Janisary's horse could gallop there, he seemed much disgusted at paying the Hire.

This account of Mackittrick would seem to identify him as James Mackittrick (1729–1802). If so he was a native of Inverness who graduated with an MD (Edinburgh) in 1766 and practised medicine both before and after that date in Antigua.[17] Mackittrick is reported to have had a high reputation as a doctor, although he 'provoked animosity wherever he went' and was at one time in Winchester gaol for provoking a duel. Mackittrick had returned to Scotland from Antigua in 1766 to take his MD. To receive this he was required only to present and defend a thesis,[18] for by that time he had already qualified to the extent that he had completed the requisite number of prescribed medical courses. He returned to Antigua some time after his graduation. It is possible that he had known Mackenzie – an older man – in the West Indies and had followed him to Istanbul in 1769. It is unclear how long Mackittrick remained there, as Murray's letter book contains no further reference to him, but, despite his alleged personality problems and unpromising start at Istanbul, he had a successful career thereafter. On his return to Antigua, he became physician to the commander-in-chief of the Leeward Islands and to the colonial troops, and a judge on the King's Bench there. He was also a fellow of the Royal College of Physicians of Edinburgh, and a member of the Royal Medical Society.

Returning from Antigua, Mackittrick settled in England and practised medicine in Andover, Guildford and Bath. His publications include an essay written in 1799 for the benefit of his Bath clientele entitled *Regime for the Preservation of Health, Especially of the Indolent, Studious, Delicate and Invalid*, and a *Natural History of Body and Mind*. More controversially, he wrote a paper setting out 'Unanswerable arguments against the abolition of the slave trade' in support of the European residents of Antigua. In 1783 Mackittrick took to calling himself James Mackittrick Adair, adopting what was probably his mother's maiden name. He died in Harrogate on 24 April 1802.[19] No publication relating to his time in Istanbul has come to light.

No mention has been found in Murray's surviving correspondence of there being a resident doctor at Istanbul in Murray's time after Mackittrick. One incident that Murray reported to London at the end of 1773 indicates that, at that time, he probably had no doctor living in his residence and was relying on his own resources. Over a period of several months there had been many deaths in Istanbul from 'a Distemper' that caused people to spit blood. From the European community, the Prussian envoy's secretary had been obliged to leave the country having contracted this disease.

By December, the sultan was indisposed and unable to go to the mosque on the first day of the Bairam festival, much to the disappointment (Murray records) of Lord Winchelsea and his party, who were visiting Istanbul at that time and had been looking forward to this occasion as 'the best show of the year'. That same evening, 'an old Turk physician' came to Murray's house asking for medicinal bark with which to treat the sultan. Murray gave him all he had in the house, but when the man found that it was in powdered form he would not take it unless Murray packaged it up himself and sealed it with his personal seal. As the physician explained, the grand signor would not take the bark unless it came from the English ambassador. This was no doubt partly a security measure, but it was surely also an extraordinary compliment to Murray personally, indicating that he was trusted and respected, and also a recognition – justified or otherwise – of the validity of European medical skills. Sadly, the bark had little effect, for the sultan died on 21 January 1774.[20]

Izmir

Little information has come to light on the physicians who attended the English factory at Izmir in the eighteenth century. For the late seventeenth century we have a lively account by Sonia Anderson of Dr Benjamin Pickering, a physician at Izmir during the consulship of Paul Rycaut (1667–78). Pickering, who was accompanied by his English wife and two sons, was the son of a Sussex rector and holder of an Oxford BA degree. Although Anderson records that he became an extra-licentiate of the Royal College of Physicians, and that his library contained works by all the major medical and botanical writers, no evidence has come to light that he had a medical degree.[21] We know too that in 1693 the Dutch community there employed two Jewish physicians. These were 'Portuguese Jews', descendants of a group expelled from Portugal who had settled in London in Tudor times, and were thus effectively Englishmen who had presumably received their medical training in England.[22] The availability or otherwise of their services to the English factory was no doubt related to the vagaries of Anglo–Dutch relations.

One colourful indication of how the English community coped with its medical problems at the end of the seventeenth century can be found in the biography (by his brother) of Dudley North, a merchant of the company who served in both Izmir and Istanbul during that period. It contains descriptions of various ailments he suffered there, including twin 'fungous excretions' on his knees, a possible after effect, it is implied, of his having felt obliged to sit cross-legged for many hours at a formal audience with 'a great man', during which his legs went quite numb. These growths became so big that North could barely walk, and he was advised to have them removed. Fearing the loss of his legs, or even his life, he instead dealt with them himself, squeezing them until all the 'curd' they contained had issued 'and so made an unexpected but perfect cure upon himself'. On another occasion, we are told, North had for long been indisposed and 'complained to one of their quacks, whom they called doctor'. Such terminology would seem to indicate that there was no reassuring compatriot physician to hand at the time who might be consulted (although it does not rule out the presence of one or more who did not inspire confidence).[23]

DR ANDREW TURNBULL

There was certainly a physician attached to the factory at Izmir in October 1759, when a list of the English nation and those under consular protection was usefully inscribed in the Register of Assemblies.[24] He was another Scot, Dr Andrew Turnbull, who is listed as being married to a French lady. Listed also as coming under the consul's jurisdiction is 'An Hospital belonging to the English nation, for Sailors in time of Sickness'. No hospital staff members appear on the list, and the hospital gets only one other mention – not clearly dated, but probably $c.1770$ – in the register, to the effect that its beds and quilts were in disrepair and should be replaced. The existence of this latter entry in the official records would seem to indicate that the costs of replacements would be met from company funds, with the further implication that the company entirely financed the hospital. This would make it all the more odd that the doctor was not on the official payroll, but the hospital may only have functioned on an *ad hoc* basis during an epidemic. There was a severe outbreak of plague in both Izmir and Istanbul in 1770, which could account for the need to replace the old beds and bedding.

We have a description of the hospital, albeit 30 years later, from John Howard, who visited Izmir around 1786 as part of a tour of the Mediterranean lazarettos to assess the usefulness of building one in England. He recorded that the city then had several hospitals, including one 'recently' built by the English factory for sick sailors. It had three rooms, all on one floor, one unfurnished, one containing three patients and the last furnished but with no patients. There were also two small unfurnished rooms in the back courtyard, intended for people infected with the plague. Howard said that, at the time of his visit, the Dutch had almost finished building a similar hospital opposite the British one, and there were in addition hospitals belonging to the Venetians/Italians, French, Jews and Greeks at Izmir.

Dr Andrew Turnbull later became well-known as a colonizer in the Americas and the prime mover behind the establishment of the settlement of New Smyrna in Florida.[25] In 1759, he was about 43 years old and had recently married Maria Gracia, the daughter of a Greek merchant of Izmir. She was considerably younger than her husband was and regarded as a lady of spirit and determination.[26] By 1764 the couple had already been back in London for some years and must therefore have returned from the Levant soon after their marriage. Dr Turnbull had become established in London as a wealthy and successful physician, and the couple moved in high social circles, numbering among their personal friends the Earl of Shelburne and Lord Grenville, both secretaries of state.

In 1766, Turnbull obtained from the British government a land grant for 20,000 acres of his choosing in Florida. He chose fertile land, excellent for agriculture, and augmented his holding by purchasing from his own resources a further large area, which he designated as a cotton plantation. Turnbull arrived in Florida with his wife and seven children in November of the same year, settling them initially at St Augustine. He then returned almost immediately to London to embark on a bizarre plan to colonize his land with Greeks. As colonists he wanted people who were accustomed to a warm climate and who would work his land for him. He felt that Greeks, of whom he had much personal experience from his time in the Levant, would be ideal and would, moreover, welcome the opportunity to escape from Ottoman rule. Setting sail from London in spring 1767 in a converted sloop, manned and provisioned at his own expense, he headed for Greece (then, of course, part of the Ottoman territories). Despite opposition to his plan from the Ottoman authorities, he managed to persuade '200 wild tribesmen' from the Mani area of the southern Peloponnese to take up his offer of a new life.[27]

Turnbull was in Greece until about November 1767. His 'very delicate' activities made Ambassador Murray in Istanbul decidedly nervous. Lord Shelburne, who knew Turnbull personally and declared confidence in him, supported the project as 'meritorious', while making it clear to Murray that Turnbull was acting entirely on his own initiative and not under any 'Commission from His Majesty'.[28] Nonetheless, there was considerable relief in Murray's reaction to news from his consul at Izmir that Turnbull had finally departed from their parish.[29]

Turnbull had not finished his recruiting, however, and went on to collect 110 Italians at Leghorn and 1000 Minorcans before finally setting sail from Gibraltar with 1500 souls in eight ships, all of which arrived safely in Florida in June 1768. Within eight years, half these immigrants were dead, mainly from malaria. The traditional local name for Turnbull's land was Mosquito Inlet, but this was long before medical science linked mosquitoes with malaria and no warning bells rang with Turnbull, despite his being a physician by profession. Nonetheless, the settlement ultimately flourished, and Turnbull named it New Smyrna after his wife's home city. The

Turnbull family prospered also, later moving to Charleston in South Carolina where Dr Turnbull died on 13 March 1792 and Maria Gracia on 2 August 1798 at the age of 68.

ALEPPO

In the case of Aleppo, we know that the community was blessed, for a continuous period of more than forty years from 1740, by the presence of three Scottish doctors, all of whom were later to attain eminence both as physicians and as botanists. The half-brothers Alexander and Patrick Russell of Edinburgh served the English factory at Aleppo from 1740–53 and 1750–71 respectively, residing there together for a period before Patrick took over his brother's post. Patrick Russell was in turn succeeded by Adam Freer – almost certainly another Scot, although his place of birth has not been established – who graduated with an MD from Edinburgh University in 1767. Patrick Russell recommended Freer to the factory and the latter remained in Aleppo at least until 1779 and possibly until 1780–81.

We know that other Scottish or English doctors preceded Russell at Aleppo, because his brother Patrick writes in the 1794 edition of *Natural History* that Alexander, unlike his predecessors, had taken the trouble to learn the local language. It has been impossible to discover the names or other details of doctors who were there in the early part of the eighteenth century, before Alexander. There is an indication, however, that a Dr Brown may have been one of them, or had at least visited Aleppo.[30] This was possibly Dr James Brown (1682–1733), MD (Rheims) and Fellow of the Royal College of Physicians of Edinburgh who is listed as having practised at Kelso in the Scottish Borders, Istanbul and Barbados. The Revd Mr Harrington Yarborough, who held the post of chaplain at Aleppo for three years from 1703, held a degree in medicine, and may also have acted as physician to the factory. Patrick Russell observes that little is known of the 'medical gentlemen' who may have resided at Aleppo in the seventeenth century.[31]

GEORGE STRACHAN

There is one intriguing report of a Scot who was in the region in 1615 and who practised as a doctor although he had no formal training. Sir Henry Yule told his story in an 1888 article based on information taken from the diaries of the seventeenth-century Roman traveller, Pietro della Valle.[32] The man in question was George Strachan, originally from Brechin in the Mearns region of Scotland (and not, as Crawford wrongly deduced, from Mearns in Kincardineshire). Della Valle had crossed paths with Strachan on a number of occasions during his travels, and knew him quite well. What he related was thus based on personal acquaintance. He described Strachan as an educated Catholic gentleman of noble birth, little wealth and a talented linguist. Brought up and educated in Paris, Strachan had entered the Scots College in Rome in 1602. Ten years later he was in Istanbul, where he spent several months as the guest of the French ambassador before moving on to Syria with a view to learning Arabic. While in the city of Aleppo in 1615, he heard that a local tribal chieftain needed a physician and, borrowing some books and prescriptions from a Flemish doctor he knew there, Strachan presented himself to Emir Feiad (della Valle's spelling) and was appointed despite having no medical training. His assumption that, as an educated man, he could cope, was doubtless less extraordinary in the early seventeenth century than it would be today. In fact, he did succeed. He spent two years in the desert between Baghdad and Aleppo with Feiad's nomadic tribe, became a 'court favourite' and much revered figure and, according to della Valle, had more patients than any doctor in Naples. Strachan adopted Arab dress and, della Valle further records, so good did his Arabic become that he could pass for a Bedouin. He also put great effort into studying Islam.

Under increasing pressure from Feiad, who had given him a Muslim wife and was urging him to convert to Islam, Strachan escaped from the tribe near Baghdad and eventually made his way to Persia. There he attached himself in June 1619 to the small EIC factory at Isfahan. It would seem that Strachan had meanwhile maintained his contacts with Aleppo, for the English consul there, Libby Chapman, wrote to the Levant Company in September 1618 recommending the employment as a physician of 'Strahanna, a Scotsman residing at Bagdad'.[33]

The EIC factory at Isfahan was the company's first in Persia and had been founded just three years previously in 1616. The Englishmen stationed there, who included a chaplain (Matthew Cardrow), had reservations about Strachan, not least because he was a Catholic. They found him more of a Frenchman than a Scot, and certainly not an Englishman, and they wondered if he were even a good subject of His Majesty, and could be trusted with knowledge of EIC business. The personal qualities that endeared him to the Bedouin, however, clearly worked again for Strachan, for they eventually welcomed him, gave him board and lodging and soon employed him both as their physician and for his linguistic skills, at a company salary equivalent to £40 a year.

It was in Isfahan that Pietro della Valle became well-acquainted with Strachan, although he had heard tell of him during his years with the nomads. The two were fellow Catholics, and each found the other congenial company. Such was their friendship that della Valle even invited Strachan to be godfather at his nephew's christening in the city in April 1620, although Strachan was ill on the day in question and an English merchant stood proxy.

Within a year of his appointment, however, Strachan fell out with the Englishmen and the company, from which he had demanded a salary of £100 rather than the £40 offered, dismissed him. He took lodging for a while at the convent of the Barefoot Carmelites in the city, and was last encountered by della Valle in

Gombroon (Bandar Abbas) in November 1622, where he claimed to be in 'confidential employment of the English'. Strachan was ill, and declared his intention to seek recovery in the healthier climate of Lar to the north and then make his way back to Isfahan. Nothing is known of what became of him thereafter, although Yule believed that he may eventually have returned to Europe.[34]

THE EIGHTEENTH-CENTURY SCOTTISH DOCTORS

The presence of Scottish doctors in the Levant Company factories in the eighteenth century needs to be set in context. As we have seen in the short history of the company contained in the introduction to this book, the Levant Company was a quintessentially English – as opposed to British – organization. Founded in 1603, 22 years before Scotland and England came together under a single crown, it was the creation of a powerful corporation of wealthy London merchants. Although there was no ban on provincial merchants joining the company, very few did. Londoners applying to join, that is anyone who lived within 20 miles of the City, had to be freemen of the City before they were admitted.

By 1595, the merchants in London each had their separate factors established in the Levant. Apprenticeship to a 'Turkey merchant', as they called themselves, was expensive and these young men were almost invariably relatives of company members, the sons of their friends and acquaintances, or the younger sons of the English aristocracy. This pattern was to continue until 1753 when, in response to a surge of anti-monopolistic protest in England, most restrictions on entry to the company were lifted by an Act of Parliament. One further consequence of the company's very English nature was that all the chaplains appointed to the Levant factories were Church of England clergymen, and themselves Englishmen.

For more than 150 years, the Levant Company was thus effectively an English 'closed shop', an elitist club for the wealthy and well-connected. Indeed, company records show that the terms 'English factory' and 'English nation' were still being used even at the end of the eighteenth century to describe its overseas establishments. Following the Union of the Parliaments of England and Scotland in 1707, there was an unsuccessful attempt to encourage the use of the term 'North Britain' in relation to Scotland. But, as one historian observes,[35] whereas by 1750 most thinking Scots were prepared to see themselves as British as well as Scots, the English on the whole continued to think of themselves as English.

Although there is no evidence that Scottish merchants ever penetrated the Levant Company, even after the relaxation of entry regulations in 1753, some Scots were to become involved during the eighteenth century in non-trading roles as administrators and, most famously, as physicians to the factory at Aleppo. This was the era of what came to be known as the Scottish Enlightenment, a period when the economic benefits of Union began to be felt and when the intellectual life of the country flourished to the extent that Scotland gained a reputation in the eighteenth century as an important centre of Western culture.

The capital city of Edinburgh, despite having suffered the loss of the Scottish parliament and the consequent shift of political power to London, was at the centre of this cultural upsurge by virtue of its wide and solidly professional middle class and by the strength and reputation of its university.[36] Edinburgh was awash with lawyers and doctors. During the eighteenth century, almost half the students at the university were studying medicine. It was inevitable that many would have to leave Scotland to find employment, and there had long been a tradition that newly-qualified doctors sought to expand their knowledge by spending time in the great European centres of medicine such as Leiden and Paris.

THE EDINBURGH MEDICAL SCHOOL

When Alexander Russell began his studies at Edinburgh University's medical school in 1733, it had been established barely ten years, although lectures in medical subjects had been available for some time before that and the university's first MD degree was awarded in 1705. In the 1730s, the curriculum of the school was undergoing radical reform under the leadership of a progressive group of professors trained in Leiden by the renowned Hermann Boerhaave (died 1738), who was considered the greatest medical teacher of the age. The reputation of these men attracted students from England, Scotland and Ireland, and even from the new 'plantations' in the West Indies and North America, who came to secure in Edinburgh what was becoming seen as the best medical education obtainable outside continental Europe.

Leiden, although a Protestant foundation, was open – uniquely in seventeenth-century Europe – to students of all religions and had attracted many dissenters from Britain.[37] At this time, the English universities were in the grip of the Church of England, and admission was barred to dissenters. Under the 1707 Treaty of Union, Scotland had retained its own separate established Church, which was Presbyterian, and there was no such ban on attendance at Scottish universities.[38] Alexander Russell would thus have been exposed to the influence of fellow students whose experiences ranged from far beyond his native Edinburgh.

Medicine was also taught at King's College at Aberdeen University and at Glasgow, where the first MD degrees were granted in 1696 and 1703 respectively, but in the 1730s Edinburgh was the flagship of Scottish medical training. In August 1734, six young men studying medicine there, including Russell, who were friends 'in the habit of spending social evenings together at a tavern'[39] formed a little medical society that would meet fortnightly to listen to readings of medical dissertations by its members. By the following summer, five of the six had left to go their separate ways, but the society flourished and was later granted a Royal Charter as the Royal Medical Society of

Edinburgh, a body that survives to this day, albeit reduced to a student body within Edinburgh University.

THE RUSSELLS

To view in perspective the achievements of the Russell brothers, and to assess the validity of their accounts of Aleppo in the eighteenth century, some study of their background is required. While every scholar with an interest in Aleppo is aware of them, and has delved into and much quoted from their major work, *The Natural History of Aleppo*, written by Alexander Russell and published in 1754, then edited and updated by Patrick Russell 40 years later, there is as yet no biography of the Russells *per se*. Nonetheless, because they both reached positions of eminence in their field and in London society, a certain amount is at least known about their professional lives.[40]

Alexander (*c*.1715–68) and Patrick (1727–1805) Russell were born into a respectable (by today's standards middle-class) Edinburgh family with a tradition of adherence to the legal and medical professions, which their own generation continued. They were half-brothers, the sons of an eminent lawyer, John Russell of Braidshaw, who married three times and had numerous children, all boys. We are told (albeit in a eulogy to one of his sons) that John Russell:

> enjoyed the singular happiness of bringing up seven of [his boys] to man's estate without ever inflicting chastisement … and lived to the age of 86 … to the last attended, whenever he pleased, (which was most of the time) with cheerful company of both sexes, and of all ages.[41]

The eldest of the seven brothers, John Russell of Roseburn[42] became a lawyer like his father, and stayed in Edinburgh.[43] Another brother, William, is recorded as being secretary to the Levant Company in London in 1777, when he was admitted – apparently on the strength of his position – as a Fellow of the Royal Society. In fact the post of secretary rotated among the company's officials and senior merchants, and was usually held for just one year at a time. The traveller Wood, who documented Palmyra, names Russell in the post of secretary also in 1746. Such a long association with the Levant Company indicates that William must have been either a London-based merchant (which would have been unusual for a Scot at that time) or simply a non-trading employee who served them for many years, eventually attaining a reputation that made him Royal Society material. In either case, it is reasonable to assume that he was instrumental in attracting his brothers to seek related employment.

Another brother, Claud, joined the East India Company and rose to become administrator of Vizagapatam on the Coromandel Coast. Of one brother, David, nothing has come to light. The remaining three sons – Alexander, Patrick and Balfour – all became physicians. The youngest, Balfour (born 30 October 1733), practised as a surgeon-apothecary for three years from 27 March 1752, and graduated with an MD from Edinburgh in 1759. He is understood to have died shortly after taking up an appointment as a physician at Algiers, possibly also in some connection with the Levant Company.[44]

ALEXANDER RUSSELL (8 SEPTEMBER 1714–28 NOVEMBER 1768)
Of the two brothers whose careers took them to Aleppo, let us look first at Alexander, the son of his father's second wife, Ursula, who died in 1717 when Alexander was an infant. John Russell had married Ursula in 1706, a year after the death of his first wife, Maria. All the children of his first marriage died in infancy. Maria's father was Andrew Russell, a merchant in Rotterdam, who might later have influenced his son-in-law's children towards the Levant Company. Two other children of this union, out of a total of nine born between 1706 and 1717, survived to adulthood: these were

John, born 1710, and William, a year older than Alexander. After attending the High School of Edinburgh – a traditional place of education for sons of the city's better-off – and two years of general classes at the University of Edinburgh, Alexander was apprenticed to an uncle, probably Francis Russell, one of Edinburgh's leading medical practitioners, and then attended two years of lectures by the professors of medicine at the university.

Aged about 20, and without collecting his degree (not at that time obligatory), Alexander headed off in 1735 for London – perhaps to join his brother William – and from there embarked on a period of travel in Europe and the Levant, which took him to Aleppo in 1740. A recent article on the Russells[45] suggests that Alexander knew of an opportunity 'for further training' in the factories of the Levant Company through his brother William. Alexander settled at Aleppo 'at the unanimous request of the gentlemen of the English factory in that city'. We are told that when he arrived, he immediately applied himself to the study of the language (Arabic is what is meant here, rather than Ottoman Turkish) and 'soon overcoming every difficulty, commenced practice at Aleppo with greater advantages than had ever before fallen to the lot of any Christian physician'.[46]

A less partial personal description of Alexander Russell is contained in a fragment of a gossipy private letter written by Jasper Shaw, a factor at Aleppo, in 1753, in which he describes his fellow compatriots at the English factory. According to Shaw, Alexander bore some physical resemblance to his brother, William, in London; he had been very successful in Aleppo, but spoke of leaving the following spring; the book he intended publishing would show his 'ingenuity and close application to business'. Alexander was facetious and fond of gently teasing his friends at the factory. He also had a fine singing voice and was only too willing to provide entertainment when asked.

Both he and his younger brother Patrick played the flute and 'a grand Concert of Musick'[47] was held once a fortnight at Alexander's house. Well-educated and congenial as he clearly was, Alexander Russell must have fitted quite well into the small factory community. He was much the same age as the young Englishmen stationed there and the consul for his last few years at Aleppo was a fellow Scot[48] from Edinburgh, Alexander Drummond. Alexander was not, as we have seen, an official employee of the company, and consequently kept his own independent establishment in the city, a fact that, together with his knowledge of Arabic, gave him (and the doctors who succeeded him) more contact with the local inhabitants than was possible for any of the company's men.

The Natural History is an objective account of Aleppo and in no sense an autobiography. Neither Alexander Russell in the original nor Patrick in the later version writes much about his personal experiences there. The book does, however, reveal indirectly how they practised and how, being independent and without any guaranteed salary, they earned their living. Medical practitioners, we are told, were numerous in the city and were generally respected. They kept shops at their houses, or in separate premises, where they prepared medicines and saw the sick at appointed hours. Advice was free to all, but there was a charge for medicines and treatment.

The clinics were packed, with separate consultation rooms for men and women.[49] Like other European doctors (mostly French or Italian) in the city, especially those who had learnt Arabic, the Russells attracted plenty of custom from 'natives of all ranks ... [including] the Grandees'.[50] As an indication of the level of access doctors enjoyed, Alexander records that any physician with the slightest pretext of business was readily granted privileged entry to Aleppo's citadel, the headquarters of the city's large Ottoman garrison, the commander of which was answerable directly to the Porte rather than to the local pasha. This was where military personnel and their families lived although, in Alexander's opinion, there was nothing worth climbing up there for save the view.[51]

7. Dr Alexander Russell by T. Trotter, after N. Dance (Wellcome Institute).

Alexander enjoyed the approval and trust of Ismail Pasha, who served as pasha at Aleppo for several years instead of the more usual one year and who, according to Fothergill, even sent gifts to Alexander's father in Scotland.[52] European doctors were expensive and thus consulted only after cheaper alternatives had been found wanting. Instant cures were expected and patients were rarely prepared to follow a recommended treatment for long before moving on to try their luck with some other doctor. Although much respected for their skills, the Europeans were generally considered to employ 'violent' medicines, none more so than the English. Any deaths were blamed on the medicines or treatment provided, so Europeans clearly had to tread carefully. They were thus inhibited from treating local patients as they would wish and it was often found expedient 'to prescribe where no medicine was required, as well as where there were no hopes of its being of service'.[53] Patrick made it a rule never to tell his patients how ill they really were, although he claims never to have concealed the truth from their relatives.

Similarly, surgery was a dangerous undertaking for a European doctor and was left to the Muslims, who were less susceptible to *avanias*[54] should a patient die. Surgery, moreover, was regarded as a rather low-class activity and physicians of eminence did not practised it.[55] It was, indeed so risky and the citizens of Aleppo so inclined to litigation, that delicate operations such as the removal of cataracts were left to 'itinerant practitioners of more courage'.[56] Patrick further observes that the dissection of dead bodies was not permitted at Aleppo.[57] Nonetheless, Ragab Pasha, whom Patrick describes as unusually liberal, offered Patrick Russell written authority to open up anyone who had died of something unexplained. He considered this altogether too risky a prospect and declined, but it is an indication of his local standing that this extraordinary offer was made.[58]

During 'sickly seasons'[59] at Aleppo (namely periods when some or other illness was rife in the city) the services of the European doctors were particularly in demand. As well as continuing to care for their own regular patients, whom they treated according to European methods, they were often called to visit patients under the care of 'native' doctors. In such instances, it was not uncommon for the European, opposed to local practices, to be 'constrained to remain an inactive spectator'. Alexander Russell admits that, at times of plague, he employed someone to go and visit the sick for him. This would seem to have been more out of concern for himself or fear of bringing the disease into the English community rather than mere pressure of work, for he adds that he did not do so in 1744 when the outbreak was less dangerous.[60] Patrick was more courageous in 1760 when on several occasions he visited three Armenians who had contracted the plague in a khan near the English Consulary House. They died and as a result the doctor found himself 'in a kind of Quarantine with respect to our own Gentlemen'. [61]

Both Russell brothers witnessed severe outbreaks of plague in the city. It raged in 1742, 1743 and 1744, and then did not return to Aleppo until 1760, again recurring in three successive years. Treatment was limited to the supposed cure-alls employed for virtually all ailments – bleeding and evacuation, the latter involving laxatives such as rhubarb and senna, or the promotion of vomiting by emetics. Muslim doctors, according to Russell, saw the plague as a curse from Allah that had to be endured, while Christian and Jewish doctors were afraid of catching it. The sick were thus largely left to survive as best they could.[62] The Europeans in Aleppo adopted a self-imposed quarantine known as 'shutting up' for the duration of each outbreak, which was very successful. Alexander writes that local Christians and Jews followed suit where they could, or fled the city. Muslims whose principle of predestination constrained them from taking overt precautions, found excuses to stay at home as much as possible, depart on a pilgrimage, or make a commercial journey to a distant city.[63] It seems clear that avoidance of the disease by whatever ploy offered the best, perhaps only, hope of survival, given that the treatment doctors could offer was unlikely to have been effective.

Alexander Russell remained in Aleppo until 1754, having scarcely set foot outside it in 14 years. He later described his journey home as extremely agreeable, although he could have wished for a few more months in Italy where, as well as taking some recreation, he spent time in the lazarettos of Naples and Leghorn as part of his research into the plague. By February 1755 he was back in England; he visited family and friends in Scotland before settling in London. Throughout his years in Aleppo, Alexander Russell had – at the suggestion of his friend Dr John Fothergill – recorded his observations and experiences, and this work was published on his return to London as *The Natural History of Aleppo and Parts Adjacent*. The title is explained by the passionate interest of both Fothergill and Alexander Russell (and, as we shall see, of Patrick Russell) in botany. This was a period of intense interest in finding effective cures from plants and many doctors were also botanists, some, including Fothergill, with their own experimental gardens. *The Natural History*, conceived as a work on the plants and herbs of Aleppo, contains exquisite drawings of some of these.[64] However, such was Alexander's fascination with every aspect of the place that the range of the book expanded to include not just the natural world but descriptions of the city, of the local population and of many aspects of life there in the mid-eighteenth century.

The Natural History was received with great acclaim and in May 1756 Alexander was elected a fellow of the Royal Society. For four years he practised medicine in London, before joining the staff of St Thomas's hospital in 1760. He was made a licentiate of the Royal College of Physicians that same year. He held his post at St Thomas's until his rather premature death 'of a putrid fever' in November 1768. John Fothergill, a fellow student from Edinburgh, provided a postscript to what we know of Alexander's character and reputation. Having tried unsuccessfully to pull his old friend through his final illness, he recorded the following tribute: 'For my own part, when I recall what I have lost in him, the sensible, firm and upright friend, the able, honest and experienced physician, the pleasing, instructive companion of a social hour, expression fails me.'[65]

PATRICK RUSSELL (7 FEBRUARY 1727–2 JULY 1805)

Alexander Russell was joined in Aleppo in 1750 by his half-brother,

Patrick, who was 12 years younger and at that time 23 years old. They remained there together until 1754, when Alexander resigned and Patrick succeeded him as physician to the English factory. Patrick's mother was Mary Anderson, the daughter of a Church of Scotland clergyman. She married John Russell on 15 October 1719 and died on 27 January 1759. Patrick may have studied medicine at King's College, Aberdeen, before taking his MD in Edinburgh. He, Claud, David and Balfour were the surviving sons (two others, Thomas and James, died in infancy of smallpox) of this, his father's third marriage. Patrick was to spend a further 18 years in Aleppo, where, like his brother, he appears to have achieved high personal standing in the community.

The correspondence of John Murray, who was ambassador at Istanbul from 1766 to 1775,[66] reveals that he was in occasional communication with Dr Russell, for whom – despite his general impatience with 'itinerant Scotch doctors' and his own bad experiences of them – he clearly had both liking and respect. As we have seen in Chapter 2 above, Murray was often at odds with the gentlemen of the factory at Aleppo, whom he thought a rather bizarre and ill-mannered lot. In letters to the consul there, however, he frequently asked for his compliments to be passed to Dr Russell, saying that he valued his friendship and describing him as a sensible man and one who seemed capable of humanity. In July 1768, having heard that the doctor might be leaving Aleppo, Murray wrote to the consul, Henry Preston, saying, 'I am sorry he leaves you so soon, as good men are scarce in the Levant.'

As he does for Alexander Russell, Jasper Shaw provides us also with a personal description of Patrick in 1753. He also reveals that, while the brothers were together at Aleppo, Patrick was a member of the consul's household, presumably as personal physician to Alexander Drummond – another Edinburgh man – and his family. Shaw paints a picture of Patrick as a humorous, good-natured, charming young man, of a lively and merry disposition, and immediately likeable. He went by the local nickname of 'Shadow' for some supposed resemblance to the apothecary in Shakespeare's *Romeo and Juliet*, and Shadow, we are told, was 'one of the most conversible men among us'. Both he and his elder brother wore 'Turkish Dress' and Patrick had the reputation of being the best Arabic-speaker in the factory (although, as Shaw points out, few others of them were in a position to judge).

There is no indication that the routine of life in Aleppo was any different for Patrick Russell than it had been for his brother before him. Like Alexander, he was referred to in official and personal correspondence from within the factory as 'our doctor', but remained independent and self-employed, his services available to all comers, although he no doubt gave priority to the English community of which, socially, he was a member. A number of original letters have survived from Patrick to company personnel stationed elsewhere in the region, to whom he was clearly in the habit of providing both medical advice and drugs on request. A letter to Cyprus, for example, in 1760, enclosed pills and rhubarb, and recommended cold baths as a treatment for fever, to be taken in the cool of the morning.[67] Treatments for all complaints remained predominantly bleeding or some sort of purging, used in conjunction with a variety of herbal concoctions.

One of the Aleppo factors, Colville Bridger, records consulting Patrick Russell in May 1762 about an eye disorder that flared up several times each year and that was rife in Aleppo. Bridger's eyes became sensitive, so that the cold air of winter blinded him, as did the brightness of the sun in summer, and he was thus unable to enjoy to the full the riding, hunting and other outdoor pleasures pursued by many of his colleagues. In this case 'our Worthy Doctor' advised him to drink asses' milk, which seemed to ease the condition.[68] The unfortunate Bridger was possibly grateful not to have been prescribed goats' milk, for the local goats were fed on garbage, and their milk tasted of garlic or cabbage leaves.[69]

Like his brother before him, Patrick Russell gained the confidence and respect of at least one of the ruling pashas during his time at Aleppo, who granted him the privilege of wearing the turban. There is a portrait of him so attired at the Wellcome Institute Library in London. Such favour was no doubt something of a two-edged sword for both brothers, for Patrick writes, in his foreword to the later edition of *Natural History*: 'amid the fatigues of an extensive practice ... much time must be sacrificed to the medical attendance expected by persons of the higher class.' Rather surprisingly, he records later that it was not unknown for 'women of the harem' to come to the doctor's premises when their illnesses did not necessitate a home visit.[70]

The doctors' high level of daily contact with local people of all ranks, and at such intimate level, together with their personal prestige, must have been unique in the English factory community, and can only have been positive factors in its relations with the ruling hierarchy and, more generally, with the local population of the city. Official contacts with the Ottoman elite were limited to occasional formal audiences granted to the consul by the pasha, the head of the judiciary, and the collector of taxes, and were heavy with ceremonial; only the last of these three ever returned a call. Whether the consuls and other company personnel recognized the value of the doctors' greater local insight and made good use of it is not recorded. Certainly no instance has come to light of either of the Russells being invited to attend any assembly, but their advice could well have been sought informally.

During Patrick Russell's time at Aleppo, the fortunes of the Levant Company and consequently of the factory declined. Trade became sluggish in the 1750s and 1760s in the face of competition from the French, and there was a spate of bankruptcies among the English merchants at Aleppo in 1763. Whereas in 1751 there had been ten merchants at the factory, numbers had dropped to eight in 1753 and by 1772 were reduced to only four.[71]

There is no indication that either of the Russell brothers ever engaged in any trading activity and, since the factory community provided only a fraction of Patrick's clientele and therefore of his income, it is unlikely that he was much affected professionally by the vagaries of trade. This independence, enjoyed also by Alexander, which would have allowed him to form his own opinions rather than having to adhere to any company line may be the key to the Russells' marked objectivity in their writings about the city. They were notably sympathetic to and appreciative of cultures and beliefs that were very different to their own, but no less worthy of respect because of it. Both had gone to Aleppo voluntarily, and, unfettered by contracts, each in his turn chose to spend many years there. It must be assumed that they did so because they found personal contentment and professional satisfaction in the city.

Patrick Russell left Aleppo in June 1770, taking advantage of his journey from the city to the port of Iskenderun, several days' ride away, to collect specimens of mountain flowers. He writes that his brother Alexander had never travelled in Syria with botany as an objective,[72] and that both brothers had collected plants only from the surroundings of Aleppo. Patrick had handed over his position at Aleppo to a young Edinburgh-educated doctor and botanist, Adam Freer, who had been in the city at least since 1769. He settled back in London in 1772, by which time his brother Alexander had been dead for four years. There is no indication that the two saw each other again after 1754, and this would seem unlikely, but they remained in touch. For example, an original letter survives from Alexander at his house in Walbrook (City of London) in 1762, under cover of which he sends a parcel of newspapers to Patrick at Aleppo.[73] And for 14 years until Alexander's death the brothers kept in regular correspondence with a view to expanding and updating *The Natural History*.

Patrick inherited his brother's papers, which included a diary of

8. Dr Patrick Russell by W. Ridley (1811)
after L. Vaslet (Wellcome Institute).

the progress of the plague in Aleppo in the years 1742, 1743 and 1744, and in due course began – declaring with great modesty his own inadequacy for the job – the huge task of expanding and updating Alexander's work. From 1772 Patrick Russell practised medicine in London and in November 1777 followed again in his brother's footsteps by being elected as a fellow of the Royal Society.

148

Among his sponsors was his older half-brother William, once again in the post of secretary to the Levant Company and by this time himself a fellow. Patrick was also sponsored by the distinguished botanist, Joseph Banks, and by Banks's close associate the Danish botanical artist, Daniel Solander, both of whom had returned in 1771 from their three-year voyage around the world aboard Captain Cook's ship *Endeavour*.

In 1781, at the fairly advanced age of 55, Patrick left London for India, initially to act as personal physician to his brother Claud and his family. The East India Company had appointed Claud, who was six years younger than Patrick,[74] as administrator of Vizagapatam on the Coromandel Coast, to the north of Madras. While there, Patrick made a study of local plants and fish, and in 1785 was formally engaged as a naturalist to the East India Company and member of the Indian Medical Service, with responsibility for the Carnatic plain to the south of Madras.

It seems probable that, in the spirit of the times, the EIC was seeking to identify plants with potential commercial benefit. King George III, who was a keen gardener, had recently authorized Banks to undertake research at the Royal Botanical Garden at Kew. His brief covered all the plants of the colonies, with the objective of identifying any that might bring economic benefit to Britain. Following his official appointment, Patrick continued living in Vizagapatam, but travelled extensively thereafter, gathering information and specimens. He held the position until his resignation in 1789.[75] When Claud returned to England, Patrick went back also, having placed his collections in the company's museum in Madras.

His reputation firmly established in contemporary eyes as a great botanist, Patrick settled in London and resumed his work on *The Natural History*, the second edition of which was eventually published in 1794, this time in two volumes, and 40 years after the original version. Alexander's original bore the dedication 'to Alexander Drummond, Esq., Consul, to the gentlemen of the

British Factory at Aleppo, and those now in England who have formerly served there'. Alexander Drummond, who served as consul at Aleppo from 1751 to 1758, and thus knew both the Russells, was, as we have seen, a fellow Scot from Edinburgh. He apparently shared their interest in botany, for he sent back home to his brother George, the Lord Provost of Edinburgh, some cedar seeds that were planted and grew into trees that survive today in the city's Spylaw Park. Patrick had meanwhile also written *A Treatise of the Plague*, which was published in 1791. After a further outbreak of the plague in the Levant, the Privy Council consulted him about quarantine arrangements. In 1791 also, a new statute, the 'Act to Encourage the Trade to the Levant Seas' finally abolished the 1753 requirement for ships coming to England from countries where plague had been reported to spend time *en route* in quarantine in one of the Mediterranean lazarettos. Patrick Russell died in London on 2 July 1805, aged 78.

ADAM FREER (C.1747–1811)

As we have seen, Patrick Russell left Aleppo in 1770 and Adam Freer took over his position as physician to the English factory. From a subsequent entry in the assembly book for Aleppo[76] we know that Dr Russell recommended him for the job. While the Russells are invariably mentioned in any literature on the history of Aleppo, Adam Freer would seem to have been eclipsed by his predecessors since his name does not appear at all. Investigation has revealed that he was a student of medicine at Edinburgh University and graduated with an MD in 1767, indicating that he was probably born around 1747. Although there is every indication that Freer was a Scot, it has not been possible to prove this absolutely. In the lists of Edinburgh medical graduates for the year 1767, written in Latin, he is described in the spirit of the age merely as 'Brito', in contrast with earlier entries that distinguish between Scottish and English students, and no record of his birth has come to light. His thesis on venereal disease – '*Dissertatio medica inauguralis de syphilide venerea; nec non de morbo Sibbens dicto*' – was published in Edinburgh[77] in 1767.

While at university, Freer made a reputation for himself as a botanist studying with Dr John Hope (1725–86), the illustrious professor of botany and *Materia Medica* who, from 1760 until his death was also Regius Keeper of the newly-founded Royal Botanic Garden of Edinburgh. Freer was something of a *protégé* of Dr Hope. In a letter of 19 August 1764 to a fellow-botanist (Dr Pulteney), Hope writes 'Now for Botany. Mr Freer has been staying with me all summer and has collected nearly 100 plants which were not in my collection.' The following year, the *Scots Magazine* contained the following announcement: 'A gold medal for promoting the study of botany, given annually by Dr Hope, Professor of botany in the University of Edinburgh, was adjudged on the 20th of May to Adam Freer, for the best collection of individual plants. [Adam Freer is] a student of medicine in the University.'[78]

A short biography of John Hope, written in 1986,[79] mentions that Adam Freer made a collection of plants in Aleppo. It has recently been established that, among John Hope's papers, which his grandson bequeathed to the Royal Botanic Garden of Edinburgh in 1865, is a 'List of the plants growing in the neighbourhood of Aleppo prepared ann. 1769', which undoubtedly is that of Dr Freer. The date of this list confirms an indication in a surviving assembly record book for Aleppo covering the period from 1768[80] that Dr Freer had been in Aleppo since at least 1769. He must therefore have known Patrick Russell there for a year or more prior to succeeding him as factory physician. It is reasonable to assume that some eighteenth-century networking, leading from the Edinburgh connection, was instrumental in taking him to Aleppo. The Russell brothers were certainly known to Professor Hope, for Alexander was one of his sponsors for a fellowship of the Royal Society in November 1766. Freer is known to have been in London in 1768 (from where he corresponded with Hope) and could well have met Alexander Russell before the latter's death in November of that year.

Early on in his career at Aleppo, the young Adam Freer achieved prominent mention in the assembly record book referred to above as a result of two incidents involving him that were the subject of discussion and investigation by the assembly in June 1772. They caused quite a furore and are recorded in detail and at some length. These records are of interest because they reveal some of the nervousness officials at Aleppo felt about the inexperience of the young Dr Freer compared with his two trusted predecessors. They confirm that the doctors were indeed independent of the Levant Company and that they maintained houses, consulting rooms and pharmacies outside the confines of the factory, where they treated anyone who sought their services. They also provide a valuable insight into the problems that the job could present. These accounts are further remarkable in that nothing similar covering the daily work of the Russells or of any other Levant Company physician has come to light in the official records.

The first of the two incidents was triggered when, on 18 June, Dr Freer informed the English consul, John Abbott, that a Jewish woman in the town was believed to have the plague. This news created consternation in the factory because an English ship, the *Tigris*, had just been loaded with cargo in the port of Iskenderun and was due to sail for home that day. It was the responsibility of the consul to issue it with a clean bill of health, but an outbreak of plague would paralyse trade, and a lengthy shipping delay could mean huge financial losses.

The ship's imminent departure was suspended, and an assembly was immediately called at which John Clark was asked to investigate and report on the matter. John Clark was the only one of the English merchants with no direct personal interest because 'he has neither just despatched a ship, nor does he have one waiting for despatch, nor one as per concern [*sic*] in either the *Tigris* or her cargo'. On 29 June 1772 he read out to the assembly a lengthy declaration, in which – in a clear case of 'shooting the messenger' – he is savagely critical of Dr Freer for breaking this disagreeable news, although the latter had candidly admitted that he had never actually seen a case of the plague.

Freer had based his report to the consul on the accounts of other doctors who had visited the woman, on descriptions of the disease contained in a local copy of Alexander Russell's *Natural History*, and on notes about the plague he had inherited from his immediate predecessor, Patrick Russell. This discredited his advice in the eyes of Clark, who said that Freer owed it to his own reputation, and to the consul and nation, to have informed himself better, presumably by going personally to examine her. Nonetheless, Clark magnanimously declared his belief that the young doctor had not acted out of any malice.

Clark then went on to produce attestations by three other doctors – one Jewish, one French and a Dr Bimbini, described as a Frank doctor who had long resided at Cairo – all of whom had actually visited the woman and declared that she did not have the plague. There is no reason to believe that Freer was reluctant to examine her out of fear, or even out of revulsion or squeamishness. He had, after all, written a dissertation on venereal disease. It seems likely that he simply bowed to the opinions of other doctors, probably older and more experienced than he was.

Arguing that cases of the disease did not happen in isolation and that, under Levant Company rules, any declaration of an outbreak should be taken only with the consensus of the French and Venetian consuls, Clark recommended that the English consul go ahead and issue a bill of health to the *Tigris*. If he did not do so, he explained, the honour of the Levant Company in the eyes of other nations, as well as the interests of many individuals, would lie entirely at the mercy of 'a young, unexperienced [*sic*], credulous

Doctor'. He then added for good measure that the factory should not allow a situation to develop in which 'the Doctor, tho' Independent of the Levant Company, becomes the most consequential man in one of the most essential points regarding the company's trade from Aleppo'.

By his own admission, Clark was young and perhaps given to speaking too freely. He claimed he meant 'no personal affront' to Dr Freer, but there was perhaps some rivalry between the two that led him to speak so disobligingly. Consul Abbott, to his credit, was not won over. He declined to issue a bill of health without further investigation. He further said that Freer's opinion on the case ought to be preferred to that of any other, since Dr Patrick Russell had recommended him to the factory as a person well skilled in his profession, and had been found to be a man of honour and probity. Abbott, for one at least, seems to have recognized that, if you have a professional on hand, you might as well listen to his advice.

Discussion and extensive investigation continued frantically over the following few days. Interested parties, including Dr Freer, were called before the assembly and questioned. The factory's chief dragoman was sent into the city streets to listen out for talk of plague, and reported that there was none. Reports were sought also from Antioch and proved negative. The three doctors who had attested that the Jewish woman did not have the plague were discredited when it was discovered that none of them had been permitted to examine the suspicious swelling in her 'privy parts', and they had been able only to look at her tongue and feel her pulse, both of which were healthy.

It was established that none of the Jewish community had stayed away from the synagogue on the previous sabbath for fear of a case of plague in their midst. The leaders of the Armenian, Maronite, Greek and Suryani Christian communities were required to sign declarations that they knew of no cases of plague among their flocks. The panic eventually subsided, and on 2 July

Consul Abbott concluded that it was safe to clear the *Tigris* to set sail.[81]

The ship finally left harbour with a clean bill of health on 13 July. By this time, the Jewish woman had made a full recovery and it had been concluded that she had suffered only 'a putrid fever'. Moreover, it had been recognized that she was one of a family of 15 to 20 people, all of whom had visited her and none of whom had fallen ill. One of the English factors, David Hays, was so incensed by the losses he incurred as a result of what he regarded as a pointless delay in the departure of the *Tigris* that, on 16 July, he took the exceptional step of drawing up a 'Publick Instrument of Protest'. In it he declared Consul Abbott, his heirs, executors and all others concerned with the detention of the ship liable for all losses, expenses and damages. The text of this document was copied into the assembly register. The original was presumably sent to the Levant Company, but no information has come to light on how it was received or on whether the matter reached the English courts. Abbott and Hays continued at Aleppo together into the 1780s, an indication, perhaps, that they managed to resolve their differences.[82] By a quirk of fate, Hays's widow, Louisa, later married Abbott's son, Robert.[83]

The second incident involving Dr Freer, which was not unconnected to the first, occurred on 30 June while the first was raging. That morning, Freer rushed from his house to the consul's residence in the Great Khan to report to Consul Abbott that a 'Greenhead'[84] had made a formal complaint against Freer for allegedly attacking his elderly father. Freer was accused of seizing the man by the throat and insisting that he should assert that there was plague in the city. The doctor was said to have then poured brandy all over the man, who as a result was claimed to be dangerously ill. Dr Freer admitted that he knew the alleged victim, whom he had indeed asked about the plague, the man being employed as a washer of dead bodies and attendant at funerals. The man had come to Freer's house that morning to give him some information, but had been seen by a number of bystanders and queuing patients to leave it again perfectly content. Several of these witnesses, including one Hamid Effendi who was the owner of Freer's house, attested that no such attack had taken place.

The English factory closed ranks around Freer. The chief dragoman accompanied him to call on the *kehya*[85] at the seraglio that very day, where both parties were called to account and the Greenhead's story totally discredited for lack of evidence. To show their recognition of Freer's innocence, the English merchants of the factory requested the consul to spare no pains in bringing the Greenhead to justice. He was to meet 'the Whole of the Expenses that may attend the process as also the procuring such satisfaction which is esteemed essentially necessary for the Honour of this Nation, as well as the deterring of others from attempting anything of the like Nature against any of the Factory in the Future.' It was unanimously agreed that all expenses should be paid out of 'the Right Worshipfull Levant Company's cash'.

It is clear from this that, although Dr Freer may have been 'independent of the company', and had, only the previous day, brought the factory the most unwelcome news, he was regarded very firmly as one of their own. Not only did they offer him their full support, but they also allocated company funds to obtain justice for someone who was not a company employee. This incident further appears to illustrate even-handedness on the part of the Ottoman administration, with the *kehya* taking the part of a Christian Frank over a Muslim who was moreover a member of the respected *ashraf*. Although this could conceivably suggest that Freer had some standing with the Ottoman officials because they were his patients, it is perhaps more of an indication that the *ashraf* were not in fact universally popular.

Alexander Russell writing *c*.1753 mentions the use by Europeans of the term Greenheads. He tells us that there were a great many of them in Aleppo, the wealthy congregating in the district of Bankufa and forming a 'numerous and formidable body including persons of all ranks'. They wore a distinctive green sash around their turbans, and were led by their chief, 'the Nakeeb', whom the Porte nominated. They enjoyed extraordinary privileges. Anyone who married the daughter of a 'Greenhead' could adopt the green sash and children of such marriages became 'Greenheads' through the matriarchal line.[86] Ambassador John Murray also used the term from the 1760s in his official correspondence from Istanbul, by which time, through common usage, it seems to have lost any pejorative implication it might originally have had, although Murray does on occasion refer to 'Greenheads' as 'a troublesome breed'.[87]

These hiccups in his early career apparently did no lasting harm to Dr Freer's standing in the eyes of the Aleppo factory. By the end of the following year, it was clear that he was by no means entirely 'independent of the company', for he sought the 'Licence and Permission of the Consul and the Gentlemen of the Factory' to travel out of Aleppo to Latakia to tend to the ailing English consul there, John Murat, who had asked for him.[88] Permission was immediately granted at an assembly meeting and Freer was able to spend some time with poor Murat before the latter died. This incident is interesting because it is the only instance that has come to light of such a mission of mercy. Certainly, Patrick Russell and possibly also Alexander offered a mail-order medical service to company personnel stationed elsewhere in the region, and several letters survive that contain medical advice and clearly accompanied supplies of drugs, addressed to men at Acre, Iskenderun, Tripoli and Latakia, but neither of them travelled away from their base.

Dr Freer's local standing clearly continued to grow, for in May 1776 it was agreed at an assembly meeting that he be recommended to the Levant Company to have an annual salary, 'he being thought a very necessary and useful man to the Factory in general'. The chancellor advised Dr Freer of this decision, but there is no further reference to the matter in the assembly registers until nearly three years later. An entry dated 5 February 1779, referring to an application from Dr Freer to the consul the previous November, records that the consul now planned to write to the Levant Company asking it to grant Freer a gratuity of $400 a year.[89] No evidence that he wrote the letter or that the request was ever granted has come to light, but it is noteworthy as the only indication found of any thought that a physician might become a salaried employee of the company. How much longer the doctor remained at Aleppo thereafter is not clear, but just two years later he had left the Levant and was in Bengal. Perhaps he had been threatening to leave Aleppo for some time, and the promise to request a salary for him was no more than a carrot to entice him to stay; or maybe the request was made in good faith but fell on deaf ears in London.

In moving from the Levant to India, Freer was following a trend that seemed to have started in the 1780s and no doubt reflected the downturn in the Levant Company's fortunes and the growing prosperity of British India.[90] For that reason it is interesting to include here details of what became of him there. In Bengal Adam Freer took up an appointment as assistant surgeon with the Indian Medical Service (IMS) on 6 July 1781. He was still a young man, at that time aged about 34. Records show that he was appointed locally, rather than in London, and it would seem therefore that he went there speculatively, hoping to find employment, and possibly directly from Aleppo.

Bengal was at that time the centre of British power in India and the seat of the British army. Medical personnel were there primarily to support the army, which, at this time of British territorial expansion in India, was frequently engaged in conflict. Members of the IMS held military rank. In 1785 there were 4 surgeon-majors, 52 surgeons, and 93 assistant surgeons attached to the Bengal army.

They were not then considered officers and for Adam Freer, with his medical degree from Edinburgh, this new career seems to have meant taking an initial backward step in terms of status. Bengal had three general hospitals outside Calcutta, at Barhamphur, Dinapore and Cawnpore, two more being commissioned in 1786.[91] Adam Freer apparently spent the rest of his life in Bengal.

One significant event of Freer's time in India was his participation in an expedition into Nepal during February and March 1793.[92] This expedition, led by Captain William Kirkpatrick of the Bengal Infantry, was mounted in response to a request from the Nepalese for British assistance in dealing with a Chinese army that had marched through Tibet and taken up a position near Kathmandu, providing a view over British-controlled territory in the Ganges valley.[93] Kirkpatrick set off with a brief to mediate, but a Nepalese greeting party that rode out to meet him at Patna advised him that the matter had meanwhile been resolved. By his own admission, Kirkpatrick decided this opportunity to enter Nepal was too good to miss and, exploiting the good manners and gratitude of the Nepalese, he insisted on carrying on to Kathmandu on what had effectively become a British reconnaissance mission.

His party consisted of two other British officers, two companies of Sepoys (Indian soldiers), one native employee of the EIC and a surgeon who was Adam Freer. In Kirkpatrick's subsequent *Account of the Kingdom of Nepal*, not published until 1811,[94] the botanical expertise of Adam Freer is clearly reflected in the many detailed and erudite descriptions it contains of the trees and plants discovered *en route*. There is learned comment, too, on their medical uses, which point also to Freer. While there is no indication in Kirkpatrick's account that Freer's medical expertise was called for to save life or limb during the expedition, his promotion in March 1793 may well reflect his undoubted scientific and botanical contribution to the usefulness of the mission. He was further promoted to head surgeon in May 1806 and died at Barhamphur in 1811 at the age of about 64. No will by Freer has been traced, nor any official gazetting of his death.

CONCLUSION

The Levant Company's apparent shortcoming in providing medical care at its overseas factories must be seen in the context of the times. The indications are that, even by the eighteenth century, doctors did not enjoy any great repute, but fell into the category of 'worth a try' when the need arose. Clergymen were regarded by the less pious in much the same way, and there remained indeed a certain blurring between the two professions and little specialization in either. Divinity or medicine were the only subjects, besides law, that universities had to offer, and, faced with such a limited choice, it is reasonable to assume that for many, perhaps the majority, vocation had little role to play in the direction their education took.

Innes Smith, writing about medical students at Leiden in the eighteenth century,[95] comments that many students were dilettantes who studied medicine as part of the education of a gentleman. In 1761, Oliver Goldsmith (1728–74), an essayist, poet, novelist and playwright, but not as far as can be established in possession of any medical qualification, applied to succeed Alexander Russell as physician to the factory at Aleppo, but lost out to Patrick Russell.[96] Even in the case of the respected Russells, there is no evidence that they were particularly successful as medical practitioners. Their contemporaries in Aleppo refer to their congeniality rather than their professional skill, which excluded surgery and consisted mainly of bleeding, purging and administering herbal concoctions. There is no evidence they even assisted at childbirth, although it was usual for physicians to be consulted about contraception and barrenness; midwives dealt with abortions.[97]

The conceived risks of service in the Levant must be considered also. There is nothing in the primary sources to suggest that health was a particular worry to the Britons who served there. Outbreaks of plague were an exception, but the British had learnt to protect themselves and few Europeans succumbed. Had the communities felt any real concern, they would surely have approached the company to provide medical support, but no such evidence has come to light. Alexander Russell recorded that, except for ophthalmic problems and plague, local diseases such as 'general inflammatory fevers, catarrhal fevers, rheumatisms, quinsies, dysenteries, pleurisies and peripneumonies' were neither more acute than they usually were in Britain nor more frequent. Of the common British diseases only gout was rare in Aleppo.[98] The evidence points to there being no conceived need, or demand, for doctors to be on the company payroll, although the factory communities were happy to consult any who were on hand, provided they were also liked and respected. Given the limited scientific knowledge available at this period, there must be some doubt whether the doctors, however conscientious and willing, were capable of providing their patients – British or otherwise – with efficacious treatment. To the factory communities at least, their presence must on occasion have been a comfort, while the help they could offer would be as much as that then available in Britain.

The wider benefits that accrued to Britain through these freelance physicians will be discussed in the overall conclusion to this work. Their most important potential contribution to the Levant factories, especially at Aleppo – their extraordinary access to local people of all ranks and religions – seems to have gone largely unrecognized and unutilized by company officials. The doctors were not 'company men', and there is no indication in the records that the Russells, for example, were consulted for either their privileged local insight or their linguistic skills, neither of which was equalled by any other Briton in the community.

5

Family Life and Recreation

In this chapter the focus turns on the way in which the company's changing fortunes during the eighteenth century may have affected the domestic and personal lives of the communities living at the Levant factories. While in some respects the Levant Company was family friendly in that it was quite small, close-knit, exclusive, and involvement in it for many family trading houses spanned several generations, unlike the East India Company (EIC), it never actively encouraged domestic family life at its overseas factories. Although company attitudes to the presence of dependants fluctuated over time, living conditions at the three principal Levant stations of Istanbul, Izmir and Aleppo remained virtually unchanged throughout the more than three centuries of its existence.

These were not easy places for European women and children whose mere presence introduced additional worries and responsibilities. Contemporary accounts reveal that the hazards of the long journey out from England, the dangers from disease and natural disasters, local security considerations and the constraints of factory life were as hazardous at the close of the eighteenth century as they had ever been in the past. Nonetheless, officials and merchants alike did raise families in the Levant and some remained there for several generations. Unmarried men, who included the majority of chaplains and doctors, also frequently chose to stay at their posts for decades. It would seem clear, therefore, that the Levant undoubtedly had a lot more to offer besides mere monetary gain to counter the difficulties and inconveniences of moving to an unfamiliar environment.

BACKGROUND

Virtually everyone writing about the Levant factories from Wood in 1935 through to the present day has observed the essentially collegiate, even monastic, nature of the living arrangements. To describe them as collegiate is perhaps accurate enough, but monastic is surely an exaggeration, and a reflection of the perpetual reiteration by later writers of Alexander Russell's description of the Aleppo factory in 1752. At that time, Russell noted that none of the Englishmen at the factory were married. There was little or no social intercourse between Europeans and the local population. Aleppo's relative isolation attracted few visitors to the factory and 'in such a recluse situation, the manner of life, in some respects, resembles the monastic.'[1]

Alexander Drummond, on first visiting the factory in 1745 (he was to return as consul a few years later) wrote of it that 'Our consul has by far the best apartments, yet they so much resemble the cells of a convent, that I could not help fancying myself immured, while I tarried in town.' However, he does go on to correct this rather dreary image by continuing, 'though I was always sure of enjoying such cheerful and agreeable conversation as is not to be found in a cloister.'[2]

Certainly, when young factors went overseas at the age of 19 or 20, they were accommodated simply within the confines of the factories and took their meals at a common table. They arrived as bachelors and their objective was to make as much money as possible in the shortest possible time so that they could return to England in comfortable circumstances and settle down. These were young, well-educated men who were sufficiently resourceful to have chosen to venture into the Levant and there is plenty of evidence to show that they found ways of making life amusing for themselves.

164

They must also have felt some relief at having been freed from the social constraints of polite eighteenth-century English society. Russell's comment on the lack of social intercourse during his time at Aleppo (1740–52) seems to be an exaggeration. As we have seen in earlier chapters, he practised medicine from a surgery outside the confines of the factory and treated all comers, while Alexander Drummond took various Englishmen from the factory with him on the lengthy recreational journeys he made from Aleppo.

In the early years, senior salaried officials of the company, like ambassador and consuls, occasionally brought their families overseas with them and had sufficient living space to accommodate them. Until the middle of the seventeenth century, there were apparently no company guidelines in place on accompanying families or on local marriage. We know that many of the English factors at Izmir had wives in the 1650s. Joseph Edwards, for example, had married Abigail, one of the five daughters of the English ambassador at Istanbul, Sir Thomas Bendysh. She was young and beautiful and the couple hosted lavish social events at which local Ottoman subjects of all religious persuasions and Europeans mingled as guests.[3]

However, these parties, which had included dancing and supper and were sufficiently remarkable to warrant mention in the Chevalier d'Arvieux's[4] *Memoirs*, stopped on Joseph Edwards's death in 1668, and the company thereafter discouraged any repetition.[5] Similar concerns resurfaced in 1671 when the company instructed Paul Rycaut, the then English consul at Izmir (1667–77), to engineer the speedy departure of two English ladies, a Mrs Mason and her daughter, who had turned up in the city independently and attached themselves to the factory.[6]

Deprived of female company of their own kind, and forbidden by the Ottoman authorities on pain of death to have anything to do with Muslim women (a constraint that was evidently flouted on occasion), the young English bachelors found entertainment in the taverns and brothels of the cities, the port areas of Galata and Izmir being especially rich in both. While the foreign communities at Istanbul, Izmir and Aleppo were generally expected to keep to their own areas of the cities, there were fewer physical constraints on movement at the first two.

At Aleppo, the English factory was housed in a khan within the city walls and at night, in accordance with local practice, the gates to both the khan and the walled city were locked and guarded. Being situated inland, Aleppo lacked the concentration of facilities that thrived on the custom of foreign seafarers in port cities. It was nonetheless a great caravan destination and regional trading centre, so attracted strangers requiring accommodation and entertainment, and no doubt provided an enterprising young man with plenty of opportunities for adventure. The Revd Henry Teonge, a naval chaplain who visited Aleppo in May 1676 describes one such example in his diary written during the time of Rycaut's tenure at Izmir.

On the local Muslims, he notes that 'their choice women never come out into the streets, but they have their peep-holes'. Then, with evident enjoyment he goes on to describe the experiences of 'a noble English man' who had come to the city some six months previously. Newly arrived there, this man had been walking the streets to familiarize himself with the place, when he was talent-spotted by 'one of the chief Turks' ladies', who subsequently sent one of her servants to summon him to her house. Advised by the English consul, Gamaliel Nightingale, that refusal could cause serious offence, possibly even with fatal consequences, he visited the lady on several occasions and was 'entertained above what was promised ... and was after safely conveyed back, and with a great gratuity.' But the lady, Teonge tells us, was 'insatiable', and began taking ever greater risks to receive her lover, so that, after narrowly missing being caught by her husband, the Englishman became fearful of the outcome of the affair and abruptly left the city. His departure 'was much lamented by the lady, as was after known to the Consul by the Turk which used to come for him; and this shows they love the English'.[7]

In the seventeenth century some of the young factors, certainly at Izmir and presumably also at Istanbul, Aleppo and elsewhere, married or entered into less formal relationships with local Greek and Armenian Christian women. Dudley North, for one, took the view that a little recreational sex helped him concentrate on his business. He kept lodgings at the house of a Greek woman on the shores of the Hellespont, an area well-known for its 'houses of pleasure'.[8] Although such liaisons, and even marriages with non-Muslim citizens of the sultan, were not actually proscribed by the Ottomans, the company was nervous of their potential for trouble and embarrassment.

The French consul had similar fears, and in 1670 had proposed to his government that French citizens who took local wives should forfeit consular protection. Clearly, so too did the Ottomans, for in 1677 they issued an edict declaring that thenceforth Europeans who married any subject of the sultan would be considered Ottoman subjects and treated accordingly. In effect, they would lose the protection and immunities they enjoyed under the terms of the capitulations.

According to a contemporary account by the English merchant, Dudley North, who was treasurer of the factory at Istanbul at the time, this edict came about as a result of local resentment of privileges enjoyed by the Franks. The Galata area of the city, which was home to all the Europeans and many Ottoman Christians, belonged to a lady whom North referred to as 'the queen-mother' – presumably a dowager sultana – who derived her income from its revenues. With so many of Galata's occupants exempted under the capitulations from paying local dues and enjoying other privileges, all of which extended to native wives and employees, others who were less privileged inevitably received higher demands, and resentment grew until the grand vizier was forced to instigate an enquiry. The appointed inquisitor, annoyed by not receiving the bribe he expected, chose to come down hard on the dragomans and native wives of the foreigners.

He found that about forty French watchmakers were married to Ottoman subjects, along with the chief of the French merchants, three leading Dutch merchants, and of the English community only one surgeon. It was also found that each of the European nations employed large numbers of dragomans. Reacting to the inquisitor's findings, the grand vizier promptly withdrew all privileges enjoyed by dragomans, and forbade each European nation to employ more than three, whose privileges should be reassessed. Moreover, it was declared that thenceforth all Franks married to Ottoman subjects should be looked on as such themselves, and become liable to pay local dues.[9]

Despite vehement protests by the French and Dutch ambassadors, who were supported in this by other European colleagues, the private pleas of individual merchants, and offers of bribes much larger than the dues involved, the grand vizier refused to move and the decree remained in place. Although the capitulations held by the English declared that an Englishman, whether married or single, should be exempt from paying local dues, the Ottoman authorities chose to interpret exemption in this case as applying only to those who arrived accompanied by their wives and no others. This was a reasonable stand for the Ottomans to take, given that modern rules of diplomatic immunity, too, set limitations on the extension of privileges to dependants, but it is understandable that a European merchant might resent the withdrawal of privileges he had initially enjoyed.

The unpopular decree served also to legitimize the confiscation of all property left by a deceased European merchant to his native wife and children. Under Islamic and customary inheritance laws, reflected in Ottoman legislation, a deceased person's declared personal wishes were not necessarily valid. He could not simply choose his inheritors and the property had to be distributed in certain designated proportions among all generations of his surviving relatives. According to North, there had long been resentment that a non-Muslim Ottoman subject, married to a European and protected by his privileges, had been able to keep all her husband's possessions, thus, in Ottoman eyes, 'defrauding others of their rights'. Presumably, the 'others' in such cases included the tax collectors. North further observed that, 'Upon this ground it hath been always esteemed [by the company] unsafe to employ married men as factors, and hath ever been avoided by all persons; their estate being purely at the discretion of their heirs.'[10] It would seem to be 'married to locals' that is implied here.

North in fact recorded, as an example, how English merchant Samuel Pentlow had soon fallen victim to the pitfalls of the edict when he died in 1678 at the age of 52. He had lived in Izmir for about 30 years, overlapping with North's time there, and about six years before he died had married a Greek woman with whom he had children and with whom he lived in a house with gardens he had bought in the town. Pentlow was a notorious penny-pincher, known to the other merchants as 'Sorry Sam' and even the Ottomans, who following the 1677 edict claimed him as one of their own, called him by that nickname.[11]

He had appointed two other English merchants – Gabriel Smith and John Ashby – as his executors and had instructed them to send his wife and children to England after his death. His family were, however, subjects of the sultan and Pentlow had omitted to seek permission from the Ottoman authorities for them to emigrate. The then English ambassador, Sir John Finch, advised the executors to do things properly and seek such authority, albeit belatedly, which they did. This gave rise to a lengthy bureaucratic wrangle, with demands made on the English for hefty bribes, which culminated in the Ottoman authorities confiscating the estate some five months after Pentlow's death. Smith and Ashby were commanded to produce their account of the estate, which (at $85,000, equivalent to about £17,000) was far less than Pentlow's reputation as a very wealthy man had given the Ottomans to expect. In fact, this was explained by Pentlow's will, which showed he had been remitting to England a considerable proportion of his income to his sister, Susanna, for her to invest on his behalf in real estate.[12]

Many months ensued of implicitly shady mishandling of the affair by Smith and Ashby with the apparent objective of tax evasion, and they both ended up in prison. Ambassador Finch in Istanbul took the view that they had brought this on themselves and declined to get involved. Through the mediation of the English chaplain at Izmir, John Luke, and the concerted efforts of English merchants there who, between them, raised sufficient money to pay what the Ottomans believed they were owed, the two were eventually bailed out. But the estate was not restored to Pentlow's widow, Anne, who had travelled personally to Istanbul with one of her children to appeal against the injustice of its seizure and had been shown little sympathy. She was awarded only his house and gardens – worth $3500 (£700) – and some money for living costs, and presumably was never permitted to leave for England, if indeed she wanted to do so. Whether or not she applied to her sister-in-law, Susanna, in England for help is not known.

Smith and Ashby, meanwhile, according to North, were quite unabashed and resumed their business in Izmir as if nothing had happened.[13] Ambassador Finch left Istanbul in 1681. Paul Rycaut, the former consul at Izmir (1667–77) who would have known Samuel Pentlow well, once back in London had raised a petition to the king for the recall of Finch for, among other things, not having done enough to protect Pentlow.[14] When the new ambassador, Lord Chandos, arrived in Istanbul to take up his appointment, he carried stern letters from King Charles II to the sultan and grand vizier protesting at past ill-treatment of the English.[15]

After the issue of the 1677 edict, the Levant Company took firm steps to prevent Englishmen in its service overseas from entering into such marriages. The ambassador and other salaried officials were instructed to prohibit them and were threatened with dismissal if they disobeyed this rule. Factors were required to take an oath not to marry Ottoman subjects.[16] While it is unrealistic to imagine that these stringent disincentives would inhibit relationships of a less formal kind, they seem to have had the desired effect in discouraging local marriages for many decades. For example, in 1753, none of the gentlemen of the English factory at Aleppo was married and, at the French factory, only the consul and one dragoman had wives. By the middle of the eighteenth century things were changing. One traveller to the region in the 1760s[17] records that the Englishmen he encountered there were by that time once again intermarrying with local Greek women. Throughout the eighteenth century, as we shall see below, there began to be also an increasing number of English families present in the factories, although it tended to be the older and more experienced merchants rather than the young factors that had wives and children with them.

THE POSITION OF THE EAST INDIA COMPANY

The Levant Company's approach to dependants was very different from that of the East India Company, although the directors of the two companies had concerns that to some extent overlapped. Both organizations were firmly Protestant and, in the mid-seventeenth century, their exclusivist policies and attitudes reflected the dislike of Roman Catholics then prevalent in England. Roman Catholic missionaries had long been active in both the Levant and India, and both companies were particularly anxious to prevent their young factors being corrupted by Catholic women. The Levant Company also feared repercussions from the Ottoman authorities in the event of Englishmen forming personal relationships with the sultan's female subjects, repercussions that might harm trade, damage bilateral relations and give rise to extortionate fines. The dangers in the Levant lay rather more with local Greek and Armenian women than with Catholics. Fears of cross-cultural pollution were no doubt real enough, but there is a marked absence of any indication that the Levant Company either recognized or understood that the Ottomans reciprocated their concerns in full measure.

Having little to fear from local authorities, the East India Company took a lenient view on extramarital liaisons with non-Catholic native women, which were so common that they scarcely drew comment.[18] What caused great concern among EIC directors, however, was that such relationships might be formalized into 'unsuitable' marriages, particularly where the Englishmen in question were 'gentlemen of good family'. While 'good family' would have been the norm in the elitist Levant Company, the EIC – at least in the seventeenth century – had operated a deliberate policy of recruiting from the lower end of the social spectrum. One of its earliest resolutions had been 'not to employ any gentleman in any place of charge' for fear that aristocrats and the gentry might wrest control of the company from the merchants. By the end of the seventeenth century, this policy seems to have fallen away, and by 1719 in Madras concern was felt because 'many of the young gentlemen in the company's service, being of good families in England, ... would be very much scandalized at such marriages'.[19]

The greatest danger came, in the eyes of the EIC directors, from the Portuguese women present in the great trading ports, especially Surat and Bombay. It had long been Portuguese government policy to dispatch an annual shipload of marriageable Catholic women out to Goa as wives for government officials there. The women were provided with substantial dowries and many ended up in other parts of India. Since Englishwomen were scarce in EIC factories, Portuguese women were, on special occasions such as Christmas, allowed to join the English merchants at table. Such concessions were rare and not officially encouraged, however, for fear that a marriage might result in which the children would be brought up as Catholics, 'to the great dishonour and weakening of the Protestant religion'.[20]

By the 1670s the EIC had adopted the Portuguese government custom of shipping out supplies of suitable women to its overseas posts. This fascinating development would warrant a dissertation of its own, but for the purposes of the present work a brief summary must suffice. The women in question[21] were classified into two separate groups of 'gentlewomen' and 'other women', and were at first few in number, although numbers grew in the early eighteenth century. They were given a free passage, one-way only, to India, and were guaranteed board and lodging there for one year. They got no dowry from the company, but some could and did provide their own.

Not surprisingly, difficulties ensued if women found themselves, at the end of the year, with no husband, no return ticket and no means of support. The company declined further subsistence and the women were obliged to earn their keep as best they could, which usually meant prostitution. EIC officials at the overseas factories, annoyed at being left with these problems, complained to London, but received little support. In 1675–76, one deputy-governor was told: 'Whereas some of these women are grown scandalous to our nation, religion and Government interest, we require you to give them faire warning that they do apply themselves to a more sober and Christian conversation.' When that advice did nothing to improve matters, 'the sentence is that they shall be confined totally of their liberty to go abroad and fed with bread and water.'[22]

By the middle of the eighteenth century, the establishment of British political supremacy had led to increased settlement there and a safe environment in which accompanying families had become the norm and, consequently, the EIC communities expanded and flourished. The Levant factories, on the contrary, remained for the entire lifetime of the company precarious foot-holds on the doorstep of the Ottoman Empire.

FAMILIES IN ISTANBUL

Daniel Goffman has observed that available sources tell us prac-tically nothing of the lives of the women who inhabited what he calls 'the early modern Anglo-Ottoman frontier'.[23] Certainly, besides the letters of the renowned Lady Mary Wortley Montagu, no memoir, diary or letter emanating from any woman stationed at a Levant Company factory has come to light, at least for the seventeenth and eighteenth centuries. In the surviving official correspondence, references to dependants are scant, usually appear-ing only if an individual is thrust into the limelight for some reason, as in the case of Samuel Pentlow's widow.

We know very little even of the wives of the ambassadors to Istanbul. After Lady Mary Wortley Montagu's account of her time there in 1717–18, there is nothing similar until the still unpublished papers came to light of Henrietta Liston, who accompanied her husband, Sir Robert Liston, during his second tour of duty at Istanbul from 1811–21. For most of the other wives and children of ambassadors, or indeed of other salaried officials or merchants of the seventeenth and eighteenth centuries, we know little beyond the facts of their existence, and often not even that. Although their experiences have for the most part gone unrecorded, we can safely assume that they were not uneventful. No one travelling to the Levant during that period can have entirely escaped enduring at least some of the trials and heartaches – as well as the pleasures – illustrated in what follows.

Seventeenth century

The English ambassador's residence at Pera was from time to time home to young families. There are a number of seventeenth-century examples of this. When Sir Peter Wyche, the sixth son of a wealthy London merchant, sailed 'with a trading fleet' in November 1627 to take up his appointment as ambassador, he left behind his pregnant wife, Jane, who travelled to join her husband the following May after the birth in London of their son, Peter. The couple had another son, Cyril, born in Istanbul in 1632, and named after his godfather, the patriarch of the city. They also had two daughters, Jane and Grace.

Lady Wyche is recorded as having caused a sensation during her time in Istanbul by calling with her entourage on the reigning sultana in the harem, on which occasion each side was intrigued by the other's mode of dress.[24] The Wyche family returned to England in 1641, where the ambassador died in Oxford in 1643. His wife survived until 1660. The young Peter Wyche was also in due course knighted and became the English ambassador to Russia (1669).[25] A James Wyche, perhaps from another branch of the family, is recorded as living in Pera as a Levant Company merchant, and having a warehouse there, in 1648.[26]

Sir Sackville Crowe, who held the embassy from 1638 until 1647, had a wife and children with him. In 1647, Crowe refused to accept his letters of recall from Cromwell on the grounds that the king and not he had appointed him and he declined to vacate the embassy for several months after the arrival of his successor, the protectorate's nominee, Sir Thomas Bendysh. Bendysh, having tried all manner of persuasion and reason to get Crowe to leave, ultimately called in the support of the Ottomans.

A crowd of Ottoman soldiers and servants eventually dragged Crowe from the house, in the presence of and supported by the English community who greatly disliked him. He was then hastened onto an Ottoman coastal boat that took him to Izmir. There, penniless, without proper clothing and with no servant to attend him, he was placed aboard an English ship, the *Margaret*. A day or two later, the Ottomans expelled his entire retinue, along with Lady Crowe who had been left unsupported, pregnant and with two small children in tow. (Sympathetic to her predicament, English merchants at the factory collected the substantial sum of £1000, which they secretly gave to her.) She and her entourage were also transported to Izmir and placed aboard the *Margaret*, which sailed in December 1647 and reached London the following March or April, after a delay in Alicante, where Lady Crowe had to be put ashore because of illness related to her pregnancy. It is not clear whether she had to be left there or was able to reboard the ship on recovering. Crowe, who later complained bitterly about his violent expulsion from the embassy without an opportunity to make provision for his wife and children, was thrown into the Tower of London where he remained until 1656.[27]

Sir Thomas Bendysh, Crowe's designated successor, received his Royal Commission as ambassador to the Porte in February 1647. He arrived in Istanbul on 26 September that year after a long and harrowing journey of violent storms and confrontations with enemy ships. He had left England with his wife, eldest son and five daughters, but delayed their journey for a while in Italy to see his eldest daughter married to a Mr Philip Williams at Leghorn. She presumably remained there with her husband, who was a leading merchant of that city. After their arrival in Izmir in August, Bendysh left his family in the care of the English consul there[28] and proceeded alone, overland, to Istanbul, to effect Crowe's departure.

Bendysh's family continued their journey by sea and joined him in Istanbul in December. Two further sons, John and Andrew, came to Istanbul separately at a later stage. In 1649, however, tragedy hit the family when the eldest son, Thomas, who had travelled from England with them, was drowned soon after starting out on a pilgrimage to Jerusalem. The ship on which the young Thomas was travelling became involved in battle with a French vessel and both he and his travelling companion, his father's personal physician Dr Reyner, who had also come with the party from England, lost their lives. Not long after that, Bendysh suffered a further grievous blow when his wife died in Istanbul, leaving him with just two daughters and the two younger sons.[29]

Of the four daughters who had come to Istanbul with their father, the two eldest must by this time have married and left home. We know that Abigail Bendysh was by the 1650s married to a leading factor at Izmir, Joseph Edwards, while another daughter, Anne, returned to England where she married her father's former treasurer at Istanbul, Sir Jonathan Dawes. Bendysh himself left Istanbul on 11 March 1661. Abigail was still in Izmir when her husband died in 1668, and Anne is known to have been a widow in England by May 1677.[30] Both John and Andrew Bendysh remained in the Levant after their father's recall. Andrew was a factor at Izmir in the summer of 1663, and his father later tried, unsuccessfully, to create a consulship for him in Cairo. Despite much support and encouragement from his father, Andrew proved a disappointment. By 1666 he was in India.[31]

With the arrival in Istanbul in 1661 of Sir Heneage Finch, second Earl of Winchelsea, it would seem that the ambassador's residence again became home to a large family. Winchilsea married four times during his life, and had 27 children, of whom we are told 16 survived 'to some maturity'. Although the names of his wives are known, the dates of the marriages are not, but the Countess of Winchilsea who accompanied him to Istanbul was his second wife, Mary, daughter of the Marquis of Hertford. Mary had at least one child in Istanbul, a little girl – Lady Mary Finch – who died of the plague while still a baby. Her bones were shipped to England aboard the *London Merchant*, which sailed out of Istanbul in June 1667.

The same ship had arrived just a month previously bearing an unexpected passenger. This was Winchilsea's eldest son and heir, William, Viscount Maidstone, who was at that time an undergraduate at Cambridge and presumably about 16 or 17 years of age. Relatives had dispatched him to his parents following his confession that, at the age of 13 and when rather the worse for drink, he had entered into a clandestine marriage. Paul Rycaut, the English consul at Izmir, who had been on leave in England when William's indiscretions had come to light, and was placed in charge of the boy for the three-month journey to Istanbul,[32] had delivered the boy to his shocked parents. Although Winchilsea remained in Istanbul until the spring of 1669, his wife Mary left for England in December 1667, just six months after the remains of her little daughter had been repatriated, no doubt taking with her any surviving young children she may have had. Winchilsea's eldest daughter later became the wife of Viscount Weymouth, an English ambassador to Sweden.

Five years later, domestic life at the residence took a rather different turn. A first cousin of Winchilsea, Sir John Finch, took over as ambassador in March 1664, at the age of 38.[33] Sir John, who never married, was accompanied by his lifelong friend, Sir Thomas Baines, whom he had met as a student at Cambridge. Finch had an interesting background. He was the younger son of another Sir Heneage Finch (who had died in 1631) – himself a younger son of Elizabeth – who was Speaker of the House of Commons in Charles I's first parliament. This Sir Heneage had seven sons, the eldest of whom became the first Earl of Nottingham, and four daughters. John Finch, the future ambassador, was extremely well educated. He graduated with a BA from Balliol College, Oxford. He then obtained an MA from Christ's College, Cambridge, where he met Baines. The two subsequently removed to Padua, where each qualified as a physician with the degree of MD.

Finch was appointed English consul at Padua, and returned to London in 1661, where, all in that same year, he was appointed a fellow of the College of Physicians, knighted and granted an MD from Cambridge. All these honours were granted also to Thomas Baines. Both men became fellows of the Royal Society in 1663, and two years later, when Finch was dispatched to Florence as English minister to the Grand Duke of Tuscany, Baines accompanied him as a practising physician. There is some implication in the sources that Baines went in some official capacity, in a joint posting with Finch. During their time in Tuscany, the Duke of Tuscany appointed Finch as professor of physic at Pisa, although there is no evidence that he at any stage practised medicine.

Finch's appointment as ambassador to the Porte, for which his cousin Winchilsea had lobbied, was granted by the king in November 1672, and he and Baines transferred there together, arriving in Istanbul 16 months later. They remained there for more than seven years, with Baines acting as physician to the English factory. They were known locally as 'the Ambassador and the Chevalier'. Finch is said to have consulted Baines in all things, so one man was as influential as the other was and both had to be convinced before any decision was taken.

On 5 September 1680, tragedy again visited the ambassadorial household at Pera when Baines died there, aged about 58. His body was embalmed, and when John Finch left Istanbul in November the following year, he took his friend's remains with him back to England and had them buried in the chapel of Christ's College, Cambridge. Finch died shortly afterwards and was buried alongside his friend.[34] It is perhaps worth noting, as a measure of Finch's wealth and social standing, that he at one time owned the house now known as Kensington Palace, which was built in the seventeenth century. He sold it to his eldest brother, the Earl of Nottingham and Lord Chancellor of England, who renamed it Nottingham House, and made it his London seat. King William III purchased the house shortly after his accession to the throne, namely around 1690, for £20,000.

Eighteenth century
The author of the only known first-hand account by a woman who experienced life at a Levant Company factory in the eighteenth century tells us absolutely nothing of the English community at

Istanbul for which her husband, as ambassador there, was responsible. Lady Mary Wortley Montagu's famous and much-quoted letters, written during her short stay there in 1717–18, are well-known for their lively and colourful accounts of her travel experiences. In them she describes her privileged access to the intimate world of high-ranking Ottoman ladies in the harem and bathhouse, and her adventurous forays in local dress to marketplaces and districts of the city not usually frequented by Europeans. There is no mention at all, however, of the Levant Company that funded her husband's presence in Istanbul, of the trading activity he was there to support and protect, or of the English merchants and officials and their families who formed the factory community. If, from her grand position as the ambassador's wife, she took any interest in the welfare of her husband's flock, and in particular of any accompanying wives and children, we do not hear of it.

It is perhaps unreasonable, given the class barriers of the time, to imagine that such concern would be conceivable. There were some English people among the ambassador's large personal household, including a chaplain, physician and young Yorkshire woman who served as nanny to the Wortley Montagus' little son Edward, all of whom had travelled to Istanbul overland with the family. The only European friend Lady Mary mentions is the young wife of the French ambassador[35] whose pedigree as the Duc de Biron's daughter and Marquis de Bonnac's wife would have made her socially acceptable to her English counterpart. She had arrived at Edirne on her way to Istanbul about the same time as Lady Mary (early 1717), had given birth that same year and by the following January was expecting her second child. Lady Mary gave birth to her own second child, Mary, at Pera in February 1718, so the two women had much in common. Another European ambassadress, 'the Dutch madam', seems to have met with less favour. She must have passed the pedigree test, for she was Catharina de Bourg, the wife of the Dutch ambassador to the

Porte, Count Jacob Colyer, but Lady Mary nonetheless regarded her as 'a perfect mad woman'.[36]

Lady Mary always intended that her letters about her Levant adventure would be published in due course, and she kept copies of them in two volumes, which she called 'Embassy Letters'. This to some extent explains why they contain almost no intimate detail of her family or of any personal or domestic issues. In fact they were not published until May 1763, six months after her death, and then only against the will and without the permission of her stuffy daughter Mary, by then Lady Bute, who feared potential embarrassment for her husband, the Marquis of Bute, who had recently been appointed prime minister.

The letters nonetheless reveal aspects of life in Istanbul in the early eighteenth century that would have been familiar to everybody at the English factory. Lady Mary speaks, for example, of her continuing dread of fire and plague, two scourges of the city that were major concerns throughout the whole period of the factory's existence and against which her position of privilege afforded her no immunity. Fires frequently raged through the wooden houses of Istanbul and Izmir, although Aleppo, where the bazaars and khans of the old city were built of stone, was less susceptible. In fact, fires broke out so frequently that, according to Lady Mary, the local population had little fear of them and, having packed up their goods, 'they see their houses burn with great philosophy, their persons being very seldom endangered.'[37] We know from Dudley North and others that, in both cities, the European merchants took care to build warehouses of stone to protect their goods from destruction by fire.

Lady Mary does not, however, dwell on her fears and writes predominantly and with enthusiasm of the many aspects of Istanbul that entranced and delighted her. These include the views from her house at Pera over 'the port, the city and the Seraglio, and the distant hills of Asia, perhaps altogether the most beautiful prospect in the world'. She speaks of the family's summer residence at Belgrade village, with its orchards and fountains, where most of the Europeans took houses and found respite from the summer heat of the city. She mentions the pleasures of boating on the waters of the Bosphorus, which she calls 'the Canal', and enjoying the scenery and magnificent palaces along its banks.[38] These natural advantages presented by the climate and geographical situation must have brought similar pleasure to generations of other men, women and children based at the Istanbul factory.

By the middle of the eighteenth century, there were again young children in the English residence at Pera. When Sir James Porter took over the embassy in 1746, he was a 36 year-old bachelor, but in 1753 he married the daughter of the Dutch ambassador to the Porte. She was Clarissa Catherine, eldest daughter of Elbert, second Baron Hochpied, and she gave Porter five children, the three eldest of whom were born at Pera. Their eldest son, John Elbert, died there in infancy in 1756. A daughter, Anna Margaretta, was born in 1758, and a second son, George, in 1760. Porter and his young family remained at Istanbul until May 1762. His father-in-law, Baron Hochpied, stayed on as Dutch ambassador, later becoming a good friend of John Murray, and died there in 1768.

Three months before the Porters left, their successors, the Hon. Henry Grenville and his wife – Margaret 'Peggy' Banks, a celebrated beauty[39] – arrived with their little daughter, Louisa. They had made a leisurely overland journey from London to Naples, spending three months in Italy *en route*, and were accompanied on the sea voyage from Naples to Istanbul by Lord Warkworth, who was travelling in the region for his health and who made his return journey with the Porters. The Grenvilles spent only three years in Istanbul. Young Louisa survived the experience to become in due course Lady Stanhope and lived until 1829.[40] It was perhaps his unusually early recall at the king's request that led Grenville to bequeath to his successor, John

Murray, two sitting tenants, a chaplain and a doctor, who have been discussed in earlier chapters.

John Murray's letters on Levant Company business during his first three years as ambassador at Istanbul (1766–69) contain a number of indications that, as well as the European ambassadors, some of the English merchants and officials also were accompanied by wives and families at this period. Murray makes frequent mention of the large 'family' (meaning household) for which he had to provide, at least in terms of comestibles. Like his predecessors, he had a staff of servants and retainers, some of whom had come with him from Venice. The factory's chancellor, Mr Lone, lodged under his roof, as did the chaplain and an elderly Scottish doctor. His private secretary, Mr Duckett, 'a Gentleman, that has lived with me for fifteen years',[41] had a large family of 'fine' children. Murray's letters also reveal that an English merchant called Palmentier, who died in late 1768, left many debts and a wife and family. One Englishman based at Ankara had need of a chaplain to baptise his child; Anthony Hayes, consul at Izmir, lost a small son to smallpox; and Murray congratulated John Abbott at Aleppo on the baptism of his youngest child. Murray's domestic situation is unclear.[42]

Other European diplomatic representatives had their families with them at this time, although for several years from 1768, when the Ottomans went to war against Russia, security in the city was poor. Often unruly troops from throughout the Ottoman territories would converge on Istanbul on their way to and from the sultan's armies. Tensions ran high as they passed through in large numbers; pillaging and attacks on the local population were common and Europeans were not immune from random acts of violence. The French ambassador (who was a bachelor at the time) was subjected to a number of attacks to his person as well as to his properties,[43] both in Istanbul and in the country.

The Austrian resident (imperial nuncio), Monsieur Brognard, went with his wife and daughters to a house in the 'Turkish' quarter to watch, discreetly, the sultan's corps of janissaries carrying the 'standard of Mahomet' through the town. Onlookers who spotted the family were angry that Christians should look on the sight and chased the Brognards from the house, dragging them by the hair and beating them. The house in which they had been was badly damaged and they were fortunate to get back to Pera with their lives.[44] Murray's secretary was stopped outside the gate of the Pera residence and shot at when he did not understand what his assailant was saying, although the two bullets merely scraped Murray's wall.[45]

The situation worsened after the Russians, with some assistance from the British, destroyed the Ottoman fleet at Çesme in June 1770. Murray was livid at having received no advance warning of this from the government in London. The Levant Company further exasperated him by asking him to take the merchandise of the entire English factory into his own house for safekeeping, a suggestion he firmly rejected on the grounds of impracticality and the offence it would cause at the Porte. Following a violent outbreak of civil disorder in Izmir (the city closest to the location of the battle) the surviving members of the Ottoman navy – unpaid, jobless and hungry – made their way to the capital, where they roamed the streets, raping, murdering and robbing. 'They hourly rob and stop Christians, Muslims, all,' Murray reported. Sailors ran around the street at night with broadswords and pistols. They broke into the prison at Galata and 'took out some of their common women'. The following night, the authorities seized 30 of the women and 45 men; the women were thrown in the sea, and the men were sent to castles on the Bosphorus where they were strangled.[46]

During this very troubled period, the populace was afflicted by a severe outbreak of plague, which raged in the summer and autumn of 1770 in both Izmir and Istanbul, and in villages within a 20-mile radius of the capital. With Russian ships blocking the Dardanelles, allowing no ships in or out, supplies grew short in the capital and prices soared. The Porte allocated extra guards for European embassies and consulates in both Istanbul and Izmir, and ordered local officials to ensure that foreigners were protected, but this proved impracticable. In September Murray reported that the city was in the grip of plague, famine and anarchy.[47]

There is no evidence that Europeans fled the region during these turbulent years or that any country evacuated its nationals, though Britain for one kept a frigate hovering in the region of Izmir in case it should be needed for this purpose. Murray stayed on until finally granted permission in 1774, after the war ended, to plan a visit to England. The French ambassador, too, remained at his post throughout the war years and in 1775 married a daughter of the Neapolitan nuncio. The couple went on to have several children born at Pera. Murray's successor, Sir Robert Ainslie, who held the embassy from 1776 to 1794, never married.[48]

<h2 style="text-align:center">IZMIR IN THE EIGHTEENTH CENTURY</h2>

Disembarking at Izmir in October 1744 at the start of his travels in the Levant, Alexander Drummond was 'in time to dine at the British tavern' where he initially took lodgings. He later moved into an apartment in the house of two merchants of the English factory, Mr D'Aeth and Mr (Richard) Lee. Drummond spent several months in Izmir, and wrote to his brother in Edinburgh giving a useful account of the factory at that time. He found a very hospitable group of English and Dutch in the city, and records that they all lived together in utmost harmony and always included Drummond in their parties, both in town and at their country houses.

Among the English community, he mentions the consul Samuel Crawley, the chancellor George Boddington and the chaplain, the Revd Charles Burdett. He names three other merchants in addition to D'Aeth and Lee – Richard Muster, Richard Dobbs and Nicholson Lee, the latter presumably a relative of Richard above. The Dutch consul, Graf Hochpied,[49] and four Dutch merchants completed the social circle into which Drummond found himself readily accepted. Because, according to Drummond, the streets where the Europeans did business were dirty, narrow and crowded, with no space for walking, they went hunting, or took their pleasures indoors, playing cards and drinking after supper. Some clearly had more serious interests, for Hochpied was proud to show Drummond his collection of medals and other 'antique curiosities'.

The community at the time was rather unsettled because bandits had murdered a Swedish gentleman, Mr Kerman, a few months previously near Izmir. Since then, Drummond tells us, all European Christians had been very cautious and nervous, and did not go out unaccompanied, but his newfound friends generously loaned him their horses and rode out with him. D'Aeth and Lee kindly took him to see a triumphant pasha returning from a military victory over 'the Germans'. A less than gracious Drummond, demonstrating distaste for Ottomans that was to become customary in his writings, describes the procession as 'a parcel of ragamuffins' and comments disparagingly on the discordant music and the pasha's 'old withered physiognomy'.

If there were any English wives and families present at the Izmir factory when Drummond visited, he fails to mention them. Indeed, his description of one social event he attended seems to indicate that the Europeans with whom he became friendly were unaccompanied. He describes a gathering, organized – it is implied – by his friends, 'during carnival, an assembly, cruel to criticize, as it is in its infancy', where there were ladies present. These were all 'natives of the country, where gallantry and true politeness are but little known. One lady rules the roost.' Consul Crawley took Drummond along to this event, where the ladies were intrigued by Drummond and surveyed him 'with truly female attention'. One asked him to dance and he declined, but he was later persuaded by 'a pretty little blooming creature, with whom I walked seven minuets during the course of the evening'. Contemporary personal accounts of life at the factory such as this one are, sadly, rare, but it does seem clear from Drummond's experiences that the Levant Company's officials and merchants were by no means all averse to socializing with the sultan's subjects when the opportunity arose.[50]

In a surviving assembly register for Izmir, which covers the period 1757–1804, there is inscribed a list dated October 1759 of the 'English nation' as it stood at that time. It indicates that the composition of the factory had changed in the 15 years since Drummond's visit to include a number of English and European women.[51] The list is written randomly, with the names appearing in no order of any sort – certainly not of seniority – apparently just as they occurred to the writer. No explanation is given of why it was drawn up at that particular time, and no other such list has come to light in any other factory register. We can only speculate that some local reason for a roll-call must have arisen. As well as providing the names of the English people living in the city, who were by implication under the consul's protection, it gives in most cases their occupation, marital status and length of residence there.

It is clear from this list that it was not unusual by this period for Englishmen to spend long periods in Izmir, that men of varying ranks had European wives with them and that there was already a trend towards effective settlement there. The 1759 list shows that Richard Harris – a former British consul at Cairo and a bachelor – was then the community's longest serving resident, with 25 years under his belt. His closest competitors for the title were two of the merchants whom Drummond had befriended, Master (or Muster) and Lee, also bachelors, who by 1759 had been there 20 years and shared a country house and garden 'to retire to in time of Sickness'.

Of the company's salaried officials serving at the factory in 1759, the consul, Samuel Crawley, had a Frank lady for a wife, and had been in Izmir for 16 years. He was to complete 20 years there in all, almost certainly dying in post in 1762–63. We are not told how long the chancellor, George Boddington, had been in the city in 1759, although Drummond had found him there in 1744. He may even have been born there, for he was the son of a George Boddington who had served in the city as consul from 1722 to 1733 and, before that, alongside three of his brothers as a factor in Aleppo. Boddingtons had been involved with the Levant Company as merchants and officials since at least the 1660s.[52]

The George Boddington of 1759 was married to a European woman and had raised a family in Izmir,[53] remaining in office there until he died in 1789. After that the chancellor's baton passed to his eldest son, also George Boddington, who carried it into the nineteenth century and beyond the period covered by the register under discussion here. On his father's death George Boddington Jr and his mother stayed on in the Consulary House, where the family had clearly been lodged. Turning to the two final salaried positions at Izmir, the post of treasurer went in October 1759 to James Lee, possibly one of the long-serving bachelor duo mentioned above, although the list includes also another bachelor merchant named Richard Lee. The factory chaplain, also in receipt of a company salary, was at that time Philip Brown, a single man.

Only 4 of the 19 members of the English factory named in the list (excluding female dependants) are described as merchants – Master, the two Lees and an unmarried man named Jasper Chitty. This clearly reflects the great slump in English trade with the Levant in the mid-eighteenth century, for in 1704 there had been 36 merchants.[54] Five 'scrivans' are also named, two of them married to Frank women. These were the European clerks (usually Italian, but in this case all English) employed by most factors in exchange for small wages and the right to trade, on a modest scale, on their own account.[55] One of the 'scrivans' had been in Izmir for nine years, two for four years, and two for seven years. A boatman, a watchmaker, and a 'Hanoverian subject' named Richard Young, all single men, also appear on the list, together with the factory's Scottish doctor, Andrew Turnbull, who had a Frank wife.

Women members of the factory community get scant mention,

mostly appearing in the register only as 'a Frank lady', without their names or even their specific nationalities recorded. There must have been children there, but they are completely disregarded, not even their numbers being listed. Two women only, of the seven present in total, are named. These are Mrs Petronella Bobbitt, the widow of an English merchant, and Mrs Ann Bobbitt, the wife of an English tailor. Since no tailor appears on the list, these two probably warranted specific mention only because they were at Izmir without men to represent their interests, so therefore needed to be borne in mind, as Englishwomen, for some courtesy protection should the need arise. This 1759 list, it should be noted, is inscribed in a register that was to form part of the official records of the Levant Company. With its references of dependants nominal to non-existent, it suggests that the company's attitude at this period to accompanying families had not much warmed. It was still a company man's personal choice to have his family overseas with him, be he a salaried official or merchant, and it was up to him to support and take care of them.

Anthony Hayes, who was consul at Izmir throughout John Murray's ambassadorship, provides a further example of an English family that virtually settled in the Levant. Hayes, having served for 14 years in Istanbul as secretary to the embassy under Ambassador James Porter, replaced Samuel Crawley in 1762–63. When Murray died unexpectedly in 1775, Hayes then acted as chargé d'affaires at Istanbul for 18 months. He was disappointed in his ambition to succeed Murray as ambassador[56] and continued as consul at Izmir until he died there in the summer of 1794 after nearly half a century in the Levant. Hayes had a wife and numerous children living with him in Izmir.

Another long-term resident was a Dutch merchant whom Drummond had met in Izmir in 1744. David George van Lennep (1712–97) married and brought up a large family in Izmir where he remained for several decades.

9. The Dutch van Lennep family at Smyrna *c*.1770, by Antoine de Favray
(Rijksmuseum).

Although no image of the Hayes family has come to light, an
elegant portrait survives of van Lennep, together with his wife and

seven children, painted at Izmir in 1770.[57] The painting portrays a clear image of a European family living in the Levant at the same time as Hayes and his family, and almost certainly longstanding acquaintances of them, but retaining European dress.

In 1766 Hayes informed John Murray that he had lost his youngest son, aged four, to smallpox, 'the second such affecting event in ten months'.[58] Later, thanking Murray for his condolences, Hayes observed that his loss could have been worse had not four other children recovered from the disease.[59] Little is known of what became of the Hayes children, except that one of the older sons is known to have survived a dangerous voyage to England.[60] There was an Anthony Hayes resident at the Aleppo factory in 1780, probably as a factor, who might have been the eldest son.[61] Hayes was replaced as consul at Izmir in 1794 by Francis Werry, who was still in post when the Levant Company was dissolved in 1825.[62]

In 1770, the year of the post-Çesme civil unrest in Izmir, the English factory consisted only of Hayes plus four other gentlemen, one of whom had returned to England by November.[63] Clearly, the relaxation of entry requirements that the Levant Company introduced in 1753 with a view to attracting new blood and revitalizing the trade had not had the desired effect. This small community, which included the families of Hayes and Boddington, found their lives in real danger when news broke of British involvement in the destruction of the sultan's fleet. The noise of the three-day battle, which began on 5 June, had been heard in the city, and the light and smoke from the burning ships were visible, drawing people out onto the streets, their numbers augmented by some '4000' others from surrounding villages.

In a hasty letter to Murray in Istanbul, on 8 June Hayes reported that rioting had broken out in which 100 Greeks and two Europeans – a Dutch dragoman who had been looking out of his window and an unnamed imperial subject – had been killed. In his memoirs Baron de Tott later put the number of Greeks killed at 15,000 and described the killings as 'a massacre'. That so few Europeans[64] died is explained by it being a Sunday so most were indoors.[65] The English factory took on 20 extra janissary guards, as did the other European communities, but local law and order broke down completely, and they had to rely on self-preservation.

All trading stopped; shops and businesses closed; starving sailor survivors of the battle roamed the streets; and a ferocious outbreak of plague (which simultaneously hit the Black Sea coasts, Transylvania and Poland) raged in the city. 'The English were extremely odious' for assisting the Russians, so 'the English Consul and Nation were in great Danger'. Local magistrates personally seized several European ships and threatened to sink them. Not surprisingly, under the circumstances, they also harassed the foreign communities with demands for money. In an attempt at conciliation, the Franks volunteered to send a deputation, consisting of one merchant from each foreign nation, to the Russian admiral, begging him to spare the city, and the magistrates jumped at this offer, but the corps of janissaries rejected the plan as dishonourable and relative peace was eventually restored without it.

Edward Wortley Montagu was in Izmir at the time and got caught up in the troubles, but, as Murray reported to Lord Weymouth, '[Montagu] is so much enamoured with this country that he mentions his ill-usage with great reluctance.' Although 'lawless rabble' continued to trouble the city into the following year, and Hayes frequently reported great nervousness in the English factory, there are no records of any of the occupants being harmed, and no other European casualties have come to light.[66]

ALEPPO

The difficulties and dangers of travelling beyond Istanbul and Izmir to more distant Aleppo would have in and of itself been a disincentive for those stationed with the Levant Company there to bring their families with them. The final stage of the journey from the port of Iskenderun, which involved a three- to five-day ride up and over the mountains through the Bylan Pass, was particularly hazardous. When Alexander Drummond made the journey in 1746, watches and guards were posted along the route for the protection of travellers, but robberies and murders were still commonplace.[67] No records have come to light of any Englishwomen living in the city, whether or not connected to the company, before the 1750s. Dr Alexander Russell in his *Natural History* tells us that in 1751 none of the residents of the English factory, at that time consisting of the consul, chancellor, physician, chaplain, *chaoush* (a post held by an Englishman in Aleppo) and ten merchants was married. In the French factory, which had twice as many merchants, only the consul and one dragoman were married.[68]

By the end of 1753, the situation in the English factory had changed a little for the better. Part of a personal letter survives from Jasper Shaw, a merchant writing from there in November 1753, which reveals that two English women had joined the community. Shaw apologized for not mentioning them until the latter part of his letter, 'but you are to know, we think more of Business and Money than of Women in general' and he added that, moreover, they had arrived in the middle of a good silk harvest, when, it was implied, the factory men were more than usually preoccupied.[69]

These women were the sisters of the English consul at Acre, Richard Usgate, and Shaw paints an interesting pen-picture of them for his correspondent. The younger of the two, Mrs Theophila Murray, was aged about forty and the widow of a clergyman. She had a lively disposition, spoke very quickly and was the more industrious of the sisters. The other (whom Shaw referred to as Mrs Usgate but who presumably was unmarried) had a very fair complexion and had probably been the prettier one in her youth. She was very thin and 'something of a Valetudinarian'. The two had been entrusted with the care of the factory's linen. The daughters of a Shropshire clergyman, long since dead, they had let lodgings in Westminster before coming out to the Levant, via Marseilles, four years previously.

When they arrived to join their brother and his family at Acre, matters took an unexpected turn. Because either they or their brother had incurred the displeasure of a local Muslim 'prince', all three were banished to Mount Lebanon for two years, where Richard Usgate's wife and children (including, Shaw remarks, a very pretty daughter of 17 or 18) presumably joined them. During their period of exile they lived with a Christian family near a convent of Maronites. Consul Drummond from the Aleppo factory and his chaplain, Mr Crofts, visited them there during a recreational break; and Messrs Wood and Dawkins also called on them during their travels to explore Palmyra. Shaw's letter offers no clue why Richard Usgate, a company employee who should have been protected by the terms of the capitulations, was made to tolerate such extraordinary treatment for two years. The episode apparently did nothing to discourage Usgate's sisters. When the local 'prince' finally restored the family to favour, the two women accepted an invitation to Aleppo where they appear to have resided from the latter half of 1752.

It is worth noting here that the year 1753 marked a significant change with respect to accompanying dependants in both the English and French factories, though for different reasons. In that year the Levant Company relaxed its traditionally strict rules of admission, which resulted in a large intake of new members. This led, at least initially, to a reinvigoration of trade and perhaps also a fresher approach and increased confidence. Certainly, thereafter a few wives and dependants arrived at the English factory.

For the French, the same year brought a royal edict commanding the repatriation of all Frenchmen who had married locally. The edict was intended to arrest what was then seen as an unwanted trend towards miscegenation. For some time, Russell writes,

Frenchmen of inferior rank had been finding their way into the Levant and marrying native Christians, thus producing 'a troublesome half-French *mezza razza*,[70] or mixed race. Thereafter no Frenchman would be allowed to marry without a licence from the French consul, 'but several families still remained in Aleppo, of which some are visited by the Europeans, and the ladies are an agreeable accession to the public assemblies'. Russell further recorded *c.*1752 that 'the female society is very confined'. Native Christian ladies knew only Arabic and only a few *mezza razza* spoke French. In his 1794 edited edition of his brother's book, Dr Patrick Russell (who remained in Aleppo until 1771) comments, 'Circumstances are much altered in this respect since the year 1752, the female society at Aleppo having had an agreeable accession of several married ladies from Europe.'

An English merchant, Colville Bridger, who lived in Aleppo from 1754 until 1766 and was thus a contemporary of Patrick Russell, wrote lively letters to his family and friends in England. These confirm that social life was by that period becoming a little more balanced than in Alexander Russell's time. Although there were no eligible European women available, there were at least some married women resident there whose presence was agreeable. We know from Patrick Russell that both he and his brother greatly enjoyed the company of the then French consul, Monsieur Thomas, and his wife and young daughter. The popular and hospitable Thomas family spent nearly twenty years in Aleppo in the 1750s and 1760s, during which they were, according to Russell, the focal point of European social life. The daughter grew up there, and 'gave spirit to much gayer amusements than Aleppo had known for many years'.[71]

There was also a Dutch consul in the city, John Vankerchem. A Dutch merchant, Nicholas van Masegh, arrived in Aleppo in early 1755 and in September that year his English wife, Elizabeth, and their baby son, also named Nicholas, joined him. Another son,

Thomas, was born in October the following year and baptised in the chapel of the English factory on 7 November 1756. This event was sufficiently momentous to inspire the chaplain, Charles Holloway, to open a register of marriages, baptisms and burials, and to record under this first entry: 'The whole English factory were present at the ceremony, which was performed after the second lesson at the Evening Service. NB This christening was the first that had been performed in the English Chappell [*sic*] for 30 years past.'[72] The entry also records that another English lady, Mrs Elizabeth Usgate (the elder of the two sisters mentioned above), was present as the child's godmother. Sadly, later entries in the register show the death of this Mrs Usgate less than two years later on 20 September 1758, and that of Elizabeth van Masegh, in childbirth, on 10 October 1761. By that time, the latter's husband Nicholas was Dutch consul, a position he attained following the death of the previous consul, Vankerchem, in Aleppo in July 1760.

The death of a third Englishwoman, a Mrs Booth (no Christian name recorded), wife of a merchant named Thomas Booth, is entered in the register as having occurred on 19 July 1758. It is noted that, although she was buried according to the rites of the Church of England, both Mrs Booth and her husband were Anabaptists.[73] Below the notification of her death it is further recorded that the entry was made at a much later date from information on a loose piece of paper discovered among the belongings of the chaplain, the Revd Charles Holloway, who died in Aleppo on 23 September 1758.

That autumn must have been a dark time for the English factory. Soon after the loss of Mrs Usgate and of their chaplain within three days of each other, the small community suffered a further blow when their recently-arrived consul, Francis Browne, died and was buried on 10 October. A memorandum in the register after the entry for Browne's death records that, as there was no Protestant clergyman at that time in Aleppo, the British chancellor,

Mr John Brand Kirkhouse, had read the funeral service over the graves of these last three people. A new chaplain, Thomas Dawes, was in place by August 1759.

Colville Bridger, the factor to the great Levant Company trading house of the Radcliffe family,[74] arrived in Aleppo in 1754. His personal letters to his family in Shoreham and to business friends in London during the period August 1756 to December 1765 have survived,[75] and were recently edited privately. These letters reveal much about the presence of English families in Aleppo during that period and in particular about the precariousness of life there and the many personal tragedies that befell them. The letters serve also to augment and expand on some of the entries in the Aleppo register mentioned above, which successive chaplains kept up to the year 1780.

Bridger first mentions the lack of suitable female company in December 1756. Writing to ask a relative in England to send him two pairs of sheets and two 'pillow coats', he confesses that he is still using those he took for his voyage out to Aleppo two years previously, 'and those only proper for a sailor's cabin. You'll laugh at my ménage but in such a country as this where there are no ladies (at least for Franks) there is no need of a great stock of household furniture.'[76] Bridger did not actually receive this new bed linen until 18 months later, in May 1758.

Between 1759 and 1762, because of three years of plague and because, he records, his family were poor correspondents at the best of times, Colville Bridger got virtually no mail from home. When contact was resumed, he found he had a new stepmother, Ann, and a new sister-in-law, Lucy, the wife of his brother, the Revd Richard Bridger. He soon struck up a real rapport with the latter young woman, whom he had never met, and asked her to write to him regularly. If his brother complained about the expense, she should tell him that 'ladies' favours are not to be valued, and that the satisfaction they give is beyond all estimate, especially to a person at a distance.'[77] On 31 October 1762, he wrote to his stepmother: 'I hear my old acquaintance Miss Piggy is at last married, I hope to her satisfaction; her intimate friend Mrs Mascyk [*sic*, clearly Elizabeth van Masegh mentioned above], late of this place, is no more. She died in ChildBirth, greatly regretted by all that knew her.'[78]

A year later, Bridger wrote to his brother-in-law Robert Hayman about various bankruptcies among the merchants at Aleppo. In this correspondence he mentioned the van Maseghs, saying that the 'villains of warehousemen' had also bankrupted the Dutch house of the van Maseghs, adding that 'my heart bleeds for Mascyk's poor little motherless children'. Bridger went on to say that van Masegh 'is [re]married to a young lady of 18, and is daily expected with her from Marseilles.'[79] Indeed, the Aleppo register bears a reference dated 13 November that year to Madame Sophia Maria Gouverts, wife of Monsieur van Masegh, the Dutch consul, and the birth of their first child the following April.

Young Sophia, a Dutchwoman from Amsterdam, became stepmother to Elizabeth's children Nicholas, born in May 1755, Thomas, born in October 1756 and John, born on Christmas Day 1758, and possibly to others not recorded in the register. A poignant little letter survives in the childish script of young John. Writing to an English merchant about to leave for home (via Marseilles) in April 1768, when he was not yet ten years old, the boy sends his greetings to his brother Thomas and grandfather in Marseilles, and begs to be allowed to go to England, to live with his godfather, Colville Bridger. He substantiates his case by saying that 'I learn nothing here but to read,' adding that he can speak French, Arabic, Italian and Armenian.[80]

In October 1763, just before Sophia's arrival at Aleppo, Colville Bridger reports further to his sister-in-law Lucy on the subject of women, or rather the lack of them. 'We have no European ladies here', he wrote:

to brighten conversation or enliven our understanding and make society agreeable, excepting two of our own nation, one of which is an Old Maid[81] whose company is not much courted, the other a Young Married Lady lately come, but I fear will not remain long amongst us being in Deep Consumption. The Loss of her will be much regretted whenever it happens, as she is endowed with all the qualities necessary to make Life agreeable to herself and others.[82]

This lady was Mrs Elizabeth Edwards, the wife of the English chancellor, Eleazar Edwards, and she did indeed die of consumption at Aleppo in February 1764. In a letter to his sister of 29 February, Colville Bridger wrote:

I am just returned from the Funeral of a countrywoman, wife to our Chancellor. She had not been long among us, and never well, being in Deep Consumption before she left England, so her death cannot be attributed to the inclemency of the Climate, tho' it might be hastened by it. She was an exceeding sensible, facetious, agreeable woman and of course is greatly regretted by everyone and by none more than myself, as she used to divert many of my leisure hours. It is something very extraordinary but we have never been able to keep an English Lady at this Place long, tho' the air is esteemed as good as any in the World. There were two here when I came, one of which died and the other went home. Four others came since, three of which are dead; but the other I believe will stick by us, for she is a fine, crummy, healthy Dame.[83]

This last lady was probably 'the old maid', Mrs Esther Rowles, and she certainly lasted some years more, for her presence is recorded at every Christmas and Easter communion service held at the factory chapel between 1763 and 1769.[84]

Poor young Elizabeth Edwards was recently married and had been in Aleppo no more than seven months when she died there. She and her husband arrived in Iskenderun in June 1763. There they received a personal letter of enthusiastic welcome from Jasper Shaw, a close and long-term friend of Mr Edwards. Shaw sent them servants and five horses for their journey over the mountains to Aleppo. Moreover, in his letter he offered lots of cheerfully uninhibited advice to Mrs Edwards on how best to cope with the long ride (three to five days), together with a side-saddle kindly loaned by the Dutch consul, boots and a muslin handkerchief for her head. He had borrowed the last two items from Mrs Rowles, and from Mrs Vernon he had borrowed 'a pair of her drawers and some string to tie them up with'. He did not think it likely that Mrs Edwards would find the side-saddle ideal, and advised her not to be ashamed to 'wear Turkish breeches or ride a-straddling for once'.

It seemed that there was no house awaiting the Edwards' arrival and, since the consul had so far made no offer to accommodate them, Shaw said they would be welcome at his own house.[85] In a warm and friendly letter to Mrs Edwards dated 31 October of the same year, her sister-in-law Sarah Younger in London congratulated the pair on their safe arrival at Aleppo, and commiserated with them about their continuing problem of finding a house. She also expressed deep concern about the health of Mrs Edwards (whom she called Betsey), saying that she had hopes of becoming an aunt: 'I wish please God it was so, as it might be a means of recovering your health.'[86] Sadly, we know from Colville Bridger that Betsey had arrived at Aleppo with consumption and survived there only a few months.

As we have seen above, Dr Alexander Russell recorded that in 1751 there were ten English merchants at the Aleppo factory and in 1753 just eight. The Great Khan they had occupied virtually exclusively since 1680 had become too big for them and in 1754 they invited some of the French merchants to join them. They also rented out storage space to native traders. It is unclear how long they continued to share with the French, but, as merchants and officials began increasingly at this period to have wives and young children with them, more of the khan would have been required for living space. There is no indication that any of the English sought accommodation freely around the city. It is more likely that, when the Great Khan became overly crowded, they took exclusive occupation of another that could be similarly secured. The doctors were exceptions to this, maintaining their own independent premises outside the confines of the factory.

By October 1763, the number of English merchants at the Aleppo factory had decreased still further. Colville Bridger wrote a number of letters home referring to the 'Great Bankruptcies among Warehousemen', and observing that, in the space of six months, the English factory, which had consisted of the representatives of eight trading houses, was reduced to five, and he was concerned for the future of one other.

Four months previously 'poor Vernon' had declared himself bankrupt and, at the end of the previous year, Booth and Lansdowne had both gone home.[87] The optimism following the 1753 lowering of the company's entry requirements had clearly not been realized. External factors such as the Seven Years' War (1756–63) and the outbreaks of plague in the Levant (1760, 1761 and 1762) had hindered expansion by disrupting shipping and discouraging investment. The local economy, too, was in a poor state after many years of dearth. In early 1758 Bridger reported to his father that there had been a great famine all over the Ottoman Empire, which had reduced the Aleppo region to the depths of misery, and had been vastly prejudicial to trade and caused much financial loss.[88]

Alexander Russell recorded a crop failure, also in 1751, which left the populace starving and in great distress. These serious local economic problems, which were still continuing in 1764, would seem to have led the English factors to lend money to local traders in order to keep trade afloat for some at least. When they could no longer afford to do so, the locals went bankrupt and brought the English traders down with them. Bridger recorded that the reason Booth had to return home was because the crisis in Aleppo caused the failure of his merchant master, Edwardes, in England.[89]

During those bleak years Colville Bridger's usually cheerful letters reflected some of the desolation and despair that those remaining in Aleppo must have felt. In 1760 he wrote: 'I think Divine Vengeance seems to have fallen upon this Country; these that spend all their days in England are not sensible of the Happiness they enjoy. ... Famine, earthquake and malignant Disorders, and now ... the Plague.'[90] Then, in 1762, he continued: 'I observe you persuade me to stay abroad which is a piece of Cruelty I am persuaded you would not have been guilty of if you knew what a person suffers in this Country.'[91] He further observed to correspondents that 'a person can have no pleasure in this Country but that of getting money, which is what everyone comes out for,'[92] adding that there was absolutely no variety or news of any kind for Europeans except what they might pick up from year-old newspapers and magazines.[93]

In April 1765 Bridger was still feeling gloomy and told his brother-in-law: 'I assure you, what with the government of the Country (which becomes intolerable), the miseries it is subject to, and the badness of trade together, a person can scarce be said to live in it, much less to enjoy Life.'[94] But this despondency paints a distorted picture, and may in part have been due to a mood of homesickness that engulfed Bridger when he came to write to his family. The fact remains that life in Aleppo was tolerable enough for him to stay there 12 years, while accumulating a considerable fortune to console him for his pains. It is clear from the writings of the Russells and others that the English community found many pleasant pastimes – riding, hunting, picnics, parties and music among them – to balance the disadvantages of their situation.

Throughout the 1760s and 1770s, and regardless of the inter-mittent difficulties of these years, there continued to be young English and European families in Aleppo. The Dutch consul, Nicholas van Masegh, and his family were there for more than two decades and, as Protestants, were virtually honorary members of the English factory. The baptisms of their many children, and the tragically early deaths of some, fill the pages of the English chaplain's register, and the names of both Nicholas and his second wife, Sophia, appear frequently right up until 1780 as participants at other recorded events. Van Masegh stayed on as consul despite his bankruptcy in 1763.

Patrick Russell recorded in 1794 that, from 1772, the position of the Dutch consul changed so that he was no longer permitted to trade but had instead 'regular appointments', meaning, presumably, that he became a salaried employee either of his government or of the Dutch Levant Company. The latter remained in existence until 1795. The young Sophia was clearly strong and healthy. She gave her husband eight children between 1764 and 1778, three of whom died in infancy. A further tragedy hit the family when, on 10 July 1775, Nicholas van Masegh, the eldest son of the consul's previous marriage to the Englishwoman, Elizabeth, died in Aleppo aged 21. There were still van Maseghs in the city in June 1800, when two people of that name were among witnesses to a marriage in the English factory.[95]

Although settlement in the Levant had never been an objective, or indeed an option, of the merchants who went out to the Levant Company factories in the Ottoman territories, certain families maintained continuing connection with the company through many generations. On the whole, the great trading houses kept their eldest sons in London to learn that end of the business, and sent their younger sons overseas to act as factors and trade on their behalf in the Levant. The vast majority served out their training for four years as factors, and as bachelors, then stayed on until they had accumulated enough money to set themselves up back in London as Levant merchants. Most spent a total of eight to ten years overseas.

One notable exception was Nathaniel Harley, who arrived in Aleppo in 1685 as a factor aged 20, and remained there until he died 35 years later, probably as a result of plague in the epidemic of 1719–20. Harley's older brother Robert was a powerful Tory politician and had been created 1st Earl of Oxford and Mortimer in 1711 for his services to Queen Anne. With such a connection, Nathaniel Harley could surely have returned to England sooner if he had so wished, and we might be forgiven for assuming that he remained there because he enjoyed life in Aleppo. Norma Perry asserted that Harley had made a personal fortune in the Levant, but Richard Grassby contradicted that in a later work. He found that Harley had in fact incurred great losses in the 1693 Bay of Lagos disaster and had remained at Aleppo all those years, unhappily, in the vain hope of financial recovery.[96]

From the middle of the eighteenth century, when it began to become more common for merchants to be married, there were some English and other Europeans who did effectively settle in the Levant. They were not colonists or conquerors, as happened in India, but they settled in the sense that they made it their home, and lived on there for the rest of their lives, with children and grandchildren who had never known their native lands. We have already seen that the Dutch van Maseghs were just such a family in Aleppo.

As we have seen above, there were families who did likewise in Istanbul, Izmir and other factories. The Hayes, the Boddingtons and the Dutch van Lenneps of Izmir are just three examples. It is for Aleppo, however, that we have clear examples of this trend, and it may be that Aleppo's more distant situation led to virtual settlement there being more common than in the factories further west.

One such English family in Aleppo were the Vernons. Thomas Vernon, whom Davis described in *Aleppo and Devonshire Square* as the last of the Vernon family's great traders, was in Aleppo from at least 1753, and was one of those obliged to declare himself bankrupt in 1763. Nonetheless, he remained in the city for several years thereafter, accompanied by a young family. Vernon was married to Roxanne (sometimes spelt Roxana), who was probably not English, and the couple had five daughters, all born in Aleppo between 1758 and 1764, the two eldest of whom died in infancy. Thomas Vernon's death is not recorded in the chaplain's register, but by 1770 Roxanne was a widow, living in Aleppo with her three little girls, by then aged nine, seven and six.

She was about to enter into a second marriage, this time to a Greek priest from Idlib who is named in the register as 'Cury'[97] Abdullah Ziyadeh. Before this marriage, Roxanne took careful steps to protect her interests and those of her children. Thomas Vernon had clearly recovered financially, for he left her a very wealthy woman. In the autumn of 1770 she requested that a copy be written into the Aleppo chaplain's register – witnessed by a merchant, David Hays, and the chaplain, Robert Foster – of an inventory of 'her Estate and Effects previous to her intended second Nuptials'. This inventory had probably been drawn up on the death of Thomas Vernon in accordance with company regulations. It was a rule that, on the death of a factor or merchant, his warehouse, living accommodation, account ledgers and money should all be sealed up until after the burial, when the chancellor would make an inventory before the estate was handed over to the man's executors.[98]

Roxanne was taking the additional precaution of having it transcribed into the chaplain's register in case of future wrangling. In the 25 years covered by the register no other inventory was so inscribed. Roxanne's inventory listed precious jewellery, personal clothing and household effects, as well as large quantities of cloth and soap that must have been her late husband's trading stock. The total value of the goods listed is $9790 – not including any cash she may have inherited – a remarkable sum considering that her husband had been bankrupt just seven years previously. The house of Vernon had, however, enjoyed a more prosperous past than may be reflected here. In the 1750s, it had been one of three leading companies that between them handled half the total English trade to Aleppo.[99]

Roxanne Vernon – clearly a cautious and level-headed woman – further drew up 'marriage articles' that she similarly had copied into the chapel register, and in which she declared that everything listed in the inventory should 'now and hereafter and at all times' remain her own property, to be disposed of as she so wished. She set up a trust binding $6000 'Dollars Gold and lawful Money of the Grand Signor' for her three daughters by Thomas Vernon – Louisa, Sophia and Catherine – to provide $2000 for each, either on marriage or on reaching the age of 20. She committed a further $4000 to be divided after her own death between these three and any children that might result from her second marriage. The merchant David Hays was appointed executor of these instructions, and guardian of the funds.

No record of Roxanne's marriage to her Greek priest appears in the English chapel register, but there is evidence that she did marry him. Two of the witnesses at the marriage on 3 March 1778 of her daughter Louisa Vernon to David Hays were Roxanne and Abdullah Ziyadeh, the latter signing in Arabic. There would seem by this period to have been some considerable relaxation of the prohibitions on cross-cultural marriage to allow Roxanne – whose citizenship of origin we do not know, although she must have been a Christian – to marry first an Englishman and then a Greek, the latter certain to have been a subject of the sultan. Louisa Vernon was not quite 17 years old at the time of her marriage. Her husband, who had been a sponsor at her baptism and had been trading at Aleppo since 1753, must have been nearly thirty years older than she was.

Like her mother Roxanne, Louisa too had a contract of marriage drawn up, which survives, although largely illegible.[100] The couple had a daughter, Marianne, born in July 1779, and another, Harriet, in October 1780 who died aged ten months. One of the sponsors at Marianne's baptism was a Thomas Philips Vernon, British consul at Tripoli since at least 1773. If, as seems certain, this was a relative (and possibly even the eldest son of Thomas Vernon senior from a previous marriage) then this is an indication that at least one member of the Vernon family was maintaining its traditional involvement with the Levant Company, albeit as an official rather than a merchant.

Louisa and David Hays remained in Aleppo, where Louisa had spent all her life, until May 1786, when David Hays found himself in financial difficulty. A vivid and moving account survives of the tragedy that befell the family at this time, written by a Scottish physician, Dr Julius Griffiths, who was travelling in the region at the time. Griffiths enjoyed the hospitality of the Hays family in Aleppo over a period of two months. Little Marianne was by this time aged seven, and she had a two-year-old sister. Louisa Hays was 'one of the most beautiful and most amiable women', and the family had a comfortable and elegant house, where Griffiths enjoyed evenings of music and 'other social engagements of polite life'. One evening, David Hays confided to Griffiths that, for the sake of his family's future prosperity, he needed to travel to India as soon as possible and would much welcome Griffiths's company on the journey. Heartbroken at the prospect of leaving his family behind, Hays persuaded Louisa to let little Marianne travel with them.

The party set off across the desert to Basra, travelling with a small caravan and in the summer heat. The account Griffiths gives of the hardships of their journey is harrowing. Within a month, Hays died of heat exhaustion and dehydration and was buried in the desert near Najaf. Marianne survived and Griffiths delivered her into the care of the East India Company factory at Basra. A few

10. The death of David Hays, from J. Griffiths, *Travels in Europe, Asia Minor and Arabia*, London 1805 (National Library of Scotland).

months later, the little girl made the return journey to Aleppo and was safely restored to her mother.[101] Hays left no will, and no details of the financial problems that forced him to embark on such a hazardous journey have survived.

Louisa later married Robert Abbott, a merchant who was by then consul at Aleppo, and who was a brother of the late consul, John Abbott. When Robert died in 1797, the consulate had been officially closed for six years, but Louisa carried on the residual consular business for the next two years 'with great spirit', until she became overwhelmed by the amount of work generated by Napoleon's incursion into Egypt, and John Barker was sent to the city.[102]

Marianne Hays married John Barker in the factory chapel at Aleppo in June 1800. By the time of her marriage at the age of 21, the family's fortunes had clearly turned around for the better, for Marianne was a wealthy woman. She had £10,000 in the Bank of

England and as much again in jewels and landed property.[103] From this marriage came future generations of Barkers who would serve at the British consulate at Aleppo right into the twentieth century. The John Barker who married Marianne Hays belonged to a family long involved with the Levant Company, whose agency Barker and D'Aeth had represented the Radcliffes and other English trading houses in Istanbul from at least the 1740s.

John Barker was born in Izmir in 1771 and had been sent to Aleppo in 1799 as an agent for the rival East India Company, at a salary of £1200 per annum, and charged with preserving communications with the east via Mesopotamia and the Persian Gulf. In November 1803 Barker was recognized as consul at Aleppo by the Levant Company. Prior to that, the consulate had been completely closed for 12 years, and the post of chaplain suspended for 20, so that Barker's marriage to Marianne was conducted according to the rites of the Greek Church, by a Joseph Anthony Arotin, signing himself as pro-chaplain. Barker was still consul at the time of the Levant Company's demise in 1825, although for many years little or no trade had been done there and he was by then the only Englishman residing in the city.[104]

The Barker story can be followed in the writings of nineteenth-century travellers, and must be the subject of a separate study, but a few details are justified of what became of them in the final quarter century of the Levant Company's existence. In March 1807, Barker fled from Aleppo on account of a breakdown in relations between England and the Porte, and took refuge with the Druze in Mount Lebanon, having already sent his wife and children to them for protection. He continued to carry out his consular duties from his retreat at Harissa, and made a splendid return to Aleppo on 2 June 1809 after peace was declared.[105]

In 1813 John Barker's path crossed that of the wilful Lady Hester Stanhope who was travelling in the region against all official advice, British and Ottoman. Plague was rife and at one point Lady

Hester helped Barker and his family move out of Aleppo to a village outside Latakia, and had her doctor assist them. On 31 October 1813, two of Barker's young children, daughters with the rather un-English names of Harissa and Zabetta, both perhaps called after Druze villages, were taken ill with a 'malignant fever' and died within five hours of each other.[106] He remained in Aleppo until 1818, when he took his family on a two-year break to England.

It was the first time in her life that Marianne had been to Europe and her visit was enlivened by the birth of twin daughters in the spring of 1819 and another daughter a year later. At some point during their stay, the Barkers travelled to Wales to leave several older children with relatives for their education. On the way, they stayed at an inn where they were offered nothing to eat but eggs and rancid bacon. Marianne, accustomed all her life to the plentiful fresh food available in Aleppo, found this rather shocking. In 1820 they returned to Aleppo where they remained until the autumn of 1825, when, following the demise of the Levant Company, John Barker was appointed British consul in Alexandria.[107] The family retained a house in Syria, at the mouth of the Orontes River until Barker's death aged 78 in 1849. His wife Marianne outlived him.

As we have seen, Colville Bridger followed the more traditional path of a Levant Company merchant at Aleppo and returned to England, still a bachelor, in 1766 after spending 12 years there. He had made a considerable fortune and bought Buckingham Place – '440 acres, and with a fine house' – in his home town of Shoreham, on the Sussex coast.[108]

Others besides the Vernons and the van Maseghs persevered in Aleppo despite its hardships, staying for long periods and raising families, so that the increasing presence of wives and children banished the collegiate atmosphere of the factory's earlier days. One such was Eleazar Edwards, who was a Levant Company merchant from as early as 1756, later becoming chancellor at Aleppo, and was still in the city when his second wife died there in May 1781. Following the earlier loss of his first wife, Elizabeth, of consumption in 1764, he married again sometime before 1770, this time to Maria Nicoletta Parker, who had an English father and an Italian mother. His new wife gave him four children, two of whom died in infancy, before she herself died on 27 May 1781, leaving him with two sons, one aged ten years and a baby of 11 months.[109]

The Aleppo chapel register contains an interesting entry related to Edwards's second wife. She had been a Roman Catholic when he married her, the daughter of Peter Parker, an Englishman living in Apollonia (Crete) and his Italian wife. On 7 September 1774, which must have been quite an exciting day in the life of the small English factory, both she and her sister Leonora 'not only abjured the Roman Catholick Religion but [were] publickly received into the congregation of Xt's [Christ's] flock according to the Rite of the Church of England'. This happened in the English chapel, in the presence of the consul and the entire factory, with the chaplain, the Revd Robert Foster, officiating.

Furthermore, the next entry in the register is the marriage that same day of Robert Foster to Leonora Parker. It is noted that, 'there being no other English clergyman upon the place but the party concerned',[110] both the English and Dutch consuls, and all the members of the English factory, witnessed the ceremony. There is nothing to tell us whether these were conversions of convenience, made to ease the situation of two sisters married to Protestant Englishmen, or an indication that the Revd Mr Foster engaged more widely in proselytizing.

Spear tells us that, at this same period in India, the traditional exclusivist Protestantism of the EIC directors and factories had mellowed, so that Roman Catholics were no longer regarded as posing a threat, and 'the conversion of Catholics was nearly as meritorious as of Hindus'.[111] It is perhaps worth noting that Foster

211

further records in the register, in January 1776, the receiving into the Church of England of a Jew 'born in Pisa in Italy of Jewish parents and educated in that religion until now'. This young man, who was born in September 1750 and whose name was Moise Vita Iflah, was publicly baptised by the name of Eleargar in the English chapel and 'in the presence of the greater part of the English factory agreeable to his request'.

By the 1760s there began to be less distinction – at least in Aleppo – between merchants and salaried officials of the Levant Company, which perhaps represents some further adaptation to the company's generally diminishing circumstances. As noted in an earlier chapter, there had always been a certain overlap between the two, with the company choosing older and more mature merchants already there to fill the posts of chancellor and treasurer at the overseas factories.[112] Company legislation dating back to 1658 required the treasurer to have resided five years in the factory of his appointment. He received a salary of $600 in exchange for which he was supposed to give up trading for the duration of his appointment. The chancellor had similar terms of service, but got only $200 a year. Both generally supplemented their salaries by continuing to trade, albeit directly with foreign merchants rather than with the Ottomans.

More than a century later, merchants filled the posts of chancellor and consul in Aleppo. As we have seen, Eleazar Edwards, who went to the factory as a merchant probably around 1756, had by 1764 replaced John Brand Kirkhouse as chancellor, a position he held continuously at least until May 1781. Following the dismissal in 1766 of Consul William Kinloch, a series of merchants held the post until the factory was closed down in 1791 for lack of trade.

One of these, John Abbott, who was appointed consul in 1770 and held the post until his death there in 1783, had been in the city since 1759. Abbott belonged to a family with long involvement in the Levant Company. Sir Maurice (Morris) Abbott, a great trader in the reign of Charles I, had risen to become lord mayor of London in 1638, and another Abbott had been consul in Egypt in 1652. By 1772, John Abbott had a wife, Marianne, in post with him. His brother, Robert Abbott, was a merchant at the Aleppo factory from about 1774 until his death in 1797, and eventually married the widowed Louisa Hays. The register shows that John and Marianne had four sons and one daughter between 1772 and 1780, the little girl dying just a few hours after her birth. John Abbott remained in Aleppo for at least 24 years, and his second son, Peter, born there in 1774, may be the Peter Abbott who became consul at Acre in 1820 and later consul at Beirut. In the 1790s, three other young Abbots – Henry, Richard Robert, and William – were corresponding from Calcutta and Madras, where they were in business, to their Uncle Robert in Aleppo.[113]

No information has come to light that confirms whether or not by the late eighteenth century officials such as Edwards and Abbott might have been permitted to continue trading as company merchants although they had accepted salaried appointments. Wood quotes correspondence from factors at Aleppo showing that the trading situation there was increasingly desperate from the 1760s, and in 1781 'in a most deplorable situation'. Given this downturn, and the fact that both had young families to support, Edwards and Abbott were no doubt thankful for the security of a company salary. Edwards may have lingered on in Aleppo as chancellor until 1791, but when John Abbott died in 1783 the posts of treasurer and chaplain were suspended, and the company decided that it could not justify appointing a replacement consul.

For the next three years the factory was in the hands of two merchants holding the title of pro-consul, David Hays from 1783 to 1784, and Charles Smith from 1784 to 1786, and we have seen above the involvement of Robert Abbott and his wife, Louisa. Michael de Vezin, who had earlier served the company at Cyprus, acted as pro-consul from 1786 until the factory was closed for lack of trade in 1791.[114] By the time it was reopened 14 years later, with the appointment of John Barker as consul in 1803, effective control over officials at the Levant Company factories had passed out of company hands to the British government. Trading methods and patterns were changing, and the transition of Aleppo from a trading outpost to a consulate in the modern sense of the word had begun, with descendants of some of the great Levant Company merchant families staying on in the region as government employees.[115]

CONCLUSION

The Levant Company emerges from this chapter as having been largely uninterested in the personal welfare of individuals at its overseas factories. Strictly speaking, it had an employer's responsibility only for those few officials who were on the company payroll. The factors and merchants who formed the body of the factory communities were directly responsible to their principals back in England and were required only to comply with the company's conditions of service as administered by the ambassador, the consuls and other officials.

As for personal behaviour and lifestyle, service at the overseas factories must have offered (for those who sought it) some emancipation from English morality. It seems that all the company asked was that no individual – whether on the payroll or not – should behave in a way that brought discredit to the company or to the English presence in the Levant, or caused friction with the Ottoman authorities. Out of this arose an insistence on circumspection in marriage, and discretion in local liaisons, and indeed a preference for most to remain unattached.

The ambassador and the consuls, who had heavy representational responsibilities and large households to run, very often brought their wives to post with them, a practice condoned no doubt because of the useful supportive role these women could play in official entertaining and domestic management. In general, however, the company appears to have taken the view that wives and children at post were a nuisance to be discouraged, and that anyone who chose to have a family with him was personally responsible for its support and security. Dependants were not regarded as any concern of the company and are neither named nor mentioned in the official company records unless for some reason they achieved notoriety.

Nonetheless, we do not hear of British wives or children finding themselves stranded at one of the factories, or left destitute because of a death or bankruptcy in the community. Nor is any merchant or official known to have died in penury, although some may have failed to accumulate the fortunes they hoped for from their time in the Levant. For officials, there was the safety net of a regular salary, for at no time in the company's history was it unable to meet its payroll. As for the merchants, they had the cushion of their comfortable social background in England, and their education, so that if they did return penniless from the Levant, they would scarcely be in dire straits.

If the Levant Company shrugged off responsibility for dependants at its factories, in a small and close-knit community one could safely assume that should some harm befall one of the men that prevented him from caring for his family, his colleagues and business partners would rally round to help his family, at least to get back to England. One should perhaps not be too critical of the Levant Company's detachment from the personal problems of individuals. The factories were far away from London; communications were slow; there were administrators and chaplains in place to deal with social issues; and it was reasonable to expect a degree of self-reliance and self-help from the Britons at its overseas posts, not least since all were there of their own free will.

6

Conclusion: The Decline and Eventual Demise of the Company

The Levant Company would no doubt have preferred its overseas factories to be simple, functional trading posts, where its English factors could reside for as long as they chose, unencumbered by personal attachments or agendas of any kind, and with an unwavering focus on the accumulation of profit for their merchant masters in London. Securing a sound trading agreement with the Ottoman Empire, however, depended on the establishment and maintenance of good political relations, so the twin objectives came to be inextricably linked in the dual role of the British ambassador to the Sublime Porte.

An ambassador needed his personal entourage of secretaries and servants at his residence in the capital. He needed consuls to represent him at the company's other major factories in the Levant, and officials to keep order among the young factors. Personnel were needed to maintain accounts, to ensure that company regulations were implemented, and to administer the small armies of Ottoman subjects who were added to the payroll in a variety of supportive roles such as interpreters, messengers and guards. A Church of England chaplain was supplied at company expense to each of the three largest factories, and freelance physicians – mainly from Scotland – arrived in the Levant on their own initiative and attached themselves to these trading enclaves. Wives and children, although discouraged by company policy, were present too, albeit in small numbers, so that the factories, rather than being the exclusive reserves of unaccompanied factors, blinkered to all but the pursuit of commerce, were instead lively and diverse communities, remote English villages against a foreign backdrop, with their fair share of problems and personal dramas.

The wealthy London merchants who constituted the Levant Company and who financed 'the Turkey trade', did not themselves travel to the Levant, and consequently had no personal experience of life at the factories, yet it was from their ranks that the company's governor and other London-based officials were elected. All issues relating to the overseas factories were discussed, and decisions taken, at 'courts' of these officials, or at larger assemblies of all company members. The surviving records of these meetings indicate that there was little interest in any problems peripheral to commerce that might arise at the factories.

Troublesome community issues were regarded with dour Protestant irritation rather than sympathy, and no evidence has come to light of any company initiative to improve life at the factories, or indeed to recognize any corporate responsibility to do so. The British government's interests in the region depended equally on these factory communities, but it too showed no great interest in them. It did not seem to recognize that the behaviour of all the Britons present at the factories played a part in forming Britain's image in the Ottoman Empire and not just the formal representations of the ambassador and his senior consuls.

The senior company employees at the factories, along with the ambassador, constituted part-commercial and part-governmental officialdom at the factories, which gave structure and discipline to the factors' activities. Their jobs and salaries were secure so long as they put up a reasonable performance, and many remained at their posts for decades, often handing over the baton to the next generation of their own family. Their value to the company lay in the continuity they provided, and the local knowledge they accumulated over their years of virtual residence in the Levant. It is not difficult to understand why the company's relations with its factories was detached and impersonal, for such long periods of service overseas must have meant that few of these officials would have been known personally to their colleagues in London. Indeed for most of its existence the company did not actually have any physical headquarters, where anyone lucky enough to get home leave might touch base. Premises were rented for court meetings and general assemblies of members, and it was not until 1801 that it acquired Levant Company House in Bishopsgate.[1]

With no common paymaster, and no overall authority interested in them, other than to impose certain behavioural standards, the small groups of Britons who populated the Levant factories had to pull together and support each other, relying on their own resources. They enjoyed considerable freedom to pursue their private interests. For young men in search of fun and a certain release from the claustrophobic constraints of English society or familial duties, there was, as we have seen, a wide range of recreational activity, such as riding and hunting, to be enjoyed in an exciting new environment, and in the company of others of their own age and social background. Such plentiful leisure time (enjoyed by all, including also the factors and officials in between peaks of trading activity) was a benefit that must have attracted at least some individuals with frivolous objectives. It also drew men of academic leanings from the Church of England and the medical profession to seek association with the Levant Company.

For the majority of the chaplains who took up appointments in the Levant, the company presented a means of achieving their underlying personal objectives. Its factories provided secure and convenient bases from which to follow their fields of study, and offered for those who wanted it the additional advantage of some limited private trading to swell the modest salaries pertaining to their posts. Moreover, their parishioners were few in number, and the chaplains' official duties light. The communities undoubtedly derived some benefit and comfort from their presence and their professional services, and there is no reason to believe that these chaplains were not conscientious in their official responsibilities.

Some of them, however, especially in the seventeenth century, made contributions that extended well beyond their time in the Levant, with Britain's universities and libraries the ultimate recipients of their writings and collections. It is a pity, though not surprising, that the interests of these learned men were focused overwhelmingly on the Christian churches and antiquities of the region. None of them seemed to have been drawn to study Islam, or to write about contemporary life in the countries they visited or in which they worked. Many European Christians clearly regarded the Ottoman administration, even in the eighteenth century, as an offensive annexation of what should rightly be Christendom, and 'the Turks' as usurpers of the Holy Land. Church of England clergymen would have looked upon any display of interest in them or their religion as a betrayal. It follows that the diligence of people like Pococke and Crofts in collecting 'Oriental' books and manuscripts, and in learning the languages of the region, was more through a quest to find out more about the history of Christianity than through any real interest in the Ottoman or Muslim world.

The physicians who on their own initiative attached themselves to the Levant factory communities – as opposed to those who formed part of the personal entourage of an ambassador or consul – enjoyed a unique position. As self-employed men who had made their own way to the locations where Britain had an official presence in the Ottoman territories, they had no obligation to the company, nor any right to expect employment.

The factory welcomed the best-documented of these doctors, the Russells of Aleppo, for their personal attributes as congenial adjuncts to the community and for the services they provided on a private basis. Alexander Russell, the first to arrive in 1740, must have had a personal recommendation, possibly from a predecessor, but most probably through his brother, William, who was an employee of the Levant Company in London. While it is likely that on first arrival he was accommodated informally within the factory, he set about learning Arabic, and rented a house in the city where he set up a surgery open to all comers. His brother Patrick, who succeeded him, followed this practice, as in turn did Adam Freer.

The range and depth of the social contacts in which these doctors engaged gave them an insight into the daily lives of Ottoman subjects of all religions and ranks that extended well beyond the experience of other Britons at the factory. Because they were not dependent on the company, or indeed on the factory, for their livelihood, they were unaffected by the vagaries of trade and detached from any institutional prejudices. Both Russells were educated men of great common sense and integrity. They were dispassionate and enlightened observers who left a valuable legacy in their admirable and fascinating *Natural History of Aleppo*. This book contains wide-ranging and detailed accounts of everyday life in the city for each of the many cultural and religious communities that made up its citizenry. Unlike their fellow Scot and contemporary, Alexander Drummond, the Russells were non-judgemental throughout and never patronizing or disparaging in their comments. They wrote with appreciation and humility, from the standpoint of men who knew that they were privileged to experience such a place.

Despite their many talents, it is difficult to judge whether the Russells could be described as great doctors, for their writings contain no tally of the successes and failures of the treatments they dispensed, and they are not known for any ground-breaking medical discovery. The Britons at the Aleppo factory trusted and respected them throughout their many years there, so they must therefore have provided as good a service as would have been available back home in the eighteenth century; they took few risks and so could have done little harm.

Their passion for botany was closely linked to medicine for its importance in the preparation of drugs. Both Russells indulged in it to good effect in Aleppo by sending specimens and drawings of the plants they discovered there back to the leading botanists of their day, such as Joseph Banks at Kew. This brought them considerable honour and acclaim when they returned to London in later life. So, too, did their careful observations of the diseases they encountered at Aleppo, in particular their studies of the plague, which struck the city for three successive years in Alexander's time there, and returned for a further three years during Patrick's tenure.

Social interaction between Britons in the Levant and local Ottoman subjects was clearly far greater than Alexander Russell's much-quoted comment that life in Aleppo at times resembled the monastic might suggest. Perhaps he was speaking very personally. Certainly, the French factory had taken steps to avoid such deprivation, for Russell's contemporary, Alexander Drummond, tells us that the young women of a very pretty village called Kefteen, near Aleppo, 'have made a very agreeable summer retreat for the French gentlemen'.[2]

Drummond also described an incident that occurred on a journey he made from Cyprus to Iskenderun in May 1745, which revealed a high level of trust between the pasha of Aleppo and the British. He found that his ship was also carrying the pasha's harem, which a black eunuch and a little white boy, who had lost his nose and was 'otherwise very disagreeable to the view', guarded. On arrival at Iskenderun, these women were accommodated at the 'British House', the best building in the town and the residence of the company's factor marine. There they promptly commandeered all the best rooms. Drummond, who was also accommodated there, described how he was teased by the sight of these 'pretty prisoners, dear little playful creatures, peeking and giggling, skipping, frisking and dancing like so many wanton kittens'. When the pasha later received Drummond on his appointment as British consul at Aleppo, the latter found that the pasha regarded him as a protector of his women and gave him a chair to sit on, an honour which, he smugly observed, had been denied the French consul who was merely offered a stool.[3]

Even before wives and children came to the factories, there must have been constant social interaction between the British gentlemen and local suppliers and artisans such as tailors, cobblers and food sellers. They had landlords with whom to deal; and they needed people to clean their houses, do their laundry and look after their horses. The accompanying families, who were present in the factories in increasing numbers from the mid-eighteenth century, must have increased still further the level of local interaction, with their need for dressmakers, midwives, jewellers, hairdressers, help with looking after their children and perhaps language teachers for themselves. Such contacts, small and insignificant in themselves, but often sustained and strengthened over many years of residence, must collectively have been valuable steps towards greater trust and mutual understanding, and it is in this area where the factories' non-traders could make their greatest contribution to British interests in the Levant, both commercial and political.

As the eighteenth century drew to a close, the Levant Company and its monopoly of 'the Turkey trade' would soon pass into oblivion as anachronisms, but trade did not die with it, nor did Britain's diplomatic relations with the Ottoman Empire. Following Napoleon's incursion into Egypt of 1798, after which Britain and the Ottomans were on common ground against the French, the importance of Britain's embassy at Istanbul grew, and financial responsibility for representation in the region was removed from the company, which had borne the burden of it for more than two centuries, and assumed by the crown. Commercial and political relations took on a new order, in which many a descendant of the old Levant Company families would play a part.

Appendix

Chaplains at Istanbul, Izmir and Aleppo in the Eighteenth Century

Chaplain WILLIAMS elected 10 December 1691. Still in post in 1706–07.

Laurence HACKET preached before the company in 1707. Lincoln College, Oxford. Pauper. Matriculated 24 May 1693. BA 1697. Nothing further known. Timing indicates that he could have gone to Istanbul between Williams and Crosse; no vacancies at Izmir or Aleppo at that time.

William CROSSE arrived *c.*1712. Went there for a second stint in 1717, travelling with the Wortley Montagus who appointed him, and apparently returned to England with them in 1718.

Thomas PAYNE arrived *c.*1718. Lady Mary Wortley Montagu records that he arrived on the *Greyhound* at Izmir on 7 or 8 March 1718.

In 1766, which was when John Murray was ambassador, there was a chaplain in post. When Murray arrived in Istanbul in June of that year he found the incumbent in residence. He was apparently engaged by Grenville, Murray's predecessor, so may have been in the post since 1762. The man left in disgrace a month or so later and no replacement seemed to have been appointed for some years, and possibly not at all during Murray's time (1766–75).

James DALLAWAY was in post in 1794–97 under Sir Robert Liston. Appointed as both chaplain and physician. Born 1763. Son of James Dallaway, gentleman, of Bristol. Matriculated 4 June 1778 aged 15. BA 1782. MA 1784. B.Med 1794. On his return to England became secretary to the Duke of Norfolk, the Earl Marshall of England, a post that he still held in 1825. Edited the letters of Lady Mary Wortley Montagu in 1803. Author of *Account of Constantinople, Ancient and Modern,* 1797 and *History of Sussex.* Died 8 June 1834.

Philip HUNT was appointed chaplain in 1799, to accompany Lord Elgin. Born *c.*1772. Son of Thomas Hunt, of Newcastle. Trinity College, Cambridge. Scholar 1791. BA 1793. MA 1799. Vicar of St Peter's, Bedford, 1798–1833. At Elgin's bidding, travelled to Athens where he arranged the removal from the Parthenon of what would become known as 'The Elgin Marbles'. Assisted Professor Carlyle who had been sent from England to examine manuscripts held in the libraries of Istanbul. Accompanied Carlyle to Greece where they also examined the libraries in the monasteries of Mount Athos. Died at Aylsham on 17 September 1838.

IZMIR

Edmund CHISHULL was at Izmir from 1698 to 1702. Son of a clergyman of Bedfordshire. Educated at Winchester, then Corpus Christi, Oxford. Matriculated 14 July 1687 aged 16. BA 1690. Fellow and MA 1674. BD 1705. Appointed vicar of Walthamstow, canon of St Paul's, then chaplain to the Queen. Died Walthamstow 18 May 1733.

John TISSER was elected 11 December 1701. In Izmir 1702–11.

Son of James Tisser, gentleman, of London. Oxford. Matriculated 6 April 1682 aged 16. Postmaster 1682. BA 1686. Fellow 1688–1719. MA 1691. Incorporated at Cambridge 1693. Rector of Keddington, Suffolk 1711–50.

Bernard MOULD was in post in 1716, possibly until 1724. Son of John Mould, gentleman, of London. Hart Hall, Oxford. Matriculated 8 August 1700 aged 17. Exhibition Wadham College 1701. Scholar 1703. BA 1704. MA 1707. Fellow 1711. Incorporated at Cambridge 1712. Various ecclesiastical posts in England from 1725.

Charles BURDETT arrived *c*.1724. Born 1700. Son of Charles, gentleman, of St Helen's, London. Matriculated 10 November 1715, Lincoln College, Oxford. BA 1719. MA 1722. BD and DD 1764. Still at Izmir in 1744 and may have remained until 1759. Rector of Guildford by 1760. Preached sermon to House of Commons 30 January 1760.

Philip BROWN was resident in Izmir in October 1759. Bachelor. Identified as *either* (1) son of Christopher, of Millum, Cumberland. Queen's College, Oxford. Matriculated 21 May 1724, aged 22. BA 1728. MA 1731. BD 17 March 1747–48, *or* (2) son of John, of Millum, Cumberland. Queen's College, Oxford. Matriculated 21 October 1743 aged 17. BA 1748. MA 1751.

Beveridge CLENDON was resident at Izmir in 1768. Son of Revd John Clendon of Boxley, Kent. Born *c*.1739. Educated at St Paul's, then Emmanuel College, Cambridge.

Robert FOSTER was previously chaplain at Aleppo. Seems to have transferred to Izmir with his wife Leonora. They left Aleppo on 18 October 1778, and are recorded in Izmir in August 1780.

ALEPPO

Henry MAUNDRELL was in post from 1696. Son of Robert Maundrell, plebeian, of Compton, Wilts. Exeter College, Oxford. Matriculated 4 April 1682 aged 16. BA 1685. Fellow 1686–1701. Died Aleppo 1701, aged about 35.

Hon. Henry BRYDGES was in post 20 June 1701 to 22 February 1703. Younger son of Lord Chandos, who, fearful for his son's health, requested his early recall. Later Bishop of Rochester.

Harrington YARBOROUGH was appointed 25 March 1703. Recommended by ambassador at Istanbul, Sir Robert Sutton. Son of John Yarborough of Newark-upon-Trent. Brasenose College, Oxford. Matriculated 7 July 1688 aged 16. D.Med. BA from Trinity College 1692. MA 1695. Died Aleppo before 18 June 1706.

Thomas OWEN was elected 17 October 1706. Died at Aleppo on 12 August 1716.

Joseph SOLEY was in post approximately 1718–23. Gentleman, of Shropshire. Balliol College, Oxford. Matriculated 16 March 1705–06 aged 16. BA 1709. MA from Corpus Christi, Cambridge, 1718. Held various ecclesiastical posts in Hampshire from 1723 until his death on 25 November 1737.

John HEMMING was in post from about 1743 at least until 1748. Son of William. Born at Ringwood, Hants. A scholar from Eton College. Matriculated at Kings College, Cambridge, 1735. Fellow 1738. BA 1739–40. Ordained deacon of Lincoln 17 June 1739. Priest, 14 March 1741–42. MA 1743 (admitted to degree 1750). Aleppo 1743. Rector of Waterden, Norfolk 1759. Vicar of Holkham 1750. Dean of Guernsey for seven years up to his death on 5 June 1765.

Thomas CROFTS was recorded in post 1750–53. Son of John of Monmouth (town). Wadham College, Oxford. Matriculated 29 March 1740, aged 17. BA 28 February 1743–44. MA 1746. Chancellor of Diocese of Peterborough 1769–83. Died 1783.

Charles HOLLOWAY was in post by 1756. Son of Ambrose Holloway, gentleman, of Winchester. Trinity College, Oxford. Matriculated 27 February 1735–36 aged 17. Died Aleppo 22 September 1758, aged about 39.

Thomas DAWES was in post by August 1759. Son of William Dawes, clergyman, of Burghclere, Hants. Queen's College, Oxford. Matriculated 11 December 1745 aged 19. BA 1749. Remained at Aleppo until about June 1769.

Robert FOSTER was in post 29 May 1770 to 18 October 1778. Son of James Foster of Horton, Yorks. Attended school at Bentham, Yorks. Trinity College, Cambridge. Admitted 13 March 1766 aged 19. Matriculated Lent 1766. Scholar 1766. BA 1770. Aged only 23 when he arrived at Aleppo. Married Leonora Parker in Aleppo on 7 September 1774. Later transferred to Izmir.

John HUSSEY was in post 9 June 1779 to 10 June 1782. Born 21 April 1751. Son of Thomas Hussey of Ashford, Kent. Hertford College, Oxford. Matriculated 7 April 1778 aged 27. Arrived in India March 1799, and was posted to Fategar, but died *en route* at Allahabad on 11 October 1799. Married 17 June 1796 to Catherine (died Ramsgate July 1837). Son, born April 1797.

Notes

1. Introduction

1. SP 110/87.
2. This subject is covered in Chapter 5. It had been more common practice in the seventeenth century for families to accompany their menfolk, but the company discouraged this from around 1670.
3. This was a consequence of political disarray in Persia lasting for several decades from 1722.
4. This was not in itself an indication that Montagu was disgraced. Company records indicate that the provision of safe passage was an honour accorded to returning ambassadors when practicable.
5. Cited by D. B. Horn, *Great Britain and Europe in the Eighteenth Century* (Oxford: Clarendon Press, 1967) p. 360.
6. Bruce Masters, *The Origins of Western Economic Dominance in the Middle East: Mercantilism and the Islamic Economy in Aleppo, 1600–1750*, (London: London University Press, 1988) p. 73.
7. Masters, *Origins,* pp. 36 and 48.
8. Daniel Goffman, *The Ottoman Empire and Early Modern Europe* (Cambridge: Cambridge University Press, 2002) p. 198.
9. Horn, *Great Britain and Europe*, p. 353.
10. Ibid.
11. Ibid., Chapter 13.
12. This was a tax that Sultan Ahmet I (ruled 1603–17) imposed on all Frank merchants for the maintenance of a hospital at Istanbul, and it was levied according to the weight or measure of the goods imported into the Ottoman territories. In 1740 the tax was two and one-sixth dollars per bale of cloth and one and 0.5 per cent of the value of all goods sold by weight. See A. C. Wood, *A History of the Levant Company* (Oxford: Oxford University Press, 1935) p. 143.
13. The Venetians called the island Candia, although this was properly the name of the main city, now Heraklion.

14. Wood, Wood, *Levant Company*, p. 2.
15. Richard Hakluyt, *The Principal Navigations, Voyages, Traffiques and Discoveries of the English Nation* (Glasgow: Maclehose, 1904) vol. 5, pp. 62–3, cited by Wood, *Levant Company*, p. 2.
16. Wood, *Levant Company*, Chapter 1.
17. Ibid.
18. Ibid., p. 6.
19. Ibid., p. 2.
20. There was some variation in the appointment of these consuls. It is clear that some were chosen from among the resident traders to hold the role of consul for a specific period, and were forbidden to trade during their tenure in exchange for a company salary.
21. To negotiate these concessions, Finch suffered five uncomfortable months under canvas at Adrianople (Edirne), where the sultan was camped with his armies. See The Hon. Roger North, *The Lives of the Norths* (London: Henry Colburn, 1826) vol. 3, p. 34.
22. Ralph Davis, *Aleppo and Devonshire Square: English traders in the Levant in the eighteenth century* (London: Macmillan, 1967) p. 27; Wood, *Levant Company*, Chapter 6.
23. Wood, *Levant Company*, p. 111.
24. Ibid., Chapters 8 and 9.
25. Ibid., p. 145.
26. Ibid., Chapters 9 and 10.

2. The Administrators

1. William Hussey 1690–91 and Everard Fawkener 1735–46.
2. Wood, *Levant Company*, Chapter 5.
3. See Sonia Anderson, *An English Consul in Turkey: Paul Rycaut at Smyrna, 1667–1678* (Oxford: Clarendon Press, 1989) pp. 92–8; and Wood, *Levant Company*, Chapter 11.
4. For further details, see Wood, *Levant Company*, Chapter 11.
5. This was a levy, imposed by the company on all company goods imported or exported through a Levant port. It was collected at the port in question, and rates fluctuated according to the company's need for revenue to finance the factories. The usual rate was around 2 per cent, but, when trade was poor – as in the

middle of the eighteenth century – it had to be raised to as much as 10 per cent to meet continuing overheads.

6. A *berat* was an Ottoman title of appointment, the holder of which was called a *beratli*. Both terms were used freely in English and accorded English plurals.

7. The ambassador's personal household included also a private secretary. brought from England to handle his political and diplomatic correspondence, as well as his private affairs.

8. SP 97/51, Murray to Rochford, 18 April 1775.

9. Wood, *Levant Company*, p. 222.

10. The unit of account used by European merchants in the Levant was the dollar. This was in principle the equivalent of the 'Turkish' piastre, a silver coin containing six drachmas of silver which was first issued in 1690 and produced only in very small quantities. The Dutch lion dollar was the most common currency. The true lion dollar contained nine drachmas of silver and was worth five shillings (that is four to the pound) in mint condition, but debased imitations containing only six drachmas of silver circulated in the eighteenth century, which exchanged from 1720 onwards at eight or even nine to the pound (Davis, *Aleppo and Devonshire Square*, pp. 188–92).

11. J. B. Pearson, *Biographical Sketches of the Chaplains to the Levant Company, 1611–1706* (Cambridge: Deighton, Bell & Company, 1883) pp. 49–50. The charge had been entered by the Istanbul treasurer, John Wolfe, whose subsequent inability to cover company liabilities in 1645 was one of the many upsets of Sir Sackville Crowe's ambassadorship. See Daniel Goffman, *Britons in the Ottoman Empire: 1642–1660* (Washington: University of Washington Press, 1998) p. 75; and Wood, *Levant Company*, p. 90.

12. SP 110/87, Murray to company, 15 September 1768.

13. SP 110/87, Murray to company, 3 March and 17 April 1769.

14. SP 110/87, Murray to company, 1 September 1766.

15. For the consuls at Izmir and Aleppo the sum required was £5000 (Wood, *Levant Company*, p. 218).

16. Davis, *Aleppo and Devonshire Square*, p. 195.

17. See footnote 15.

18. Chequins, sequins, or zecchini, as they were variously spelt, were Venetian ducats, which exchanged at around two to the pound. (Sevket Pamuk, *A Monetary History of the Ottoman Empire* (Cambridge: Cambridge University Press, 2000) p. 193.
19. Wood, *Levant Company*, pp. 89, 134–5, 177–8.
20. SP 97/57, Company to Murray at Venice, 17 January 1766.
21. Philip Mansel, *Constantinople: City of the World's Desire, 1453–1924* (London: John Murray, 1995) p.191.
22. Wood, *Levant Company*, p. 177.
23. SP 110/87, Murray to company, 1 June 1768. See map at illustration 1.
24. Ibid., 14 July 1768.
25. Wood, *Levant Company*, p. 177.
26. SP 105/121, Company to Liston, 22 May 1795, cited by Wood, *Levant Company*, p. 178.
27. SP 110/87, Murray to company, 17 October 1768, 3 February and 17 March 1769.
28. SP 110/87, Murray to Hayes, 27 June 1768.
29. SP 110/87: Murray to Hayes, 27 December 1766; Murray to Preston, 13 January 1767; Murray to Stevenson, 14 February 1767; Murray to Hayes, 25 February 1768.
30. Wood, *Levant Company*, p. 135.
31. Wood, *Levant Company*, pp 217–22.
32. Aside from Izmir and Aleppo, there were numerous small company outposts at east Mediterrranean ports such as Larnaca, Acre and Thessaloniki. Discipline was similarly a problem for the Ottoman administration at Istanbul, which could do little to control erring officials in distant parts of the empire.
33. Percival Spear, *The Nabobs: A Study of the Social Life of the English in Eighteenth Century India*, revised edn (Oxford: Oxford University Press, 1963) Chapter 1.
34. This kind of boycott (or 'battalation', as it was called, from the Arabic *battal*, meaning negate, or make unemployed) was also applied to any local merchant who reneged on a contract or refused to pay debts. See Masters, *Origins*, p. 66.
35. Both these cases are discussed in Chapter 3 below.

36. John Howard, *An Account of the Principal Lazarettos in Europe* (Warrington: Printed by W. Eyres and sold by T. Cadell, 1789) p. 63.

37. SP 105/119, Company to Kinloch, 1 July 1766, cited by Wood, *Levant Company*, p. 219.

38. It is unclear when Kinloch finally left. He was either still in Istanbul, or he returned there in July 1767 when Murray consulted him about some events at Aleppo and when he referred to Kinloch as a friend and correspondent of Dr Russell. SP 110/87, Murray to Aleppo, 11 July 1767.

39. SP 110/87, Murray to Hayes, 15 March 1767.

40. This is discussed in Chapter 4 below.

41. John Ingamells (compiler) *A Dictionary of British and Irish Travellers in Italy, 1701–1800* (Newhaven: Yale University Press, 1997) p. 669.

42. This subject is discussed further in Chapter 5 below.

43. Cited by Ingamells. *Dictionary*, p. 691.

44. SP 110/87, Murray to Hayes, [illegible] April and 27 June 1768.

45. There was clearly some kind of Levant Company post at the Dardanelles (possibly at Cannakale or Gallipoli) for Murray writes often to the Levant Company seeking a pension for an employee who has been sacked by Porter, Murray's predecessor, and who is referred to only as 'the Jew at the Dardanelles'. The man's family had been in company employment for a century and had originally come from England. It was thought necessary to keep someone at the Dardanelles to deal with the occasional British ship that passed by there.

46. SP 110/87, Murray to Hayes, 23 July 1768.

47. Now called Zakinthos.

48. Howard, *Lazarettos*, p. 10.

49. Cited by Ingamells, *Dictionary*, p. 691.

50. SP 110/87, Murray to Preston, 24 September 1767.

51. Horn, *Great Britain and Europe*, p. 341.

52. D. B. Horn, *The British Diplomatic Service 1689–1789* (Oxford: Clarendon Press, 1961) p. 18.

53. Ingamells, *Dictionary*, p. 691.

54. Another member of the Milbanke family was Annabella (only daughter of a later Sir Ralph Milbanke) who made a disastrous marriage in 1815 to the poet, Lord Byron; the couple spent part of their honeymoon at Halnaby Hall. The house has now been destroyed, but 100 acres of its landscaped parkland remain, near the village of Croft, where generations of Milbankes lie buried in the churchyard.

55. Cited by Ingamells, *Dictionary*, p. 691.

56. Ingamells, *Dictionary*, pp. 713–14.

57. Cited by Christopher Hibbert, *The Grand Tour* (London: Methuen, 1987) p. 138.

58. One Manx historian, unreliable in other detail, claims that Murray actually died in his sister's house, but legal annotations on Murray's will (q.v.) make clear that this is untrue. (A. W. Moore, *Manx Worthies: Biographies of Notable Manx Men and Women* (Douglas, Isle of Man: S. K. Broadbent, 1901).

59. Demolished in 1899.

60. For example that he was appointed ambassador at Constantinople during the reign of George I (who died in 1727, when Murray was only 13 years old).

61. There is an area called Landican in the Wirral, by Woodchurch, just south of Birkenhead.

62. Manx National Heritage Library; the only reference it bears is 'Episcopal 1741 vol. 3'.

63. The second son, William, inherited Ronaldsway. The third son, Revd Thomas Murrey of London, inherited and sold the Douglas house.

64. Cited by Ingamells, *Dictionary*, p. 691.

65. Ibid.

66. R. Halsband (ed.) *Complete Letters of Lady Mary Wortley Montagu* (Oxford: Clarendon Press, 1965–67) vol. 3, p. 127, letter to Lady Bute, 30 May 1757. It is unclear what is meant by the reference to smuggling, unless Lady Mary was harking back to the trading carried out by Murray's father and grandfather. She could be implying here that Murray abused the diplomatic mail system to repatriate items of his collection.

67. Halsband, *Complete Letters*, vol. 3, p. 147, letter to Lady Bute, 13 May 1758.

68. Cited by Ingamells, *Dictionary*, p. 689.
69. See illustration 3.
70. Halsband, *Complete Letters*, vol. 3, p. 262 *et seq.*
71. George III was to become famous for appointing Scots to influential positions. It was observed of him in 1773 that 'Nothing will Gentle George's nose well suit, But Burrs and Thistles from the Isle of Bute'. Cited by Horn, *British Diplomatic Service*, p. 119.
72. Moore, *Manx Worthies*, p. 154.
73. This girl should not be confused with Murray's niece, also named Catherine, mentioned earlier.
74. Ref. MD 20. The museum holds also extracts from a private paper on the Murrays produced in 1982 by Herr Rudolf Otto of Vienna, who claims descent from Murray's daughter Catherine (Ref. 12838 G90/MUR).
75. PRO, Prob. 11/1035, an English translation.
76. 'Natural' used here in its meaning of 'illegitimate, born out of wedlock'.
77. SP 110/67, Murray to company, 1 October 1766.
78. A small oval silver box, plain except for the government crest on the lid.
79. See illustrations 2 and 3.
80. The artist West was born in Philadelphia in 1738, but had settled in England by 1760. He travelled to Venice with the ill-fated Northamptons, and is known to have completed two portraits there, one of Murray and the other of the Countess of Northampton and her little daughter. Murray commissioned from him also a painting that would show the costume of an American Indian; the resulting work, 'Savage taking care of his family', is now owned by the Royal College of Physicians in London.
81. Oliver Millar, *The Later Georgian Pictures in the Collection of Her Majesty the Queen* (London: Phaidon, 1969) pp. 13–14.
82. He is recorded as owning *inter alia* several works by Titian, a Raising of Lazarus by Veronese, and a small Conversion of St Hubert by Dürer (Ingamells, *Dictionary*, p. 691).
83. See illustration 4.
84. But the artist was not entirely delighted by the outcome of this

prestigious commission, which he confessed a few years later had been an honour he wished had been conferred on someone else, 'but it was not possible to foresee that what Mr Murray intended to be of the utmost servis to me, shou'd be of so very contrary an effect.' He had difficulty in obtaining payment for the original and for the several copies he was commissioned to produce, and complained to a friend 'I am told that I am only to have 35 Zichines for Each Copy, and seventy only for the Orriginal.' Cited in Millar, *Georgian Pictures*, p. 13.

85. No will of Lady Wentworth has been traced.

86. Millar, *Georgian Pictures*, p. 13.

87. His opposite number in the Ottoman fleet was similarly inexperienced; the newly-appointed Ottoman *kapitanpasha* (admiral of the fleet) had never been to sea, and had been placed in charge of the fleet because the sultan dreamt that the man had delivered a great naval victory. (François Emmanuel de Guignard, Comte de Saint Priest, *Mémoires*, Paris: Calman-Lévy, 1929, pp. 133–6).

88. SP 97/46, Murray to Weymouth, 17 July 1770; Weymouth to Murray, 27 July and 18 August 1770.

89. That is sufficient income on which to live.

90. SP 97/58, Murray to Ritchie, Venice, 3 September 1770.

91. SP 97/46, Weymouth to Murray, 30 October 1770.

92. SP 97/58, Rochford to Murray, 10 October and 25 December 1772.

93. SP 97/47, Murray to Rochford, 3 June 1771; SP 97/58, Rochford to Murray, 14 February 1772.

94. SP 110/87, Murray to Murat, 8 May 1769.

95. Saint-Priest, *Mémoires*, vol. 1, p. 131 *et seq.*

96. SP 97/58, Rochford to Murray, 25 July 1774.

97. SP 99/70.

98. SP 99/76, Udney to Rochford, 16 August 1775; SP 97/51, Murray to Rochford, 5 July 1775.

99. Girolamo Asranio Giustiniani, who declined the responsibility.

100. SP 99/76, Strange to Rochford, 11 and 18 August 1775; Udney to Rochford, 16 August 1775; Rochford to Strange, 1 September 1775.

101. SP 99/76, Udney to Rochford, 16 August 1775.
102. The ultimate fate of these children would be a fascinating subject for further study. The Otto family, now living in Vienna, claims descent from Murray's daughter. They believe she married an Italian aristocrat, but they claim also that the Archbishop of Canterbury intervened to wrench young Catterina from her mother and restore her to Murray's family in England. They do not mention his other children, of whom they seem to be unaware.
103. Horn, *British Diplomatic Service*, p. 275.
104. The Crellin family, present-day descendants of Murray, were unable to find his grave, and believed him to have died in some disgrace. Research for this book has shown that this was not so.
105. A. L. Bagis, *Britain and the Struggle for the Integrity of the Ottoman Empire: Sir Robert Ainslie's Embassy to Istanbul 1776–1794* (Istanbul: Isis Press, 1984) pp. 5 et seq.

3. The Chaplains

1. K. N. Chaudhury, *English East India Company: The Study of an Early Joint-stock Company, 1600–1640* (London: Frank Cass & Company Ltd, 1965) pp. 33–4; Wood, *Levant Company*, p. 42.
2. Company minutes for 16 January 1633 and 17 December 1635, cited by Pearson, *Chaplains*, pp. 48–9.
3. Pearson, *Chaplains*, p. 9.
4. Sermon of John Luke, chaplain-designate to Izmir.
5. The British Library has a good collection of these, but scrutiny of their subject matter revealed nothing of interest to this book.
6. Spear, *Nabobs*, p. 10.
7. S. J. McNally, *The Chaplains of the East India Company* (commissioned for India Office Records, London, 1976) p. 69.
8. Hugh Goddard, *A History of Christian–Muslim Relations* (Edinburgh: Edinburgh University Press, 2000) p. 117.
9. McNally, *Chaplains*.
10. Pearson, *Chaplains*, p. 9.
11. Ibid., pp. 46–50.
12. Anderson, *English Consul*, p. 6.
13. Wood, *Levant Company*, pp. 222–3.

14. Pearson, *Chaplains*, p. 56.
15. These were Christian slaves, many of them English, held by the Ottomans or by pirates.
16. Anderson, *English Consul*, pp. 100 *et seq*. Temple's will was in fact rather sensational in that he did not leave the usual $50 to the doctor, Benjamin Pickering, but left instead a vast sum of money and property to Pickering's wife, with whom he had clearly had some close involvement.
17. Anderson, *English Consul*, p. 217. See illustration 5.
18. Pearson, *Chaplains*, p. 16.
19. Covel is mentioned in the biography of the Hon. Dudley North, brother of Lord North and a company factor at Izmir and later Istanbul during Covel's time. It seems that North once composed a Turkish dictionary, which 'was pirated out of his house, and he could never find who had it: perhaps it may now be in England, in the hands of Dr Covell' (North, *Lives*, vol. 2, p. 373).
20. The particular interest of these three successive Izmir chaplains – Denton, Smith and Covel – in the Greek church, is explored in a doctoral thesis by A. N. Pippidi entitled 'Knowledge of and Ideas on the Ottoman Empire in Western Europe and Britain in the Sixteenth and Seventeenth Centuries with Special Reference to Thomas Smith and his Friends', D.Phil. thesis (Oxford, 1985), cited by Anderson, *English Consul*, p. 216.
21. Pearson, *Chaplains*, p. 22.
22. In the Royal Society of Great Britain's series *Philosophical Transactions*, vol. 19, no. 217, London, 1695 (printed for Samuel Smith and Benjamin Walford).
23. Revd Henry Maundrell, *Journey from Aleppo to Jerusalem, at Easter, AD 1696* (Edinburgh, 1812).
24. Pearson, *Chaplains*, p. 125.
25. Edmund Chishull, *Travels in Turkey and Back to England* (London, 1747).
26. North, *Lives of the Norths*, vol. 2, p. 356.
27. At that time William Cave.
28. The Disruption is the name given to the period of civil war in England in the mid-seventeenth century when the monarchy was

overthrown and Charles I executed. Cromwell's 'protectorate' held power until the restoration of the monarchy in 1660. For an account of this period see Goffman, *Britons in the Ottoman Empire*.

29. Wood, *Levant Company*, p. 89.
30. G. Wheler, *A Journey into Greece* (London, 1682) cited in Anderson, *English Consul*, p. 102.
31. It is not hard to see that some might have regarded this as unseemly conduct for men of the Church, although no specific examples of such disapproval have come to light.
32. Pearson, *Chaplains*, p. 34.
33. Anderson, *English Consul*, p. 102.
34. SP 110/74.
35. McNally, *Chaplains*, p. 38.
36. Spear, *Nabobs*, p. 107.
37. McNally, *Chaplains*, p. 69.
38. Pearson, *Chaplains*, pp. 56 and 61.
39. Wood, *Levant Company*, pp. 125–27.
40. Ibid., pp. 162–3.
41. How far Catholics may have targeted Muslims, if at all, is a subject that requires research way beyond the scope of this book. That the Ottomans tolerated a substantial Catholic presence up to and beyond the end of the eighteenth century would seem to indicate that they took care not to offend.
42. Bruce Masters, *Christians and Jews in the Ottoman Arab World* (Cambridge: University Press, 2001) pp. 69 and 80.
43. Eldhem Eldem, Daniel Goffman and Bruce Masters, *The Ottoman City between East and West: Aleppo, Izmir and Istanbul* (Cambridge: Cambridge University Press, 1999) p. 54.
44. Goddard, *Christian–Muslim Relations*, pp. 117 et seq.
45. This was George Strachan. See following chapter.
46. North, *Lives*, vol. 3, pp. 37–8.
47. Goddard, *Christian–Muslim Relations*, p. 122.
48. Spear, *Nabobs*, p. 109.
49. SP 110/59, 30 September 1778.
50. Philip Anderson, *The English in Western India* (London: Smith, Elder, 1856) p. 336; Spear, *Nabobs*, p.106.

51. This was what the English usually called the particular khan, or caravanserai, where they themselves lived and worked, but here probably refers to a different location.

52. Alexander Russell, *The Natural History of Aleppo and Parts Adjacent* (London, Printed for A. Millar, 1756) p. 235.

53. Abraham Parsons, *Travels in Asia and Africa, Including a Journey from Scanderoon to Aleppo, and Over the Desert to Bagdad and Bussora* (London: Longman, Hurst, Rees & Orme, 1808) p. 28.

54. Parsons, *Travels*, Chapter 1.

55. See illustration 6.

56. A. Drummond, *Travels through Different Cties of Germany, Italy, Greece and Several Parts of Asia, as Far as the Banks of the Euphrates* (London: Printed by W. Strahan for the author, 1754) Letter X, dated 26 October 1747.

57. Ibid., Letter XI, dated 2 December 1748.

58. Ibid., Letter XII, dated 25 March 1749.

59. The Scottish equivalent of lord mayor.

60. Ibid., Letter XI, dated 2 December 1748.

61. Sarah Searight, *The British in the Middle East* (London: East-West Publications, 1969) pp 39–40.

62. Charles Robson, *Newes from Aleppo* (London: Printed for M.S., 1628) p. 16.

63. *Dictionary of National Biography*, vol. 17, p. 60.

64. Chishull, *Travels*.

65. SP 110/74, Shaw at Aleppo to Edwards, 8 November 1753.

66. A possible indication that Crofts, like Hemming, was educated at Eton, or that at the very least the appointments of the two men were in some way related.

67. Ingamells, *Dictionary*, p. 255.

68. Bibliotheca Croftsiana, London, 1782.

69. A copy of this catalogue can be found at the British Library.

70. SP 110/74, 11 October 1773; 27 September 1775.

71. SP 110/74.

72. SP 110/74, 19 September 1775.

73. SP 110/70.

74. It is possible that 'German' was used here as a synonym for Lutheran.
75. SP 110/74, fragment of letter from Dawes at Aleppo to someone in Latakia, 1 May 1764.
76. SP 110/74. It is unclear whether this was an innovation, or merely the continuation of an established practice; no other such record has come to light.
77. Bobbit had presumably been a merchant stationed at Aleppo; two ladies with the surname Bobbit were present at Izmir in 1759 (see Chapter 5). It was not unusual for merchants to leave a number of small bequests.
78. SP 110/59.
79. See Chapter 5 for further details.
80. McNally, *Chaplains*, p. 57.
81. SP 110/87, Murray to Company, 15 July 1766.
82. SP 97/57, Company to Murray at Venice, 21 March 1766. A similar complaint had been lodged by the chancellor, Mr Lone, whom Murray also inherited as a sitting tenant.
83. SP 110/87, Murray to Clendon, 12 November 1768.
84. SP 110/87, Murray to Abbott at Ankara, 25 November 1768.
85. SP 105/337, Assembly register for Izmir, 1757–1804.
86. Drummond, *Travels*, Letter V, dated 4 March 1745.
87. R. Walsh, *An Account of the Levant Company, with some Notices of the Benefits Conferred upon Society by its Officers* (a short tract, London, 1825).
88. Richard Grassby, *The English Gentleman in Trade: The Life and Works of Sir Dudley North, 1641–1692* (Oxford: Oxford University Press, 1994) p. 65.
89. Drummond, *Travels*, Letter XI, dated 2 December 1748.
90. See Appendix for list of eighteenth-century chaplains at Istanbul, Izmir and Aleppo.

4. The Physicians

1. Wood, *Levant Company*, p. 225.
2. Chaudhury, *English East India Company*, pp. 33–4; Wood, *Levant Company*, p. 42.

3. Ingamells, *Dictionary*, pp. 428–9, 978–9.
4. SP 97/49, Murray to Rochford, 3 December 1773.
5. SP 97/58, Rochford to Murray, 8 January 1774.
6. Ingamells, *Dictionary*, pp. 314, 1010. This man should not be confused with the Alexander Drummond who was earlier consul at Aleppo.
7. SP 97/50, Murray to Rochford, 8 May 1774.
8. See also Chapter 5.
9. Ibid.
10. Halsband, *Complete Letters*, p. 80; Timoni is described as a Fellow of the Royal Society (FRS) although no record of him as such has come to light. He had already published an article on the process of inoculation in the society's *Transactions* in 1714. See Christopher Pick (ed.) *Embassy to Constantinople: The Travels of Lady Mary Wortley Montagu* (London: Century, 1988) p. 94.
11. Letter to Lady Mary, 10 March 1718, cited by Pick, *Embassy to Constantinople*, p. 161.
12. On his return to England, Maitland disappeared into relative obscurity, and history has, perhaps rightly, accorded more credit for inoculation to Lady Mary than to her doctor.
13. SP 110/87; Hochpied was the Dutch consul at Izmir; a relative of the same name was later the Dutch ambassador at Istanbul.
14. It has not been possible to identify this man positively. He could be Alexander Mackenzie, MD (Aberdeen) 1755–80, who served at some time in Kingston, Jamaica.
15. The dictionary definition of a gallipot is a small earthenware pot used by pharmacists as a container for ointments. Here Murray seems to be using the word as *pars pro toto* for the profession.
16. SP 110/87, Murray to Hayes, 14 June 1769.
17. P. J. Wallis and R. V. Wallis, *Eighteenth Century Medics* (Newcastle-upon-Tyne: Project for Historical Biography, 1985); s.v. *Dictionary of National Biography*, vol. I, p. 70.
18. The subject of Mackittrick's degree thesis was the yellow fever of the West Indies.
19. See entry under 'Adair' in *Dictionary of National Biography*, vol. 1, p. 70.

20. SP 97/49, Murray to Rochford, 17 August and 17 December 1773; 3 February 1774. Bark extract, usually in liquid form, was used as a cure for fevers.
21. Anderson, *English Consul*, pp. 105–8.
22. Eldem et al., *The Ottoman City*, p. 110.
23. North, *Lives*, vol. 2, pp. 413 *et seq*.
24. SP 105/337.
25. I am grateful to Dr Alex Murdoch of the Scottish History Department, University of Edinburgh, for drawing my attention to this.
26. She may have been Turnbull's second wife if the reference to a French wife is correct.
27. Carita Doggett Carse, *Dr Andrew Turnbull and the New Smyrna Colony in Florida* (Florida: The Drew Press, 1919).
28. SP 97/57, Shelburne to Murray, 5 June 1767.
29. SP 110/87, Murray to Hayes, 3 December 1767.
30. Russell, *The Natural History of Aleppo*, pp. 139–40.
31. Alexander Russell, *The Natural History of Aleppo and Parts Adjacent*, 2nd edn, revised and enlarged by Patrick Russell (London: Printed for G. G. and J. Robinson, 1794) vol. 2, p. 142.
32. Henry Yule, 'Some little known travellers to the east', *Asiatic Quarterly Journal*, April 1888, pp. 313–35; cited in D. G. Crawford, *A History of the Indian Medical Service 1600–1913* (London: W. Thacker, 1914) pp. 68–82.
33. Aleppo Court Minutes of 8 January 1619, cited by Crawford, *History of the Indian Medical Service*, p. 60.
34. Yule, 'Some little known travellers', p. 335.
35. Michael Lynch, *Scotland: A New History* (London: Century, 1991) Chapter 20, p. 344.
36. For an account of the Scottish Enlightenment period see Jane Rendall, *The Origins of the Scottish Enlightenment* (London: Macmillan, 1978).
37. R. W. Innes Smith, *English-speaking Students of Medicine at the University of Leyden* (Edinburgh: Oliver & Boyd, 1932).
38. John D. Comrie, *History of Scottish Medicine to 1860* (London: Wellcome Historical Medical Society, 1932) vol. 1; B. C. Corner

and C. C. Booth (eds) *Chain of Friendship: Selected Letters of Dr John Fothergul of London, 1735–1780* (Cambridge Mass.: Harvard University Press, 1971) p. 6.

39. Comrie, *History of Scottish Medicine*, vol. 1.

40. *Dictionary of National Biography*, s.v. See also Anita Damiani, *Enlightened Observers: British Travellers to the Near East, 1715–1850* (Beirut: American University of Beirut, 1979); Barbara J. Hawgood, 'Alexander Russell and Patrick Russell: Physicians and Natural Historians of Aleppo', *Journal of Medical Biography*, vol. 9, no. 1, February 2004, pp. 1–6.

41. Fothergill's eulogy on the death of Alexander Russell, in John Coakley Lettsom, *The Works of John Fothergill, MD*, 3 vols (London, 1783) pp. 15–16.

42. The family sold Braidshaw (which still stands, though now called Broadshaw, on the outskirts of West Calder, 20 miles west of Edinburgh) in 1734, and moved to Roseburn, now subsumed by the city.

43. This man's son, also John and also a lawyer, married a daughter of the Revd Dr William Robertson, principal of Edinburgh University and a leading figure of the Scottish Enlightenment.

44. Janet Starkey, 'Bagnios, coffee-houses and glistening pomegranate-thickets: Aleppo in the eighteenth century', unpublished paper presented to conference of the Association for the Study of Travel in Egypt and the Near East (ASTENE), Edinburgh, July 2001.

45. Hawgood, 'Alexander Russell and Patrick Russell'.

46. Fothergill's eulogy to Alexander Russell, in Lettsom, *The Works of John Fothergill*, vol. 2, p. 369.

47. SP 110/74, fragment of original letter dated 8 November 1753, which I identified as being in the handwriting of Jasper Shaw, to 'Sozy' (the nickname of another Levant Company merchant, Eleazar Edwards, who was later himself stationed at Aleppo).

48. Research has produced no clue as to how a Scot came to be appointed at this time. Little is known of Drummond prior to his arrival in the Levant.

49. Russell, *Natural History* (1794 edn), vol. 2, pp. 122–3.

50. Ibid., p. 141.

51. Ibid., vol. 1, p. 38.
52. Ibid., p. 215. Fothergill's eulogy to Alexander Russell, reproduced in Lettsom, *The Works of John Fothergill*, vol. 2, p. 372.
53. Russell, *Natural History* (1794 edn), vol. 2, p. 125.
54. *Avania* (from the French *avanie*, meaning insult, affront) was the word commonly used for the irregular levies and extortions imposed on Europeans by Ottoman officials.
55. Russell, *Natural History* (1794 edn), vol. 2, p. 138.
56. Ibid., vol. 2, pp. 136, 138.
57. Ibid., vol. 2, p. 130. Although not specifically forbidden under Islam, dissection was generally viewed with revulsion and not traditionally practised in Muslim countries, often for climatic as well as ideological reasons. See Emilie Savage-Smith, 'Attitudes towards Dissection in Mediaeval Islam', *Journal of the History of Medicine and Allied Sciences*, vol. 50, no. 1, 1994, pp. 67–110; Manfred Ullmann, *Islamic Medicine*, Edinburgh: Edinburgh University Press, 1978.
58. Russell, *Natural History* (1794 edn), vol. 2, p. 131.
59. Ibid., p. 125.
60. Ibid., p. 348.
61. SP 110/74, fragment of letter in P. Russell's handwriting, 26 May 1760.
62. Russell, *Natural History*, pp. 241–2.
63. Russell, *Natural History* (1794 edn), vol. 2, p. 376. Writing 250 years after Russell and also citing Ottoman primary sources, Abraham Marcus, *The Middle East on the Eve of Modernity: Aleppo in the Eighteenth Century* (New York: Columbia University Press, 1989) pp. 258–60, found Russell's account of Muslim, Christian and Jewish attitudes to the plague to be accurate.
64. By Ehret and others, and probably commissioned later from sketches.
65. Lettsom, *Works of John Fothergill*, vol. 2, p. 378.
66. SP 110/87.
67. SP 110/74, P. Russell to an unnamed patient in Cyprus, 11 October 1760.
68. Michael Norman, 'Colville Bridger in Aleppo: his personal letters

home, 1754–1766', unpublished: copy held by British Library, 1998, p. 15, letter from Bridger to his father dated 20 May 1762.

69. Russell, *Natural History*, p. 53.
70. Russell, *Natural History* (1794 edn), vol. 1, p. 254.
71. Ibid., vol. 2, p. 3.
72. Ibid., vol. 2, pp. 266–7.
73. SP 110/74, A. Russell to Edwards, 20 December 1762.
74. He was born on 7 October 1732, and registered in the Old Parish Records as Claude, a female.
75. Hawgood, 'Alexander Russell and Patrick Russell', p. 5.
76. SP 110/58.
77. By Balfour, Auld & Smellie.
78. *Scots Magazine*, vol. 27, p. 334.
79. A. G. Morton, *John Hope, 1725–1786: Scottish Botanist* (Edinburgh: Botanic Garden Sibbald Trust, 1986).
80. SP 110/58.
81. Ibid.
82. SP 110/58 and SP 110/59.
83. For an account of Hays's death, see Chapter 5.
84. The name widely used by Europeans for the *ashraf*, Muslims claiming descent from the Prophet, and relating to their green turbans. Although no doubt originally pejorative, the word appears in official correspondence from at least as early as the mid-seventeenth century.
85. An Ottoman agent of the pasha dealing with military and political matters.
86. Russell, *Natural History* (1794 edn) vol. 1, pp. 12, 159–60. Although Patrick Russell used the term 'Greenhead' in 1794, Alexander Russell in his original of 1756, p. 122, called them 'emeers'.
87. SP 110/87.
88. SP 105/343, original letter from Freer, 15 October 1773.
89. SP 110/58 and SP 110/59.
90. There are further examples of this drift to India in Chapter 5.
91. Crawford, *Indian Medical Service*, vol. 1, p. 297. The spellings of the place-names are those used by Crawford.
92. I am grateful to Mr Patrick Chaney, an amateur botanist of Edinburgh with an interest in Freer, for drawing my attention to this.

93. This would seem at first sight to be a geographical impossibility. However, I am grateful to Dr William Donaldson, who has travelled in the region, for pointing out that there is indeed a high pass to the south of Katmandu from which the Ganges valley can be seen, albeit at a great distance.
94. William Kirkpatrick, *An Account of the Kingdom of Nepal: Being the Substance of Observations Made during a Mission to that Country in the Year 1793* (London: William Miller, 1811).
95. Innes Smith, *English-speaking Students*, p. viii.
96. Sir H. C. J Luke, *Cyprus under the Turks 1571–1878: A Record Based on the Archives of the English Consulate in Cyprus under the Levant Company and After* (Oxford: Oxford University Press, 1921) p. 95. Luke regrets the lost opportunity of the vivid accounts Goldsmith would have left us of 'the Levant merchants and their consuls'.
97. Russell, *Natural History* (1794 edn), vol. 1, p. 439.
98. Russell, *Natural History*, pp. 138, 144.

5. Family Life and Recreation

1. Russell, *Natural History*, p.12.
2. Drummond, *Travels*, Letter IX dated 27 December 1746.
3. Anderson, *English Consul*, p. 6.
4. French consul at Aleppo 1679–86, with 12 years' experience of the Levant prior to that.
5. Anderson, *English Consul*, p. 6.; Goffman, *Britons*, p. 27.
6. Anderson, *English Consul*, p. 6.
7. Henry Teonge, *The Diary of Henry Teonge: Chaplain on Board His Majesty's Ships* Assistance, Bristol *and* Royal Oak *Anno 1675 to 1679* (London: C. Knight, 1825) pp. 173–5.
8. Grassby, *English Gentleman in Trade*, p. 211.
9. North, *Lives*, vol. 2, pp. 452 *et seq.*
10. Ibid., p. 452.
11. Anderson, *English Consul*, p. 81.
12. PRO, PROB 11/377, f. 117. Cited by Anderson, *English Consul*, p. 81.
13. North, *Lives*, vol. 2. pp. 452 *et seq.*
14. Anderson, *English Consul*, p. 252.

15. Wood, *Levant Company*, pp. 128–9.
16. Anderson, *English Consul*, p. 6; Wood, *Levant Company*, p. 244.
17. Richard Chandler, *Travels in Asia Minor and Greece (1764)* (London, 1817) p. 74, cited by Wood, *Levant Company*, p. 244.
18. William Dalrymple gives a good account of this in *White Mughals: Love and Betrayal in Eighteenth Century India* (London: Harper Collins, 2003).
19. Spear, *Nabobs*, p. 151.
20. Dennis Kincaid, *British Social Life in India: 1608–1937*, 2nd edn, London: Routledge, 1973, p. 25.
21. Presumably they were volunteers, although it is not possible to establish this without further research.
22. Kincaid, *British Social Life*, pp. 43–4; Spear, *Nabobs*, pp. 12–13.
23. Goffman, *Britons*, p. 226.
24. John Bulwer, *Anthropometamorphosis: Man Transform'd: or, the Artificiall Changling Historically Presented* (London: William Hunt, 1654) p 54, cited in *Dictionary of National Biography*, vol. 21, p. 1108.
25. *Dictionary of National Biography*, vol. 21, p. 1108; see also Wood, *Levant Company*, pp. 88–9.
26. Goffman, *Britons*, pp. 121, 131.
27. Goffman, *Britons*, pp. 115–20; Wood, *Levant Company*, p. 92.
28. This was John Wilde.
29. Goffman, *Britons*, pp. 98 *et seq*, 162.
30. Anderson, *English Consult*, pp. 6, 82.
31. SP 105/174, p. 513, cited by Goffman, *Britons*, pp. 260–1, 210–11.
32. Anderson, *English Consul*, p. 47; Wood, *Levant Company*, p. 246.
33. Winchilsea and Finch shared a maternal grandmother, Elizabeth Heneage, who, when she was widowed, had been created Countess of Winchilsea. Several members of the family were later to bear the Christian name Heneage.
34. *Dictionary of National Biography*, vol. 7, p. 18.
35. Pick, *Embassy*, p. 106, letter to Lady Bristol, 1 April 1717.
36. Ibid., p. 176, letter to Wortley Montagu, 23 March 1718.
37. Pick, *Embassy*, p. 158, letter to Miss Anne Thistlethwayte, 4 January 1718.
38. Ibid., p. 179, letter to Lady Bristol, 10 April 1718; ibid., p. 195,

NOTES

letter to Abbé Conti, 19 May 1718. It would seem that the embassy owned a boat, for Lady Mary writes of crossing the Bosphorus in 'my galley'.

39. Wood, *Levant Company*, p. 177.
40. Ingamells, *Dictionary*, see entry for Grenville, pp. 428–9.
41. SP 110/87, Murray to Company, 16 December 1768.
42. See Chapter 2 above. His wife, Lady Wentworth, returned to England when he was transferred from Venice in 1766. We cannot be sure that Murray was accompanied in Istanbul by his Italian Catholic mistress, Cattarina and their children, but the scanty evidence available seems to point to their having been there with him.
43. SP 97/46, Murray to Weymouth, 17 May and 27 June 1770; Saint Priest, *Mémoires*, p. 126.
44. Saint Priest, *Mémoires*, pp. 125–6; Wood, *Levant Company*, p. 234.
45. SP 97/46, Murray to Weymouth, 3 December 1770.
46. Ibid., 15 August 1770.
47. SP 97/46, Murray to Weymouth, 3 September 1770.
48. Although he had a son who predeceased him, dying in 1796 of a putrid fever (*Dictionary of National Biography*, vol. 1, pp. 189–90).
49. A relative of the Baron Hochpied who later became Dutch ambassador at Istanbul.
50. Drummond, *Travels*, Letter V dated 4 March 1745.
51. SP 105/337.
52. Anderson, *English Consul*, p. 67.
53. John Boddington, who was consul in Cyprus in 1775, may have been one of his sons.
54. Wood, *Levant Company*, p. 162.
55. Davis, *Aleppo*, p. 86.
56. SP 97/51, Weymouth to Hayes, 15 December 1775.
57. Painting by Antoine de Favray, known to have been in Istanbul/Izmir 1766–71. See illustration 9.
58. SP 97/51, Hayes to Murray, 1 November 1766.
59. Ibid., 8 January 1767.
60. SP 110/87, Murray to Hayes, 27 December 1766.
61. SP 110/58, 27 July 1780.

62. Wood, *Levant Company*, Appendix II.
63. SP 97/46, Murray to Weymouth, 3 November 1770.
64. Tott did not, apparently, consider the Greeks who died to be Europeans.
65. François Tott, *Memoirs of Baron de Tott: Containing the State of the Turkish Empire and the Crimea, During the Late War with Russia* (London: Printed for G. G. J. and J. Robinson, 1786) vol. 2, pp. 236–7, cited by Wood, *Levant Company*, p. 234.
66. SP 97/46, Murray to Weymouth, 7 July, 17 July and 3 August 1770.
67. Drummond, *Travels*, Letter IX dated 27 December 1746.
68. The French factories' dragomans, or interpreters, were often native Frenchmen.
69. SP 110/74.
70. Although Russell used this phrase, there is no indication that the wording is his own; it seems to have been an expression used by the French embassy. Colville Bridger, writing in 1763, mentions also the *mezza razza*, 'who, like images in the Roman Catholic Churches, receive the adoration of all with as much insensibility as those they represent' (Norman, 'Bridger', p. 29).
71. Russell, *Natural History*, 1794 edition, vol. 2, p. 14.
72. SP 110/70. On the front of this register is an undated handwritten note pointing to the baptism of George Worsley Lloyd, recorded in an Aleppo letter book dated 1729.
73. A radical Protestant sect that originated in Switzerland in the early sixteenth century and that denied the validity of infant baptism; the Anabaptists were forerunners of the Baptists, Quakers and Mennonites. For an account of them, see Ninian Smart, *The World's Religions*, 2nd edn (Cambridge: Cambridge University Press. 1998) pp. 334–5.
74. For an account of the Radcliffes, see Davis, *Aleppo and Devonshire Square*.
75. Norman, 'Colville Bridger at Aleppo'.
76. Ibid., p. 6.
77. Ibid., p. 18.
78. Ibid., p. 25.

79. Ibid., p. 38. The Dutch consul in Aleppo was at this time permitted to engage in trade, unlike his English and French counterparts.

80. SP 110/74, John van Masegh to Mr Edwards at Tripoli, April 1768.

81. Probably Mrs Esther Rowles.

82. Norman, 'Colville Bridger at Aleppo', p. 29.

83. Ibid., p. 42.

84. SP 110/74, Chaplain's Charity Book.

85. Ibid., Shaw at Aleppo to Edwards at Iskenderun, 10 June 1763.

86. Ibid., Sarah Younger at London to Mrs Edwards at Aleppo, 31 October 1763.

87. Norman, 'Colville Bridger in Aleppo', p. 38.

88. Ibid., p. 9.

89. Ibid., p. 38.

90. Ibid., p. 11.

91. Ibid., p. 19.

92. Ibid., p. 33.

93. Ibid., p. 44.

94. Ibid., p. 49–50.

95. This was the marriage of John Barker (later consul) to Marianna Hays (born Aleppo 19 July 1779, the daughter of David Hays and Louisa Vernon). It took place on 15 June 1800.

96. Norma Perry, 'Levant Company factors at Aleppo in the 1720s,' in F. Paknadel (ed.) *La Méditerranée au XVIIIe siècle* (Aix en Provence: University of Provence, 1987) pp. 91–112. See also Grassby, *The English Gentleman*, p. 115.

97. Probably the French *curé* (priest).

98. Roxanne seems not to have been treated like the Pentlow widow had been a century earlier, in Izmir, indicating that she was perhaps not an Ottoman subject.

99. Davis, *Aleppo*, p. 51.

100. SP 110/74.

101. J. Griffiths, *Travels in Europe, Asia Minor and Arabia* (London: T. Cadell & W. Davies/Edinburgh: Peter Hill, 1805) pp. 332–92. Griffiths's account of this journey can also be found as an

appendix to J. Barker, edited by E. B. B. Barker, 2 vols, *Syria and Egypt under the Last Five Sultans of Turkey* (London: S. Tinsley, 1876).

102. .Barker, *Syria and Egypt*, p. 29.
103. Ibid., pp. 282–3.
104. Wood, *Levant Company*, pp. 188, 196.
105. *Dictionary of National Biography*, vol. 1, p. 1124.
106. Virginia Childs, *Lady Hester Stanhope: Queen of the Desert* (London: Weidenfeld & Nicolson, 1990) p.150.
107. Barker, *Syria and Egypt*, pp. 278–83.
108. Norman, 'Colville Bridger in Aleppo', p. 2.
109. SP 110/70.
110. Ibid.
111. Spear, *Nabobs*, p 116.
112. Anderson, *English Consul*, pp. 92–105; Wood, *Levant Company*, pp. 220–2.
113. SP 110/74; SP 110/70.
114. SP 110/70.
115. Wood, *Levant Company*, pp. 179–204.

6. Conclusion

1. Wood, *Levant Company*, p. 208.
2. Drummond, *Travels*, Letter XI, dated 2 December 1748.
3. Ibid., Letter IX, dated 26 December 1746. Drummond names this man as Khur Ahmet Pasha, whom he describes as 'a decayed, squinting, ugly old letcher'.

References

ARCHIVAL SOURCES

Levant Company Archives:
The Public Records Office (PRO) in London (renamed in 2003 as the National Archives) holds the archives of the Levant Company, 1600–1825. The records consulted for this book were the following from the State Papers series (SP):

SP 97/46 Copy book of John Murray's letters to Secretaries of State (1770).

SP 97/47 Copy book of John Murray's letters to Secretaries of State (1771).

SP 97/49 Copy book of John Murray's letters to Secretaries of State (1773).

SP 97/50 Copy book of John Murray's letters to Secretaries of State (1774).

SP 97/51 Correspondence with Secretaries of State from John Murray and Anthony Hayes (1775).

SP 97/57 Correspondence from Levant Company to Murray and Hayes (1765–68).

SP 97/58 Papers relating to John Murray and Sir Robert Ainslie, includes part of Murray's copy book of letters to Secretaries of State January 1770–January 1772 (1769–79).

SP 105/337 Register of the Cancelleria of the British factory at Smyrna (1757–1804).

SP 105/343 Correspondence and papers of the British factory at Aleppo (1687–1842).

SP 110/58 Minute book of the assembly of the consul and British factory at Aleppo (1768–1776).

SP 110/59 Minute book of the assembly of the consul and British factory at Aleppo (1776–1791).

SP 110/70 Register of marriages, baptisms and burials by the chaplain of the British factory in Aleppo (1756–1800).

SP 110/74 Miscellaneous correspondence and papers of the consul and factory at Aleppo, including the account book of the chaplain for the distribution of charity money (1707–1871).

SP 110/87 Copy book of John Murray's letters to the Levant Company, his consuls and others (1766–1769).

SECONDARY SOURCES

Ambrose, Gwilym P., 'English traders at Aleppo (1658–1756)', *The Economic History Review*, vol. 3, 1932, pp. 246–67.

Anderson, Philip, *The English in Western India*, London: Smith, Elder, 1856.

Anderson, Sonia, *An English Consul in Turkey: Paul Rycaut at Smyrna, 1667–1678*, Oxford: Clarendon Press, 1989.

Bagis, A. I., *Britain and the Struggle for the Integrity of the Ottoman Empire: Sir Robert Ainslie's Embassy to Istanbul, 1776–1794*, Istanbul: Isis Press, 1984. •

Barker, J., *Syria and Egypt under the Last Five Sultans of Turkey*, edited by E. B. B. Barker, 2 vols, London: S. Tinsley, 1876.

Bulwer, John, *Anthropometamorphosis: Man Transform'd: or, the Artificiall Changling Historically Presented*, London: William Hunt, 1654.

Chandler, Richard, *Travels in Asia Minor and Greece (1764)*, London, 1817.

Chaudhuri, K. N., *English East India Company: The Study of an Early Joint-stock Company, 1600–1640*, London: Frank Cass & Company Ltd, 1965.

Childs, Virginia, *Lady Hester Stanhope: Queen of the Desert*, London: Weidenfeld & Nicolson, 1990.

Chishull, Edmund, *Travels in Turkey and Back to England*, London, 1747.

Comrie, John D., *History of Scottish Medicine to 1860*, London: Wellcome Historical Medical Society, 1932.

Corner, B. C. and C. C. Booth (eds) *Chain of Friendship: Selected Letters of Dr John Fothergul of London, 1735–1780*, Cambridge MA: Harvard University Press, 1971.

Corse, Carita Doggett, *Dr Andrew Turnbull and the New Smyrna Colony in Florida*, Florida: The Drew Press, 1919.

Crawford, D. G., *A History of the Indian Medical Service, 1600–1913*, London: W. Thacker, 1914.

Dalrymple, William, *White Mughals: Love and Betrayal in Eighteenth Century India*, London: Harper Collins, 2003.

Damiani, Anita, *Enlightened Observers: British Travellers to the Near East, 1715–1850*, Beirut: American University of Beirut, 1979.

Davis, Ralph, *Aleppo and Devonshire Square: English Traders in the Levant in the Eighteenth Century*, London: Macmillan, 1967.

Drummond, Alexander, *Travels through Different Cities of Germany, Italy, Greece and Several Parts of Asia as far as the Banks of the Euphrates*, London: Printed by W. Strahan for the author, 1754.

Eldem, Edhem, Daniel Goffman and Bruce Masters, *The Ottoman City between East and West: Aleppo, Izmir and Istanbul*, Cambridge, Cambridge University Press, 1999.

Goddard, Hugh, *A History of Christian–Muslim Relations*, Edinburgh: Edinburgh University of Press, 2000.

Goffman, Daniel, *Britons in the Ottoman Empire: 1642–1660*, Washington: University of Washington Press, 1998.

Goffman, Daniel, *The Ottoman Empire and Early Modern Europe*, Cambridge: Cambridge University Press, 2002.

Grassby, Richard, *The English Gentleman in Trade: The Life and Works of Sir Dudley North, 1641–1692*, Oxford: Oxford University Press, 1994.

Griffiths, J., *Travels in Europe, Asia Minor and Arabia*, London: T. Cadell & W. Davies/Edinburgh: Peter Hill, 1805.

Hakluyt, Richard, *The Principal Navigations, Voyages, Traffiques and Discoveries of the English Nation*, 12 vols, Glasgow: Maclehose, 1904.

Halsband, Robert (ed.) *Complete Letters of Lady Mary Wortley Montagu*, Oxford: Clarendon Press, 1965–67.

Hawgood, Barbara J., 'Alexander Russell and Patrick Russell: physicians and natural historians of Aleppo', *Journal of Medical Biography*, vol. 9, no. 1, February 2004, pp. 1–6.

Hibbert, Christopher, *The Grand Tour*, London: Methuen, 1987.

Horn, D. B., *The British Diplomatic Service 1689–1789*, Oxford: Clarendon Press, 1961.

Horn, D. B., *Great Britain and Europe in the Eighteenth Century*, Oxford: Clarendon Press, 1967.

Howard, John, *An Account of the Principal Lazarettos in Europe*, Warrington: Printed by W. Eyres and sold by T. Cadell, 1789.

Ingamells, John (compiler) *A Dictionary of British and Irish Travellers in Italy, 1701–1800*, New Haven: Yale University Press, 1997.

Innes Smith, R. W., *English-speaking Students of Medicine at the University of Leyden*, Edinburgh: Oliver & Boyd, 1932.

Kincaid, Dennis, *British Social Life in India: 1608–1937*, 2nd edn, London: Routledge, 1973.

Kirkpatrick, William, *An Account of the Kingdom of Nepal: Being the Substance of Observations Made During a Mission to that Country in the Year 1793*, London: William Miller, 1811.

Lettsom, John Coakley, *The Works of John Fothergill, MD*, 3 vols, London, 1783.

Lynch, Michael, *Scotland: A New History*, London: Century, 1991.

Luke, Sir H. C. J., *Cyprus under the Turks 1571–1878: A Record Based on the Archives of the English Consulate in Cyprus under the Levant Company and After*, Oxford: Oxford University Press, 1921.

McNally, S. J., *The Chaplains of the East India Company* (commissioned for India Office Records) London, 1976.

Mansel, Philip, *Constantinople: City of the World's Desire, 1453–1924*, London: John Murray, 1995.

Marcus, Abraham, *The Middle East on the Eve of Modernity: Aleppo in the Eighteenth Century*, New York: Columbia University Press, 1989.

Masters, Bruce, *The Origins of Western Economic Dominance in the Middle East: Mercantilism and the Islamic Economy in Aleppo, 1600–1750*, London: London University Press, 1988.

Masters, Bruce, *Christians and Jews in the Ottoman Arab World*, Cambridge: Cambridge University Press, 2001.

Maundrell, Revd Henry, *Journey from Aleppo to Jerusalem at Easter, AD 1696*, Edinburgh, 1812.

Millar, Oliver, *The Later Georgian Pictures in the Collection of Her Majesty the Queen*, London: Phaidon, 1969.

Moore, A. W., *Manx Worthies: Biographies of Notable Manx Men and Women*, Douglas, Isle of Man: S. K. Broadbent, 1901.

Morton, A. G., *John Hope, 1725–1786: Scottish Botanist*, Edinburgh: Botanic Garden Sibbald Trust, 1986.

Norman, Michael, 'Colville Bridger in Aleppo: his personal letters home, 1754–1766', unpublished: copy held by British Library, 1998.

North, The Hon. Roger, *The Lives of the Norths*, 3 vols, London: Henry Colburn, 1826.

Pamuk, Sevket, *A Monetary History of the Ottoman Empire*, Cambridge: Cambridge University Press, 2000.

Parsons, Abraham, *Travels in Asia and Africa, including a Journey from Scanderoon to Aleppo, and over the Desert to Bagdad and Bussora*, London: Longman, Hurst, Rees & Orme, 1808.

Pearson, J. B., *Biographical sketches of the chaplains to the Levant Company, 1611–1706*, Cambridge: Deighton, Bell & Company, 1883.

Perry, Norma, 'Levant Company factors at Aleppo in the 1720s', in F. Paknadel (ed.) *La Méditerrannée au XVIIIe siècle*, Aix-en Provence: University of Provence, 1987, pp. 91–112.

Pick, Christopher, (ed.) *Embassy to Constantinople: The Travels of Lady Mary Wortley Montagu*, London: Century, 1988.

Pippidi, A. N., 'Knowledge of and ideas on the Ottoman Empire in western Europe and Britain in the sixteenth and seventeenth centuries, with special reference to Thomas Smith and his friends', D.Phil. thesis, University of Oxford, 1985.

Rendall, Jane., *The Origins of the Scottish Enlightenment*, London: Macmillan, 1978.

Robson, Charles, *Newes from Aleppo*, London: Printed for M.S., 1628.

Russell, Alexander, *The Natural History of Aleppo and Parts Adjacent*, London, Printed for A. Millar, 1756.

Russell, Alexander, *The Natural History of Aleppo and Parts Adjacent*, 2nd edn, revised and enlarged by Patrick Russell, 2 vols, London: Printed for G. G. and J. Robinson, 1794.

Saint Priest, François Emmanuel de Guignard, Comte de, *Mémoires*, 2 vols, published by the Baron de Barante, Paris: Calman-Lévy, 1929.

Savage-Smith, Emilie, 'Attitudes towards dissection in Mediaeval Islam', *Journal of the History of Medicine and Allied Sciences*, vol. 50, no. 1, 1994, pp. 67–110.

Searight, Sarah, *The British in the Middle East*, London: East-West Publications, 1969.

Smart, Ninian, *The World's Religions*, 2nd edn, Cambridge: Cambridge University Press. 1998

Spear, Percival, *The Nabobs: A Study of the Social Life of the English in Eighteenth Century India*, revised edn, Oxford: Oxford University Press, 1963.

Starkey, Janet, 'Bagnios, coffee-houses and glistening pomegranate-thickets: Aleppo in the eighteenth century', unpublished paper presented to conference of the Association for the Study of Travel in Egypt and the Near East (ASTENE), Edinburgh, July 2001.

Teonge, Henry, *The Diary of Henry Teonge: Chaplain on Board His Majesty's Ships* Assistance, *Bristol and Royal Oak anno 1675 to 1679*, London: C. Knight, 1825.

Tott, François, *Memoirs of Baron de Tott: Containing the State of the Turkish Empire and the Crimea, during the Late War with Russia*, 2 vols, London: Printed for G. G. J. & J. Robinson, 1786.

Ullmann, Manfred, *Islamic Medicine*, Edinburgh: Edinburgh University Press, 1978

Wallis, P. J. and R. V. Wallis, *Eighteenth Century Medics*, Newcastle-upon-Tyne: Project for Historical Bibliography, 1985.

Walsh, R. *An Account of the Levant Company, with some Notices of the Benefits Conferred upon Society by its Officers* (a short tract) London, 1825.

Wheler, G., *A Journey into Greece*, London, 1682.

Wood, A. C., *A History of the Levant Company*, Oxford: Oxford University Press, 1935.

Yule, Henry, 'Some little known travellers in the East', *Asiatic Quarterly Journal*, April 1888, pp. 313–35.

Index